NEW LITURGY, NEW LAWS

NEW LITURGY, NEW LAWS

R. Kevin Seasoltz, O.S.B.

THE LITURGICAL PRESS

Collegeville   Minnesota

Library of Congress Cataloging in Publication Data

Seasoltz, R   Kevin.
  New liturgy, new laws.

  Bibliography: p.
  Includes index.
  1.   Liturgics—Catholic Church—History.   I.   Title.
BX1975.S4   264'.02'009   79-27916
  ISBN 0-8146-1077-3

Nihil obstat: Joseph C. Kremer, S.T.L., *Censor deputatus.*
Imprimatur: ✚ George H. Speltz, D.D., Bishop of St. Cloud. December 6, 1979.
  Quotations from the documents of Vatican Council II are taken from *Documents of Vatican II*, copyright © 1966 by The America Press, New York.
  English translation of excerpts from the Roman Missal, Rite of Christian Initiation of Adults, Rite of Confirmation, Rite of Penance, Rite of Anointing and Pastoral Care of the Sick, Rite of Marriage, Institution of Readers and Acolytes, and Ordination as Deacons copyright © 1969, 1973, 1974, 1975, 1976, 1978 by The International Committee on English in the Liturgy, Inc. All rights reserved.
  Copyright © 1980 by The Order of St. Benedict, Inc., Collegeville, Minnesota.
  Printed in the United States of America.

CONTENTS

NEW LITURGY, NEW LAWS

INTRODUCTION

In the years following the promulgation of the Second Vatican Council's Constitution on the Sacred Liturgy, there has been extensive renewal and reform in the Roman Catholic Church. There has also been considerable anguish and confusion as the Church has tried to implement the directives of the Council. The confusion has been magnified by the vast cultural developments that have taken place throughout the world. Since the Council, the Holy See has issued numerous liturgical instructions and rites whose language has been the subject of differing interpretations. In some areas of the Church, the texts have been interpreted with considerable care as living symbols meant to express and deepen the life of Christian communities. The texts have been situated in their proper context, and an effort has been made to explore and understand the theological foundations of what has been stated. Directives have been implemented in accord with the best principles of canon law. But in other areas of the Church, the texts have been looked upon as sterile directives, subject to no subtlety or ambiguity and allowing no measure of nuanced interpretation. The former interpretation has resulted in a genuine revitalization of the liturgical life of the Church; the latter interpretation has meant a continuation of the rubrical mentality that prevailed in the Roman Catholic Church from the sixteenth century down to the Second Vatican Council.

3

In a certain sense, the impression has been given on official levels that the primary goal of the Constitution on the Sacred Liturgy has been the restoration of purified ancient rites. Certainly such restorations have been most valuable. However, the constitution itself has clearly shown in its opening paragraphs that liturgical renewal and reform must go far beyond the stage of restoration: "It is the goal of this most sacred Council to intensify the daily growth of Catholics in Christian living; to make more responsive to the requirements of our times those Church observances which are open to adaptation; to nurture whatever can contribute to the unity of all who believe in Christ; and to strengthen those aspects of the Church which can help summon all of mankind into her embrace. . . . The Council also desires that, where necessary, the rites be carefully and thoroughly revised in the light of sound tradition, and that they be given new vigor to meet the circumstances and needs of modern times."[1]

The deeper meanings of liturgical renewal are also touched upon in other sections of the constitution: "Pastors of souls must therefore realize that, when the liturgy is celebrated, more is required than the mere observance of the laws governing valid and licit celebration. It is their duty also to ensure that the faithful take part knowingly, actively, and fruitfully."[2] The struggle to achieve a deepening of Christian faith and to assert the primacy of persons over things as well as the relationships that must be strengthened between persons and communities is a constant challenge to Christian ministers. The goal is clearly stated in the constitution: "In the restoration and promotion of the sacred liturgy, this full and active participation by all people is the aim to be considered before all else."[3] The uniqueness of persons and their needs is also acknowledged in the document: "Provided that the substantial unity of the Roman rite is maintained, the revision of liturgical books should allow for legitimate variations and adaptations to different groups, regions, and peoples, especially in mission lands."[4]

This relaxed and yet responsible approach to the celebration of

---

[1] *Sacrosanctum Concilium*, nos. 1, 4: *AAS* 56 (1964) 97–98.
[2] *Sacrosanctum Concilium*, no. 11: *AAS* 56 (1964) 102–3.
[3] *Sacrosanctum Concilium*, no. 14: *AAS* 56 (1964) 104.
[4] *Sacrosanctum Concilium*, no. 38: *AAS* 56 (1964) 110.

Christian faith stands in marked contrast to the anxious, suspicious, fearful, rigid attitude that inhibits both the expression and development of Christian faith. Such a healthy attitude is dependent on both excellence and expertise in liturgical leadership and planning; it is surely not fostered by untrained amateurs whose inept and haphazard efforts tend to distort the Christian mysteries and endanger the development of Christian faith.

In order that the official documents of liturgical renewal might be situated in their proper theological and historical context, and consequently be more accurately interpreted, the following pages seek to provide an overview of significant theological and historical developments in the liturgy during the years that immediately preceded, spanned, and followed the Second Vatican Council.

Chapter 1

THE LITURGICAL MOVEMENT FROM 1946
UNTIL THE SECOND VATICAN COUNCIL

Although the modern liturgical movement struggled for well over
a century to achieve the status of a genuine movement, by the end of
the Second World War it was quite firmly established in the most
significant Catholic countries of the world. On May 10, 1946, Pope
Pius XII asked the prefect of the Sacred Congregation of Rites, Cardinal Salotti, to initiate an outline for a general official reform of the
liturgy. A special commission was established on July 27, 1946, for
the purpose of studying the proposed reform. In August of that year,
at the Liturgical Congress held at Maastricht, Holland, plans were
laid for a major international liturgical meeting. Although the congress was never held because of unsettled post-war conditions, contact was established at Maastricht between the French and Dutch
leaders of the liturgical movement.

On January 28, 1947, the Holy See granted the Belgian hierarchy
an indult to celebrate evening Mass on Sundays and holy days
throughout the country. From that date, permissions of that nature
were granted more and more readily to hierarchies throughout the
world. In the same year, the Liturgical Institute was established at
Trier under the direction of Johannes Wagner, secretary of the
German Liturgical Commission. On September 18, 1947, Pope Pius
XII gave a significant allocution in the Basilica of St. Paul Outside
the Walls on the occasion of the fourteenth centennial celebration in

honor of St. Benedict of Nursia. Part of his address was devoted to various concerns of the liturgical movement and served as a prelude to the promulgation of his encyclical *Mediator Dei* on November 20, 1947.[1] Often called the *Magna Charta* of the liturgical movement, this encyclical was the first in the history of the Church to be devoted entirely to the liturgy. Although it was basically positive in tone, it contained various statements reflecting the apprehension and the spirit of unrest that the liturgical movement had initiated in various European countries. Nevertheless, the document did give the liturgical renewal decisive encouragement and a forward thrust.

Cardinal Salotti died on October 24, 1947, and was succeeded as prefect of the Sacred Congregation of Rites by Cardinal Micara. On May 28, 1948, Pope Pius XII appointed the members of the commission that would be responsible for initiating a project for a general liturgical reform. Father Ferdinand Antonelli, O.F.M., was appointed general director, Father Joseph Loew, C.Ss.R., assistant director, and Father Annibale Bugnini, C.M., secretary. The commission held its first meeting on June 22, 1948. The discussions led to the printing of a memorandum on liturgical reform. Although the document bore the date of December 30, 1948, it was not completed until June 1949. It was given to members of the new commission and to Pope Pius XII, and also to three other experts for their comments: Dom Bernard Capelle, Father Josef Jungmann, and Monsignor Mario Righetti.

During the years immediately following the publication of *Mediator Dei*, progress in the liturgical movement was rather cautious and slow. In June 1950, the first national German Liturgical Congress, dealing with the Sunday celebration of the Eucharist, was held. This was the first public conference sponsored and organized by the Liturgical Institute at Trier. Of special importance was a lecture given by Monsignor Romano Guardini, which prompted the formulation of a resolution urging the German bishops to request the Holy See to transfer the Holy Saturday liturgy from the morning to the evening or night. On November 2, 1950, the German and Austrian bishops formally submitted their petition for the transfer of the Holy Saturday liturgy. Cardinal Lienart,

[1] *AAS* 39 (1947) 521–604.

president of the Assembly of the Bishops of France, also requested the Holy See for the same indult. Their requests were favorably received, and on February 9, 1951, the Sacred Congregation of Rites issued its decree, *De Solemni Vigilia Paschali instauranda*, restoring the Solemn Paschal Vigil. The rites were approved experimentally for one year.[2] The following January, they were approved for three more years.

From July 12 to 15, 1951, the first international liturgical study week, sponsored by the Liturgical Institute at Trier and the Centre de Pastorale Liturgique in Paris, met at the Benedictine Abbey of Maria Laach. Some forty scholars, mostly from France, Germany, and Belgium, discussed the problems of the *Missale Romanum*. In 1948 a survey had been made by the editors of *Ephemerides Liturgicae* to discern which proposed reforms of the Roman liturgy were supported in various parts of the Catholic world. The first international meeting, therefore, dealt mainly with the various aspects of the rites of the Mass and also with the Easter Vigil service. Most of the conclusions from this meeting, which were in turn passed on to the Sacred Congregation of Rites, were eventually adopted and found their way into official decrees promulgating a restored order for the celebration of Holy Saturday and a simplification of the rubrics of the Roman Missal and Breviary.

In 1952 a somewhat larger group of scholars met at Sainte-Odile near Strasbourg in France in order to follow up on the work that had been done the previous year at Maria Laach. Since these meetings proved to be helpful in promoting collaboration and channeling liturgical investigations, it was decided that at the next meeting the scope of the sessions should be broadened. The scholars decided to meet at Lugano so as to encourage attendance by Italians. Organized by the national liturgical committees of France, Germany, Switzerland, and Italy, the Lugano conference was attended by Cardinals Ottaviani, pro-prefect of the Holy Office, Lercaro of Bologna, and Frings of Cologne, by various officials of the Sacred Congregation of Rites, and by bishops, priests, and lay people from approximately twelve countries, including England and the United States. The bishops agreed to submit the four major resolutions of

[2] *AAS* 43 (1951) 128–37.

the conference to the Holy See. These included a petition for a reform of the entire Holy Week liturgy, permission to use the format of the "German Solemn Mass" in other countries, permission to proclaim the liturgical readings in the vernacular, and encouragement of more active participation by the faithful.

On December 7, 1953, Cardinal Gaetano Cicognani, former apostolic nuncio to Spain, was made prefect of the Sacred Congregation of Rites. The following year, 1954, the fourth international study meeting was held in Louvain at the Benedictine Abbey of Mont César. The principal topics discussed at the conference were the system of biblical pericopes and the rite of concelebration. Since it was agreed that the subjects had not yet been sufficiently investigated, no definite resolutions were passed on to the Holy See. On November 2, 1954, Pope Pius XII gave an allocution in which he warned priests not to change anything in the liturgy on their own authority.[3]

The decree *Cum nostra hac aetate* was issued by the Sacred Congregation of Rites on March 23, 1955.[4] Quite similar to the apostolic constitution *Christus Dominus*, of January 6, 1953, which simplified the regulations governing the Eucharistic fast and the celebration of evening Mass,[5] the 1955 decree provided for a broad simplification of the rubrics. It reduced the number of commemorations and octaves, and also the number of days on which the creed was to be recited. Extensive changes in the liturgy of Holy Week were brought about the following November 16 by the decree *Maxima redemptionis nostrae*.[6]

Pope Pius XII issued an encyclical letter, *Musicae sacrae disciplina*, on December 25, 1955.[7] International congresses on church music had been held in 1950 in Rome and in 1954 in Vienna, but neither of these gatherings had addressed basic pastoral issues; they were of interest primarily to musicologists and discussed relatively minor matters such as singing by women in the liturgy and orchestral Masses. In his encyclical, Pius XII tried to set forth the true

[3] *AAS* 45 (1954) 670.
[4] *AAS* 47 (1955) 218–24.
[5] *AAS* 45 (1953) 15–24.
[6] *AAS* 47 (1955) 838–47.
[7] *AAS* 48 (1956) 5–25.

place of music in liturgical celebrations. Picking up on this theme, the Sacred Congregation of Rites made numerous practical applications in its instruction *De musica sacra et sacra liturgia ad mentem litterarum Pii Papae XII 'Musicae sacrae disciplina' et 'Mediator Dei,'* issued on September 3, 1958.[8] This latter document also contained important norms regulating the active participation of the laity in the liturgy.

In September 1956, the fifth international liturgical meeting was held in Assisi and in Rome. It was an occasion to honor Pope Pius XII on his eightieth birthday. Wide-reaching liturgical reforms had been implemented during his pontificate, and his encyclicals *Mystici Corporis* and *Mediator Dei* had done much to clarify the theological foundations of the liturgy and to promote liturgical reform and renewal. To express their gratitude to the Holy Father, the liturgical and pastoral leaders of the world came together for the Assisi-Rome Congress. Approximately twelve hundred participants from various parts of the world, including six cardinals and about eight hundred bishops, were in attendance. The Assisi-Rome Congress was structured differently from the international liturgical study weeks that preceded and followed it; it was more like a convention, whereas the others were small gatherings of specialists. The meeting closed with an allocution by Pope Pius XII in the course of a papal audience in Rome.[9] The Holy Father dealt particularly with a number of very complicated problems regarding the Eucharist that were the cause of tensions in various parts of the Church. In general, the impression was communicated that the Holy See was disturbed by the quickening pace of the liturgical movement and by the extensive demands for reform that were being made by the northern European countries. As a result, increased tensions were experienced in the liturgical movement following the Assisi meeting.

At the liturgical congress held in Strasbourg in July 1957, an attempt was made to bring together the positive developments that had taken place in both the biblical and the liturgical movements. Fortunately many liturgical scholars had come to realize that no lasting liturgical progress is really possible without a biblical catechesis of the Christian community. In various ways it was the

[8] *AAS* 50 (1958) 630–63.
[9] *AAS* 48 (1956) 711–25.

biblical movement that gave the liturgical movement the depth and authenticity it needed.

Shortly before the death of Pope Pius XII, the Sacred Congregation of Rites issued its instruction of September 3, 1958, to which reference has already been made. The instruction was prepared by the pontifical commission for the liturgical reform working in conjunction with various experts in sacred music. In addition to its treatment of the nature of the liturgy, liturgical language, and the active participation of the faithful, the document summarized the significant work that had been accomplished in the area of pastoral liturgy during the pontificate of Pius XII.

Pope Pius XII died on October 9, 1958. Following the accession of Pope John XXIII to the papacy on October 28, 1958, the commission for the restoration of the liturgy was retained. The Holy Father announced plans for an ecumenical council on January 25, 1959, and on June 5, 1960, he appointed a new pontifical liturgical commission and entrusted to it the preparation for the Second Vatican Council. Cardinal Gaetano Cicognani, prefect of the Sacred Congregation of Rites, was named president of that commission. The prefects of the various Congregations of the Roman curia were named presidents of the corresponding conciliar preparatory commissions; however, no other members of the Roman dicasteries were to be members of the preparatory commissions in order that the commissions could work freely in preparing their material for the Council.

On June 18, 1959, Cardinal Tardini, president of the general preparatory commission, had sent a circular letter to the cardinals, bishops, and heads of religious orders asking for their suggestions for the Council. On July 9, 1960, he gave Cardinal Cicognani the report listing the themes to be treated by the Council concerning the liturgy as suggested by the letters from the world's bishops and heads of religious orders. There were seven major topics: revision of the calendar, the Mass, sacred rites, sacraments, the breviary, liturgical language, and liturgical vesture. On July 11, 1960, Father Annibale Bugnini, C.M., was appointed secretary of the preparatory liturgical commission.

There was a widespread feeling that a provisional correction of the rubrics should be implemented even before the Council discussed the more basic liturgical issues. Consequently, Pope John promulgated a new code of rubrics on July 26, 1960.[10] This new code filled an immediate need for rubrics that were sounder from a theological point of view; the document also cleared the way for the Council itself to address the most important liturgical problems rather than the secondary details of celebration.

In the motu proprio introducing the new code of rubrics, Pope John stated the relation between the reforms that had begun with the memorandum of 1948 and the reforms of the forthcoming ecumenical Council:

> After we had decided, under the inspiration of God, to convene an ecumenical council, we turned over in our mind what was to be done about this project begun by our predecessor. After mature reflection, we came to the conclusion that the more important principles governing a general liturgical reform should be laid before the members of the hierarchy at the forthcoming ecumenical council, but that the above-mentioned improvement of the rubrics of the breviary and missal should no longer be put off.[11]

The basic principles of liturgical reform set forth in the 1948 memorandum formed the foundation of the schema for the liturgy that was eventually presented to the Council Fathers.

One other significant publication before the first session of the Council was a new edition of the second part of the *Pontificale Romanum*, issued by the Sacred Congregation of Rites on April 13, 1961.[12] It included, among other things, a simplification of the rite for the consecration of a church.

Unlike the other preconciliar commissions that had been established to prepare the Council agenda, the liturgical commission faced issues that had already been quite clearly formulated in the preceding fifteen years. Four points in particular had come to the surface: the desire and the need for vernacular in the liturgy, the pastoral character of the liturgy, its importance in missionary countries, and the desire for concelebration.[13]

As the liturgical apostolate had progressed from country to coun-

---

[10] *AAS* 52 (1960) 593–95.
[11] *AAS* 52 (1960) 595.
[12] *AAS* 54 (1962) 52.
[13] See P.-M. Gy, "Esquisse historique," *La Maison-Dieu*, no. 76 (1963) 7–17.

try, the general conviction had grown that the liturgy is by its very nature intrinsically pastoral. During the Assisi-Rome Congress, it had become evident that the liturgical movement had assumed universal proportions. Likewise, during discussions of missionary and catechetical topics at important congresses held at Nijmegen and Eichstätt, and through the zeal of various missionary bishops and the effective apostolate of Father Johannes Hofinger, it had become quite clear that missionary activity must incorporate vital celebrations of liturgy. As the movement spread, however, it became apparent that serious obstacles had to be overcome before renewal on a deep level could really take place. This was surely the case with the question of the use of the vernacular in the liturgy. Although bilingual rituals had been approved for use in many countries and other concessions had been made for missionary territories, the vernacular proclamation of the liturgy of the Word in the Eucharist was still excluded.

Major obstacles also stood in the way of restoring a rite of concelebration. It seems that permission for concelebration was seriously considered in 1955 for the celebration of the Holy Thursday liturgy; it was surely considered for the anniversary celebrations at Lourdes in 1957; but official action was delayed in light of the complicated theological controversies occasioned by Karl Rahner's writings, and also because of the prevalence of a rigid kind of Eucharistic piety that looked upon concelebration as an encroachment on each priest's right to celebrate Mass privately. For various reasons, then, the possible restoration of concelebration in the West was frowned upon as a disturbing innovation. Although Pope Pius XII had tried to clarify the theological foundations for concelebration in the allocution he gave to those attending the Assisi-Rome Congress, an actual rite was never formulated.

Although it would have seemed logical for Pope John to look to the countries where the liturgical reform had made the most advances when naming the personnel to serve on the preconciliar commission on the liturgy, this does not seem to have been the case. The competent liturgists among the German and French bishops and the various staff members of the liturgical centers at Paris and Trier were not included at first, but when it became evident that their assistance was sorely needed, the following were named to the commission: Bishop Jenny of Cambrai, France; Bishop O. Spuelbeck of Meissen, East Germany; Fathers A.-M. Roguet and A.-G. Martimort from the Centre de Pastorale Liturgique in Paris; and Monsignor Johannes Wagner, director of the Liturgical Institute at Trier. When the membership of the preparatory liturgical commission was first announced on August 22, 1960, there were eighteen members and twenty-nine consultants. The final membership achieved by September 2, 1961, consisted of twenty-six members and thirty-seven consultors. In recruiting the full membership of the commission, the president, Cardinal Cicognani, ultimately tried to secure the services of the most competent liturgists and also to ensure a balanced representation from the various parts of the Western Church. The choice of Father Bugnini as secretary was especially fortunate, for he proved himself to be an efficient organizer with an open mind and a sound pastoral sense.

The achievements of the commission were described by Father Bugnini in an article written for *L'Osservatore Romano* on March 5-6, 1962.[14] The work was divided among various subcommittees, which spent four months of intensive work on the thirteen divisions of the proposed schema. The preliminary text went through four drafts. At its plenary session on January 11, 1962, the preparatory liturgical commission unanimously approved the fourth draft and gave it to the president of the commission, Cardinal Cicognani.

In preparing a document to be presented to the Council Fathers, the liturgical commission had to face two serious questions. Should the text be confined to a treatment of the Latin liturgy, or should it address the other Catholic liturgies as well? The second issue concerned the general orientation of the document: Should it be cast primarily in a juridical framework, or should it attempt to provide a theological rationale for its decisions on practical matters?

The first question was of prime importance, for this was to be an ecumenical council and not a council of the Latin Church alone. The objection that an ecumenical council should not consider the reformation of a single rite in the Church seemed to be a legitimate objection. Since most of the Council Fathers belonged to the Latin rite, discussion on various topics would naturally tend to be one-

---

[14] "L'opera del Card. Gaetano Cicognani per il rinnovamento liturgico dell' ultimo decennio," p. 2.

sided. Furthermore, it was not agreed that members of other rites should take part in the discussions and vote on the reform of the Latin rite. In retrospect, however, it seems that often objections of this kind were raised not so much out of concern for the Eastern rites as out of a desire on the part of certain Western ecclesiastics to defeat a reform in the liturgy of the Latin rite. When the Council actually assembled, the Fathers from the Eastern rites expressed their willingness to consider the reform of the Latin rite, because they recognized that the theological principles underlying the liturgical reform of one rite are in some ways applicable to all rites and hence are useful for the whole Church.

The solution proposed to the second problem was readily accepted: the schema was to be both disciplinary and doctrinal, or in canonical language, it should be a constitution rather than a simple decree. In this regard, it was unfortunate that there was not collaboration between the liturgical commission and the theological commission in preparing the document. It seems, however, that the theological commission was unwilling to cooperate.

The actual style in which the schema was to be cast raised another problem. The documents that had been submitted to the Council Fathers at Trent and Vatican I were generally expressed in biblical and patristic language, and attempted as far as possible to abstract from theological disputes. However, since Pope Pius XII's encyclicals *Mystici Corporis* and *Mediator Dei* and other recent decrees of the Holy See did in fact deal with the contemporary theological aspects of the Church and its liturgy, it did not seem at all possible to maintain a discreet distance from the theological issues raised by the modern liturgical movement. It was finally agreed that the traditional conciliar style of a constitution would be adopted, but theological issues would be discussed where necessary. In other words, in its foundational language the constitution would be biblical and patristic, but certain general theological and canonical precisions would also be made.

Another problem to be considered was the amount of detail to be incorporated into the constitution. On the one hand, the enactment of a detailed disciplinary program was not the work of an ecumenical council, but on the other hand it was highly desirable to have a definite program of reform agreed upon so as to ensure implementation. The end result was a schema outlining the general principles of reform and a detailed list of *declarationes* explaining the text for the Council Fathers. Although the *declarationes* are not binding on the postconciliar Church, they are really the foundation for the schema and hence do indicate the broad lines of interpretation that should be given to the Constitution on the Sacred Liturgy.

The text that was presented to Cardinal Cicognani contained eight chapters: (1) general principles for renewal and development of the liturgy; (2) the Eucharist; (3) the sacraments and sacramentals; (4) the divine office; (5) the liturgical year; (6) sacred furnishings; (7) sacred music; (8) sacred art. Since the program of reform was so extensive, Cardinal Cicognani initially hesitated to sign the document. He finally signed it on February 1, 1962, just a few days before his death.

Cardinal A. M. Larraona, a Spanish Claretian long associated with both the canon law faculty at the Lateran and the Congregation for Religious, was appointed as Cardinal Cicognani's successor on February 22, 1962. The appointment was not a good one, since it seems that Cardinal Larraona did not possess any real comprehension of the true nature of liturgical reform. In fact, in the beginning he was clearly opposed to the reform of the liturgy and consequently often proved to be an annoying obstacle in the work of renewal.

Also on February 22, Pope John XXIII promulgated the curious apostolic constitution *Veterum sapientia*, which forbade any opposition to the use of Latin in the Roman liturgy.[15] Bishops and religious superiors were directed to see that no one wrote against the use of Latin in the liturgical rites. During the same month, Father Annibale Bugnini, secretary of the preparatory liturgical commission and its acting head after the death of Cardinal Cicognani, was removed from his teaching position in liturgy at the Pontifical Lateran Athenaeum. When the conciliar liturgical commission was named, he was not appointed secretary. The schema for the liturgy, which had been prepared under his direction, had advocated a limited use of vernacular in the liturgy.

[15] *AAS* 54 (1962) 129–35.

Chapter 2

THE SECOND VATICAN COUNCIL

The Second Vatican Council opened on October 11, 1962. The first three general congregations of the Council were devoted to the election of the conciliar commissions. Six of the bishops elected to the conciliar commission for the liturgy, including Cardinal Giacomo Lercaro and Bishop G. van Bekkum, had served as members of the preparatory commission. Father Ferdinand Antonelli, a Franciscan who had served on the commission to study liturgical reform set up by Pope Pius XII, was named secretary.

The Council began its discussion on the liturgy schema on October 22, 1962. It was presented to the Council Fathers by Father Antonelli. He outlined the general principles that had guided the commission in writing the schema. The text was then discussed at fifteen general congregations of the Council from October 22 to November 13. There were 328 oral interventions and more than the same number of written submissions. Although the debate was often repetitious and was quite poorly organized, it did have the advantage of familiarizing the Fathers who were often not informed on liturgical matters with the rationale underlying the schema, and it gave them the chance to become abreast of liturgical developments in various parts of the world. Much to the surprise of many of the Roman curial officials, it was soon apparent that the desire for liturgical reform was generally quite strong among the Council Fathers. Those who had come from missionary countries and from

17

Latin America were especially vocal in their demands for the vernacular and for adaptation of the liturgy to the diverse cultures of
the world.

The question of liturgical language was prominent in the Council
debate. In discussing communion under both kinds, care was taken
not to contradict the teaching of the Council of Trent on the matter.
There were many conflicting views on the question of the reform of
the liturgy of the hours. The topic proved especially difficult
because of the absence of clearly defined criteria to be used in
evaluating proposals. Finally, it is interesting to note that although
sacred music plays an important role in the celebration of the liturgy
and was thought significant enough by some of the Council Fathers
to claim a central place in the liturgy document, the whole question
attracted very little comment during the actual discussions, probably because the Fathers themselves knew very little about the
subject.

On November 14, 1962, the Council Fathers approved in principle the liturgy schema. The vote was 2,162 to 46. The conciliar commission then set about the arduous task of analyzing the various
written observations of the Fathers and preparing the amendments
that were generally desired. Between November 17 and December
6, 1962, the proposed amendments to articles 1 to 46 were voted
upon. Chapters 2 to 8 were then revised between the first and second
sessions of the Council.

Each chapter of the constitution was submitted to a final vote.
The terms were *placet, placet iuxta modum,* and *non placet.*
Although votes *iuxta modum* were counted as *placet,* the commission had to inform the Fathers of the nature of the various *modi.* In
several cases where there were many qualified votes, the commission
actually presented a new amendment to the Fathers for a vote. For
example, since there were 781 votes *placet iuxta modum* on the
chapter on the Eucharist, the commission decided to make a special
amendment indicating that the regulation of the discipline of concelebration in a diocese pertains to the local bishop. Likewise, since
the vote on the chapter on the other sacraments was 1,054 votes
placet iuxta modum, the commission decided to give the episcopal
conferences the right to choose the language of the sacraments. The
final vote on the whole constitution was taken on November 22,

1963. Since so much care was taken in revising and voting on the various sections of the constitution, it cannot truthfully be said that the Council Fathers did not in fact know what they were doing when they approved the document.

The various amendments made to the Constitution on the Sacred Liturgy seem to fall into two broad categories. The one class was doctrinal, aimed at ensuring continuity between the teachings of the Council of Trent and the Second Vatican Council; the other category was pastoral.

If the teaching of the Second Vatican Council seems to complement the documents of the First Vatican Council from the point of view of ecclesiology, in matters of liturgy and sacramental theology it may be compared with the teaching of the Council of Trent. In our own time there is generally little need for the Catholic Church to defend her sacramental theology against the attack of Reformers; in fact, it is generally acknowledged that a number of the liturgical insights of the Reformers were quite correct. Protestant observers at the Second Vatican Council were impressed and pleased at seeing such a manifestation of humility and truthfulness on the part of many of the Council Fathers. Ecumenical dialogues today attempt to discern the areas in sacramental theology and practice where the stands of Catholics and those in the Reformed traditions may in fact be reconciled. Nevertheless, the Fathers of Vatican II were concerned lest the impression be conveyed that the Church could reverse the positions that were taken at Trent. It was for this reason that several amendments emphasizing the sacrificial dimension of the Eucharist, asserted so strongly at Trent, were inserted into the second chapter of the constitution. Some of the Fathers were concerned lest this aspect of the Eucharist be overshadowed in the constitution by the lengthy consideration of the Mass as a meal.

From a pastoral point of view, the Fathers realized that the Council must not only provide for the immediate needs of the Church but must also anticipate future developments. Changes that are too radical can be pastorally debilitating; however, provision must be made for progressive evolution of the Church's institutions. It is in this sense that the Constitution on the Sacred Liturgy is especially pastoral. In this regard, Edward Schillebeeckx remarked that some theologians

. . . interpreted the affirmation of the pastoral orientation of the Council in a purely *pragmatic* sense, a pastoral care which is less concerned with the truth, or at any rate the formulation of the truth, than with the fully existential experience of faith, for which a vague indication of the context of belief would suffice. . . . The fact that today's modern language is "dated" tomorrow simply implies that expressing the truth is a never-ending task which has to be begun anew all the time, but it is quite out of the question that one could ever hope to promote a certain historical interpretation to the status of a timeless statement that could of itself provide an absolute formulation of the faith. . . . This . . . is the painful mistake people make who think the Church "must speak its own language" (which it must) but who then identify that language with one particular phase of the perennially new language of revelation. . . . The Catholic Church must undoubtedly speak its own language, and it should not, in the name of irenics, speak a language alien to it. But the Church's own language is the ever-changing language of the people, only cast in the idiom of the one revelation and also, as a negative norm, in the language of the Bible.[1]

During the years since the Constitution on the Sacred Liturgy was promulgated, its theological content has been analyzed in detail. The basic ecclesiology running through the document is an ecclesiology of communion in contrast to a socio-juridical ecclesiology that views the Church as a society, a supernatural society with all the characteristics of a perfect group.[2] In the Constitution on the Sacred Liturgy, the Church is a communion of divine life that the Father communicates to his people in his Son Jesus Christ through the power of the Spirit. Not only are people united with the Father through the Spirit but they are also united among themselves. The social structures of the Church exist, not because they have been clearly specified by God, but because structures are needed to support and challenge the life of communion. They should be thought of, then, not in the sense that they have been imposed by God as immutable, but as capable of adjustment so that they may achieve the end for which they were instituted in the first place. This applies

[1] "The Second Vatican Council," *The Layman in the Church* (New York: Alba House, 1963) 22–26.

[2] Cipriano Vagaggini, "Riflessioni in Prospettiva Teologica sui Dieci Anni di Riforma Liturgica," *Rivista Liturgica* 61, no. 1 (January–February 1974) 36–37.

also to symbols and rites that are meant to express and deepen the Church's life of communion.

The Church as a communion must be situated in the theological framework of the theandric concept of the Church as the Body of Christ, the incarnate Son of God. As the constitution states, "It is of the essence of the Church that she be both human and divine, visible and yet invisibly endowed, eager to act and yet devoted to contemplation, present in this world and yet not at home in it. She is all these things in such a way that in her the human is directed and subordinated to the divine, the visible likewise to the invisible, action to contemplation, and this present world to that city yet to come. . . ."[3]

It is only in the perspective of the incarnation and the Church as the Body of Christ, as the basic sacrament of salvation, that the liturgy, the seven sacraments, the communal celebrations, and the concept of the liturgy as the source and summit of all the rest make any sense. The basic concept is always the Church as the expression, continuation, and life of the Son of God incarnate. The Church is always human and divine, but the determining element is the divine, which communicates with the human in order to transform it.

The principles that were operative in the liturgical movement were certainly operative in the formulation of the Constitution on the Sacred Liturgy. They also had an effect on other conciliar documents, especially the Constitution on the Church and the Constitution on the Church in the Modern World. If the liturgy is really the cultural expression of the Church in the world, it would have been more logical for the Council Fathers first to formulate the Constitution on the Church in the Modern World, then proceed to the Constitution on the Church, and finally to the Constitution on the Sacred Liturgy. The influence was in the reverse order.

In the Constitution on the Church, account is taken of the Church as a community.[4] Likewise, importance is given to the ministry of the Word in the life of the hierarchy and in the mission of the whole Church.[5] The Decree on the Oriental Churches takes a broad ap-

---

[3] *Sacrosanctum Concilium*, no. 2: *AAS* 56 (1964) 103.

[4] *Lumen gentium*, chs. 1, 2: *AAS* 57 (1965) 5–21.

[5] *Lumen gentium*, nos. 19, 20: *AAS* 57 (1965) 22–23.

proach to liturgical questions. It approaches rite in the sense of discipline, spirituality, and theological tradition, and affirms that liturgical and ritual pluralism is a normal phenomenon in the Church, not a privilege or the result of canonical exemption.[6]

The Decree on Ecumenism touches on important liturgical problems. The document asserts that ecumenical associations have good effects. They are based on the primacy of God's Word in Christian life and faith as a dedication of the whole person to Christ, who is supreme in the life of all Christians.[7] This affirmation is important in relating the life and person of the Blessed Virgin and the saints to the total Christian economy.

Both the Declaration on Non-Christian Religions and the Decree on Missionary Activity in the Church touch on the issue of acculturation, even in the liturgical life of the Church.[8] They stress the positive value of non-Christian religions and the various cultures throughout the world.

The Decree on the Ministry and Life of Priests gives a much more balanced view of the priest than the Constitution on the Church does.[9] It reiterates the Tridentine definition of orders as the "power to offer sacrifice and to remit sins," but it widens the scope of priestly ministry to include "participation in the authority by which Christ Himself builds up, sanctifies and rules His Body." The basis of the priestly character, then, is an inner dynamic relationship with Christ as head of his Body and source of authority and unity in the Church. Standing in the place of Christ, the priest has a creative, unifying role, a service of reconciliation within the Christian community and an ordering of other ministries. He shares in the authority of Christ in the sense that he is capable of authoring God's life in others because God has first begotten the life of Christ in him through the gift of his Spirit.

The Constitution on the Church in the Modern World was the last document promulgated by the Second Vatican Council. It has many

---

[6] *Orientalium Ecclesiarum*, nos. 1–6: AAS 57 (1965) 76–78.

[7] *Unitatis redintegratio*, ch. 1: AAS 57 (1965) 91–96.

[8] *Nostra aetate*: AAS 59 (1966) 740–44; *Ad gentes*, nos. 14, 19, 22, 26: AAS 58 (1966) 966–78.

[9] *Presbyterorum ordinis*, ch. 1: AAS 58 (1966) 992.

implications for the liturgy.[10] By raising the problems that the Church must confront in the modern world and by stressing the need for a proper relationship between the Church and contemporary culture, the constitution implicitly raises issues that have become acute in the liturgical reform since the Council. These include the question of liturgy and indigenization, liturgy and secularization, and liturgy and social and political responsibility.

From what has been said, it should be clear that one looks for the ecclesiology of the Second Vatican Council not only in *Lumen gentium* but also in the Constitution on the Sacred Liturgy and the Constitution on the Church in the Modern World. Likewise, one looks for the ecclesiological, theological, and anthropological foundations for the liturgy not only in the Constitution on the Sacred Liturgy but in the other conciliar documents as well. The liturgy is incomprehensible without its anthropological and general theological framework; hence the concept of the liturgy and the principles of liturgical reform that derive from the Constitution on the Sacred Liturgy ought to be integrated with the ecclesiological, anthropological, and theological principles which, while being less apparent in *Sacrosanctum Concilium*, are more developed in the other conciliar documents. The consequences that these principles can have on the understanding of the liturgy and its reform are significant.[11]

Pope Paul VI, who as the archbishop of Milan had given the liturgy schema his support on the first day of the conciliar debate, October 22, 1962, promulgated the Constitution on the Sacred Liturgy as supreme head of the Church on December 4, 1963.[12] The final vote on the document by the Council Fathers had been 2,147 *placet* and 4 *non placet*. All the disciplinary sections of the constitution that could be implemented immediately were to go into effect on that date. Those parts that were dependent on various reform projects yet to be developed naturally had to be postponed.

On January 25, 1964, the Pope issued a motu proprio, *Sacram liturgiam*, which implemented certain additional parts of the constitution. Mystery surrounds the writing and the release of that

---

[10] *Gaudium et spes: AAS* 58 (1966) 1025–1115, esp. nos. 38, 48, 49, 52, 58, 62.

[11] Vagaggini, *art. cit.*, 40–42.

[12] *AAS* 56 (1964) 97–138.

document. The initial text of the motu proprio was drawn up by the Sacred Congregation of Rites under the direction of Cardinal Larraona and Father Antonelli. Apparently the first draft did not meet with the Pope's complete approval. When it was finally issued, the document was castigated by many liturgists in the Church as a betrayal of the Council Fathers, who had given almost unanimous approval to the Constitution on the Sacred Liturgy. The text failed to say anything about specific changes in the Mass that had been contemplated, and it actually contradicted the Constitution on the Sacred Liturgy in regard to the kind of approval needed for vernacular texts. Whereas the constitution authorized regional conferences of bishops to choose and approve such texts, the motu proprio stipulated that such translations must be submitted to the Holy See for approval. Cardinal Larraona, prefect of the Congregation of Rites, let it be known that he was not responsible for the wording of the change. He also noted that a number of members of the Holy Office had had access to the Pope while the motu proprio lay on his desk waiting for his approval.

The original text of the document appeared in *L'Osservatore Romano* on January 29, 1964. The following day the paper carried an article by the Benedictine liturgist Salvatore Marsili.[13] He said quite frankly that the motu proprio conceded very little. His article contained a number of significant insights. He noted that the constitution on the liturgy was not intended to be a code of rubrics; as a document built on contemporary theological foundations, it called for a change of outlook in ceremonial matters. He stressed the need for a certain flexibility in liturgical matters and the desirability of accommodating the liturgy so as to provide for complex and varying spiritual needs throughout the Church and the world. The whole tenor of the article gave the clear impression that it was aimed at the members of the Congregation of Rites and other curial prelates who did not seem to grasp at all the pastoral thrust of the Constitution on the Sacred Liturgy. For writing so daring an article, Father Marsili was relieved of his teaching posts and literally banished from Rome. Sometime later he was rescued by Cardinal Lercaro and restored to his former academic positions in Rome.

---

[13] "I primi passi della riforma liturgica," p. 2.

Since the French, German, and Belgian hierarchies had authorized vernacular versions of the Mass and sacraments in early January 1964, they made strong protests to the Pope about the motu proprio. After considerable wrangling within the Roman curia, a revised final version of the motu proprio was prepared and printed in the *Acta Apostolicae Sedis.*[14] In its final form *Sacram liturgiam* still skirted the issue of the submission of vernacular versions to the Holy See for confirmation, but all those phrases that had been introduced to give the impression that the basis for the liturgical changes was the Pope's kind disposition and not the liturgy constitution were deleted.

[14] Vol. 56 (1964) 139–44.

Chapter 3

IMPLEMENTATION OF THE CONSTITUTION
ON THE SACRED LITURGY

The Fathers of the Second Vatican Council left the implementation of the principles and decrees concerning the liturgy to the Holy Father, just as the Fathers of the Council of Trent had done in 1563. The plan was that the revision of the liturgical books should be undertaken by a special postconciliar commission rather than by the Congregation of Rites, which had supervised the development of liturgical books since 1588. The Constitution on the Sacred Liturgy specified that experts were to be employed and bishops were to be consulted, both groups being representative of the various parts of the world.[1]

The commission was established by Pope Paul through his motu proprio *Sacram liturgiam*, of January 25, 1964. It was called the Council for the Implementation of the Constitution on the Sacred Liturgy, or simply the Consilium. When the Pope announced the membership, most liturgists were pleased, for they recognized the competency of most of the men appointed. Cardinal Lercaro was named the first president, followed later by Benedictine Cardinal Benno Gut. Father Annibale Bugnini was named secretary.

The establishment of this commission was looked upon as an important step in acknowledging the collegial character of the

[1] *Sacrosanctum Concilium*, no. 25: AAS 56 (1964) 107.

episcopacy. The Constitution on the Sacred Liturgy stressed that the bishops are co-responsible along with the pope for directing the worship of the Church. For three and a half centuries following the Council of Trent, the Congregation of Rites had exercised almost exclusive control over liturgical matters. It was natural that various members of that Congregation should strive hard to retain their power over the Church's worship. The relationship between the Congregation and the Consilium was strained in various ways.

The association was defined in a compromise. The Consilium was described primarily as a study body. Its various experts were assigned by subject matter to specific subcommittees called *coetus studiorum*. The texts that the Consilium developed were submitted to the Congregation of Rites and were issued by that dicastery over the signatures of both the president of the Consilium and the prefect of the Congregation of Rites. In general, then, the Consilium did not promulgate the results of its own work; however, it did have the authority to carry out and permit experimentation with a view to the revision of the rites, and it was also responsible for the Holy See's confirmation of decisions taken by episcopal conferences in liturgical matters, especially the approval of vernacular translations.

In 1965 the Consilium initiated a monthly journal called *Notitiae*. In a prefatory note to the first issue, Cardinal Lercaro described the goal of the journal as primarily informative.[2] It was intended first of all to help the members and consultors of the Consilium keep abreast of the various projects undertaken by the Consilium itself. Secondly, it was meant to inform national and diocesan liturgy commissions and liturgical centers about the activity of the Consilium. Thirdly, it was to provide liturgical and pastoral periodicals with information about the progress of liturgical renewal. Fourthly, it was to carry the texts of various documents emanating from official authorities, especially the Congregation of Rites, and to explain such documents. Finally, it was to promote liturgical understanding and renewal by various studies. The Cardinal insisted that the periodical was intended primarily to be informational rather than formative. In other words, it was not official nor were its views meant to be

[2] Vol. 1 (1965) 3–5.

binding in any way. This is especially true of answers to various questions that have been given.

The principal work of the Consilium was the reform of the Roman liturgical books, since the revision of the various liturgical rites was thought to be the most effective means to bring about the liturgical renewal called for by the Constitution on the Sacred Liturgy. Since the implementation of new rites must be accompanied by liturgical catechesis, the Consilium also was charged with the preparation of doctrinal background for the proposed changes. This it did in a series of instructions that were substantially doctrinal and supporting but basically pragmatic. Two instructions were issued by the Congregation of Rites, in 1964 and 1967, and one was issued by the Congregation for Divine Worship in 1970.

The first instruction, *Inter Oecumenici*, was dated September 26, 1964, and went into effect on March 7, 1965, the first Sunday of Lent.[3] Its structure more or less followed the plan of the Constitution on the Sacred Liturgy. It provided general norms and detailed regulations on the Eucharist, the other sacraments and sacramentals, the divine office, and the building of churches. In particular, it defined more clearly the function of the bodies of bishops in liturgical matters.

Of particular importance was chapter five of the instruction, devoted to norms to be followed in the construction and adaptation of churches. Number 91 stated that the altar was to be so constructed as to facilitate the celebration of Mass facing the congregation. Number 92 dealt with the seat for the celebrant. It stated that it should be so placed that the celebrant could easily be seen by the faithful and appear to preside over the entire community.

The second instruction, *Tres abhinc annos*, was dated May 4, 1967, and went into effect on June 29, 1967.[4] A number of issues in the instruction required action by the episcopal conference, such as the use of a color other than purple or black for requiem celebrations (no. 23); addition of an intention to the prayer of the faithful throughout a country (no. 6); and the use of the vernacular in the canon of the Mass, in ordinations, and in the readings of the choral office (no. 28).

[3] *AAS* 56 (1964) 877–900.
[4] *AAS* 59 (1967) 442–48.

The rubrical provisions included both changes and optional variants left to the judgment of the celebrant. For example, the number of genuflections, kisses of the altar, and crosses over the offerings was greatly reduced. The celebrant was not required to join his thumbs and forefingers after the consecration. Provision was made for a period of silence, a psalm, or a canticle of praise after the ablutions following communion. All separate commemorations in addition to the one required collect, prayer over the gifts, and postcommunion were suppressed. Permission was given to omit the maniple and to wear the chasuble for the *Asperges*, distribution of ashes before Mass, and for absolution for the dead after the Mass.

The instruction also shortened certain parts of the divine office by permitting the omission of two of the three nocturns on first- and second-class days. It also suppressed the absolution and blessings before the readings and the conclusion *Tu autem* in the individual recitation of the divine office.

The third instruction, entitled *Liturgicae instaurationes*, was issued by the Sacred Congregation for Divine Worship on September 5, 1970, and went into effect immediately.[5] The document proposed some norms that were restrictive and inflexible. They were not really new, since they had appeared in other instructions dealing with specific liturgical matters since 1964, such as the discipline concerning communion under two species.

A very encouraging feature of this instruction was its urgent recommendation that bishops provide positive leadership for their priests and people in the area of liturgical renewal. They were reminded that they do not fulfill their responsibility simply by ensuring an integral observance of the clearly prescribed disciplinary norms in the area of liturgy. With the help of their liturgical commissions, they were directed to evaluate the pastoral situation in their dioceses and determine what fosters and what inhibits genuine liturgical renewal. In light of their findings they were instructed to engage in the wise and prudent work of persuasion and direction. The instruction noted that it is easier for priests to work together in hierarchical fellowship if the bishop is knowledgeable and is able to stimulate pastoral activity as well as to correct abuses.

Priests were reminded by the instruction that genuine liturgical

---

[5] *AAS* 62 (1970) 692–704.

renewal is not achieved by arbitrary personal innovations that tend to undermine the genuine character and unity of the Church's worship. The instruction maintained that the Roman Missal, published in June 1970, provides sufficient choice of texts to meet any pastoral situation or need. Basically this is true, but use of the new Roman Missal has shown that the repertory of texts needs to be augmented with texts that more effectively reflect the contemporary understanding and experience of Christian theology and worship. While there might well be more scope for improvisation in accord with pastoral needs, most celebrants do not have adequate theological and liturgical formation to warrant a departure from the norm and texts of the Roman Missal.

It should be noted here that the declaration on the vernacular translations of new liturgical texts that was issued by the Sacred Congregation for Divine Worship on September 15, 1969, formally stated that new texts are necessary but should be created only after the discipline of translating the Latin books has been experienced.[6] Likewise, the new ritual books, in their introductions, almost always speak of new texts prepared by authority of episcopal conferences.

From 1964 to 1970 a certain fluidity had existed in the order of Mass. During that time interim guidelines were issued, but a complete revision did not appear until the publication of the new missal in June 1970. With the instruction of September 5, 1970, the Congregation for Divine Worship wanted to ensure proper usage of the missal and to clarify its position concerning certain other rites that were either arbitrarily introduced or implemented by indult.

A number of the norms in the instruction dealt specifically with the liturgy of the Word. Number 2 specified that non-biblical readings, whether religious or secular, may not be substituted for the biblical readings, nor may the proclamation of the Word be reduced to a single reading. As a general norm this is certainly sound, but it should not have been stated in an inflexible manner. What is important is that God's Word be effectively proclaimed in every celebration. In some instances a single lengthy reading from the gospel might more effectively stir up the faith of the community than two or three shorter readings. Exception to the norm was made

[6] *Notitiae* 5 (1969) 333–34.

in the Directory for Children's Masses, issued on November 1, 1973. There number 41 asserts that a children's Mass should never be celebrated without a Bible reading, since the Scripture readings constitute the main part of the liturgy of the Word. The following norm stipulates that the number of readings on Sundays and feast days may be reduced to only one or two if the two or three readings appointed for those days seem too lengthy. The gospel reading, however, should never be omitted.

The instruction of September 5, 1970, clearly did not prohibit the addition of non-biblical readings, provided the biblical readings are retained. Carefully chosen non-biblical readings may effectively mediate God's Word and help people to realize that God speaks in their own lives, indeed in and through their own secular experience. The danger, of course, is that the liturgy of the Word will become excessively protracted or some people will come to the false conclusion that what is more is better. However, experience has already shown that the effective use of multimedia, above all within the context of the liturgy of the Word, can be a powerful way of bringing God's Word to life in a celebration.

The instruction reserves the homily to the priest and prohibits comments by the faithful. This restriction is unfortunate. It is certainly the celebrant's role to preside over the liturgy of the Word; likewise, he bears the major responsibility for mediating God's Word. The licensing of preachers is surely a valuable tradition in the Roman Catholic Church, but licensing alone does not ensure competent preaching of the Word.

Experience over the past fifteen years has shown that there are many men and women in the Church who are well trained and competent to share God's Word with his people but who are not licensed to preach. The celebrant's words are not the only words through which God may speak. Experience has also shown that in small groups and in informal settings, a dialogue homily can be a very effective way of sharing God's Word with the community. On such occasions the celebrant, as well as those who intend to dialogue, should not excuse themselves from serious preparation and reflection on the readings. Again, experience has shown that on some occasions it is more appropriate for some member of the community other than the celebrant to give the homily. This is often the case in com-

munities of women religious where sisters are highly trained in
Scripture, theology, and liturgy but the chaplain is either semi-
retired or theologically and liturgically out of date. It should be
noted here that alternatives to the formal homily by the priest or
deacon are mentioned in the Directory for Masses with Children[7]
and in the introduction to the rite for confirmation.[8]

The instruction repeats the basic teaching of the Constitution on
the Sacred Liturgy that the liturgy of the Word and the Eucharistic
action form one act of worship.[9] Although the instruction states that
they should not be celebrated separately at different times or in different places, this principle should not be inflexibly applied. Experience has shown that communities comprised of people of diverse
ages and backgrounds can experience a more effective celebration of
the Word if the group is divided into homogeneous subgroups for the
liturgy of the Word; these subgroups then come together in one
place for the Eucharistic action. It is surely a challenge today to give
an effective homily to young children, teenagers, young married
couples, middle-aged people, and those advanced in age, all
gathered together in one assembly. Furthermore, experience has
shown that in home celebrations, it is often effective to celebrate the
liturgy of the Word in one room where the people are able to sit
comfortably and then move to another room for the Eucharistic
action.

With regard to the prayer of the faithful, the instruction comments on the desirability of adding some intentions for the local
community, but it does not seem to permit the spontaneous offering
of intentions by members of the community. Again, experience has
shown that this is common and natural in small community celebrations. It is the responsibility of the celebrant, however, to ensure
that in all liturgies there is a genuinely ecclesial dimension to the
prayer of the faithful whenever it is celebrated.

In its fourth norm the instruction insists that the Eucharistic
prayer is assigned to the celebrant alone. In some places the practice
has developed whereby the whole congregation recites some or all of
the text. Certainly this is contrary to the hierarchical structure of the

[7] No. 48: AAS 66 (1974) 44.
[8] No. 18: Notitiae 7 (1971) 346.
[9] No. 56: AAS 56 (1964) 115.

liturgy, according to which each participant carries out the role that is properly assigned; it likewise violates the structure of the approved Eucharistic texts, which were never meant to be chorally proclaimed. Perhaps the common practice does indicate the desirability of creating other Eucharistic prayers so structured that the people have more involvement in the text by means of more frequent acclamations. The approved canons for Masses with children do in fact allow for more frequent involvement by those participating. Even the recitation of the doxology by the whole community seems to make the great "Amen" anti-climactic and to violate the structure of the text by making the community respond to and affirm its own doxology.

In the fifth norm the instruction insists that the bread used for the Eucharist should appear as actual food, but it must always be made in the traditional form. For most people, small white wafers do not look like food. This norm is in accord with the most important General Instruction of the Roman Missal, also issued in 1970, which is insistent that if the bread is to signify effectively the meaning it is intended to convey, it must really look like food. Experience since the publication of the General Instruction has shown that loaves, rather than small wafers, are sometimes more appropriate, especially with small groups.

The seventh norm of the instruction, in keeping with number 66 of the General Instruction of the Roman Missal, provides for some relaxation in the Roman discipline concerning the role of women in the liturgy. They may proclaim the Scripture readings, with the exception of the gospel, offer the intentions for the prayer of the faithful, lead the congregation in singing, play approved musical instruments, and serve as commentator and usher. It is curious that they may not serve the priest at the altar and yet may proclaim the Scriptures; the latter role would seem to be a much more honorable function than the former. In the last few years, many have questioned the justice of the Church's legislation concerning the role of women in the liturgy and in the Church. It seems likely that they will not only rightly claim but also be given a fuller role in the Church's worship in the years ahead.

Norms 8, 9, and 10 of the instruction are concerned with the vesture, vessels, sacred furnishings, and sacred places for the celebration of the liturgy. While allowing for greater freedom in the matter of material and designs, representing different cultures and artistic gifts, the instruction calls for durability and good quality in everything that is used. It is unfortunate that the practice of wearing only a stole over the monastic cowl is described as an abuse. The incongruity of that assertion becomes apparent in Cistercian communities, where there is little or no difference between monastic cowls and monastic albs. Furthermore, monastic communities have sought to play down the difference between priests and non-priests in the celebration of the Eucharist so as to stress the essential unity of the community, which is of its nature neither clerical nor lay. The prohibition against wearing only a stole over non-clerical clothes may also be questioned. It seems incongruent to take a full church liturgy into a home or into another informal setting. Celebrations must take account of the environment in which they are carried out. Certainly home liturgies celebrated by Jewish communities are adapted to the place; they are formal and dignified but appropriate to the situation. Experience has shown that full vesture is often not appropriate in some celebrations.

The ninth norm notes that the Eucharist is normally to be celebrated in a sacred place. For Christians of deep faith, God's presence is to be found everywhere and always; hence every place is sacred, not simply church buildings. The instruction asserts that it is not permissible to celebrate Mass outside a church without a real need, according to the judgment of the ordinary within his own diocese, but it should be pointed out that any genuine pastoral need is a real need. The norm also maintains that Mass should not be celebrated in refectories or on tables normally used for meals. Again, this seems unfortunate. If Christians are to have a deep appreciation of the Eucharist as a meal, and if they are to realize the profound relationship that should exist between the liturgy and the rest of their lives, perhaps the occasional celebration of the Eucharist in the refectory is one of the best ways to communicate these values. Furthermore, it often happens that in homes, the dining room is the most appropriate and dignified place to celebrate the Eucharist. Especially in poor families, often the only appropriate table on which to celebrate the Eucharist is the table the family normally uses for its meals.

The last three norms of the instruction deal with experimentation and adaptation in the liturgy. The document makes express provision for experimentation that may be undertaken when the bishops consider it necessary. If episcopal conferences find it necessary and useful to add other formulas or make certain adaptations, these may be introduced only after the approval of the Holy See has been obtained.

There are two difficulties here. The idea of adaptation is inadequate to express what is involved in this issue. The Constitution on the Sacred Liturgy referred to the need for adaptation in a number of places,[10] but the Constitution on the Church in the Modern World reflected a better understanding of the issue when it stressed the positive relationship that must exist between the Church and the world.[11] If the liturgy is the expression of the Church's own life in the world, the cultural and social life of the world must be reflected in that liturgy. Likewise, the world must to some extent shape the life of the Church and its celebrations. The relationship between the Church and the world is not simply accidental, nor does it exist on the external plane alone; the relationship exists on the internal plane as well. The term "indigenization" would seem to be more adequate than "adaptation," since it implies that due account is taken of all that is natural, native, and intrinsic in a culture. The term "adaptation" is more generic than "indigenization." The former is appropriate enough when the substantial unity of the Roman rite is the starting point from which change is to take place, but it is inadequate to express acculturation when that is what should be involved.

The insistence that a detailed outline of proposed changes must be submitted to the Holy See for approval before the changes are tried is curious. It is really impossible to know what changes will be effective unless people experiment with them first of all.

In general, the tone of the third instruction has prevailed in the official responses of the Holy See to the efforts at revitalization of the liturgy from 1970 down to the present time. It would seem that the Holy See has not fostered the responsibility of bishops and their conferences for continuing liturgical reform and renewal in their own

[10] *Sacrosanctum Concilium*, nos. 37–40: AAS 56 (1964) 110–11.
[11] *Gaudium et spes*, nos. 40, 44: AAS 58 (1966) 1057–58, 1064.

areas. This appraisal has been confirmed by commentaries in various parts of the world.[12]

As has been noted, there are positive elements in the instruction, but these were rather well expressed in earlier documents. The basic attitude of the Holy See reflected from 1970 onwards appears to be in contradiction to the understanding of liturgy introduced by the Second Vatican Council and the earlier postconciliar documents implementing liturgical reform. The conciliar trend away from a rubrical and legislative understanding of the liturgy has yielded in Rome to a greater preoccupation with liturgy understood as the execution of prescribed rites and rules. There has been a growing opposition toward liturgical experimentation. In practice the Holy See has been claiming sole competence in the matter of liturgical law. The national conferences of bishops and individual bishops have become simple organs of opinion. They may submit petitions to Rome and make suggestions, but their hard-won competence in the area of liturgical law seems to be more and more eroded.[13]

The third instruction was prepared and published by the Holy See with little or no collaboration or consultation with the liturgical commissions of the national conferences of bishops nor with the consultors who had been named to the Congregation for Divine Worship shortly before the instruction was issued. It would have seemed proper that the Consilium, which was originally entrusted with the revision of the liturgical books and which existed as a special commission within the Congregation for Divine Worship until the spring of 1970, should have had the responsibility for preparing the final document relative to the general implementation of the Constitution on the Sacred Liturgy. But that was not the case.

Certainly a third instruction was needed to clarify and specify certain issues, but the local churches should have been consulted in the preparation of such a document, and their experience and views should have been taken into account. The document emphasizes the responsibility of bishops and episcopal conferences in the matter of

[12] For an articulate evaluation, see the unsigned article "Sieht Rom die Liturgiereform für beendet an?" *Herder Korrespondenz* 24, no. 12 (December 1970) 557–59.

[13] See Frederick R. McManus, "The Juridical Power of the Bishop in the Constitution on the Sacred Liturgy," *The Church and the Liturgy*, Concilium 2 (Glen Rock, N.J.: Paulist Press, 1965) 33–49.

liturgical renewal, but that responsibility seems to be confined primarily to implementing the directives of the Holy See. Canon 1257 of the Code of Canon Law states that only the Apostolic See has the right to regulate the liturgy and to approve liturgical books. In spite of the clear derogation from this canon by the Constitution on the Sacred Liturgy, the episcopal conferences have in practice been judged to be in a position parallel to the preconciliar position of the local bishop, who simply had the right and the responsibility to carry out or enforce the liturgical norms established by the Holy See.

The trend toward centralization, inflexibility, and a rubrical mentality is indeed regrettable. It runs counter to articles 37 and 38 of the Constitution on the Sacred Liturgy, which emphasized that the Church does not wish to impose a rigid uniformity in liturgy but rather wants to provide for legitimate variations. It has been curious that bishops and national episcopal conferences that have exercised their initiative in attempting to respond to concrete pastoral needs have sometimes been reprimanded or their petitions begrudgingly acknowledged by the Holy See, but those that have not fulfilled their responsibility or have implemented decrees and instructions simply because they have been mandated by a higher authority to do so have gone uncorrected. Although there have been liturgical abuses, efforts to enrich celebrations through creative responses to liturgical prescriptions have in many instances sustained and deepened the faith of Christians; it is regrettable that the Holy See tends to view such spontaneity merely as a devaluation of liturgical celebration, a contempt for legitimate authority, and a pernicious manifestation of individualism.

The three instructions that have just been considered constitute the principal documents implementing the Constitution on the Sacred Liturgy as a whole. Many other important texts have been issued, referring to specific aspects of the constitution. These will be noted and commented on briefly in the pages that follow.

Chapter 4

SACRAMENTS:
CHRISTIAN INITIATION

The second and third chapters of the Constitution on the Sacred Liturgy called for a revision of the rites and norms affecting the sacraments and their celebration. That task has been basically completed, in the sense that the model rituals have been provided which must now be used creatively in the production of rituals appropriate to the diverse cultures throughout the world. In article 63 the constitution directed that territorial ecclesiastical authorities should prepare, in accordance with the new edition of the Roman Ritual, local rituals adapted linguistically and otherwise to the needs of the different regions.[1]

Shortly before the Second Vatican Council began, the Sacred Congregation of Rites issued a detailed decree, dated April 16, 1962, that modified the norms for the celebration of adult baptism.[2] The tenor of that decree was in continuity with that of February 9, 1951, which introduced the restored rite for the Paschal Vigil, as well as with the report that had been presented to the Congregation of Rites by the pontifical commission for the reform of the liturgy on May 25, 1955. The report contained a positive evaluation of the experience of the baptismal thrust of the restored Easter Vigil and prepared the way for the decree of the Congregation of Rites issued on

[1] AAS 56 (1964) 117.
[2] AAS 54 (1962) 310–38.

November 16, 1955, which introduced the reform of the Holy Week celebrations.

The decree of April 16, 1962, authorized the restoration of a genuine liturgical catechumenate corresponding to the various stages of catechetical instruction in preparation for baptism. The text was not a radical revision of the prayers for baptismal initiation, but it did provide for a profound change in the process of catechetical instruction given to adults by involving the Church community in the preparation of catechumens and by involving the candidates for baptism in the prayer life and celebrations of the Church. The norms contained in the ritual left the individual local ordinaries free to allow or prescribe the restored arrangements in place of the old single rite. Also, the episcopal conferences were given the right to establish norms for rites improperly understood in their regions, such as the use of salt. This freedom was important at the time because it manifested the Church's growing awareness that unity in the Church need not be equated with rigid uniformity. It also gave evidence of the Church's willingness to implement the principle of subsidiarity.

BAPTISM OF CHILDREN

In a sense, the baptism of infants is not a normal sacrament, since the free faith-response of the recipient is missing; it is the baptism of adults that structurally sets out the proper roles of both minister and recipient. However, it was the ritual for infant baptism that was first reformed by the Holy See. A new order for the baptism of little children was issued by the Sacred Congregation for Divine Worship on May 15, 1969.[3]

There are a number of distinctive features in the new ritual. The theology of the Church implicit in the sacrament of baptism is symbolized by the new rite of welcoming the child. The assembled community is called to experience the joy of the Church over the gift of human life and her loving concern for the sanctification of this life by Christ. The relationship between the infant and the Church is indicated in the new rite through the crucial role of the parents, who form the natural link between the local church and the child. The rite impresses on the parents their obligation to participate with the

[3] *AAS* 61 (1969) 548.

child in the total life of the Church. This stress is important. In most contemporary societies people are moving toward a concept of parenthood based on deliberate choice. In other words, the choice of parenthood is increasingly a carefully made decision on the part of couples. In the celebration of baptism, the child's birth is placed in the proper faith-perspective.

In baptism the child is received into the community of faith and becomes the responsibility of the community. The establishment of this community relationship is important because it really changes the child. This is another way of speaking about sacramental character. Just as a mother smiles at and cares for her child even though the child is not able to smile in return, establishing the foundation whereby the child will one day be able to return love and affection, so in baptism the Church commits herself to care for the child and to create an environment of faith in which the child can develop so that one day he or she will be able to respond with a faith-commitment of his or her own. This commitment of the Church through baptism establishes a vital relationship with the child, a relationship that changes the child, a change we have traditionally called "sacramental character."

Christian baptism asserts that no one can come to full explicit faith alone. The faithful person emerges out of a faithful community. Christian baptism also asserts that no one can live sinlessly in the world alone, but by the death and resurrection of Christ it has become possible and not futile for the community to strive together to live sinlessly. In the baptism of an infant, the community of believers pledges itself to welcome the child into the community effort and not leave him or her alone to struggle against the mystery of iniquity.

The celebration of the liturgy of the Word is also a welcome addition to the new rite of infant baptism. The Constitution on the Sacred Liturgy had directed that in liturgical celebrations a more ample, more varied, and more suitable reading from Sacred Scripture should be restored so that the intimate connection between rite and words may be apparent in the liturgy.[4] It is the Word, proclaimed and broken for the community, that sheds light on the ritual action and stirs up the faith of the Church that is present.

---

[4] *Sacrosanctum Concilium*, no. 35: AAS 56 (1964) 109.

The new rite also provides for the consecration of clean, fresh water. The prayer of blessing draws heavily on the baptismal theology of Paul and places baptism in the context of salvation history. The formula for the blessing omits the practice of mixing the baptismal oil with the water, thus reducing the excessively mystical significance of the rite. It also solves the perennial problem of preserving the cleanliness of baptismal fonts.

The option of baptism by immersion is given in the new rite. In fact, the order asserts that this form is more suitable as a symbol of participation in the death and resurrection of Christ. Experience in the Eastern Churches has shown that it is truly a powerful symbol of immersion into the death of Christ by the total immersion of one's life into the suffering of Christ in the world. The fullness of the baptismal symbol of emergence from the water is restored to express the Christian's participation in the life of the risen Lord, which comes through a life of dedicated suffering service to God's people. The new rite calls for the parents to hold the child, whether he or she is baptized by immersion or infusion, as a symbol of their complete involvement with the child in the ecclesial effects of the sacrament.

The customary ceremonies with the baptismal robe and candle are slightly altered in the new rite to allow greater participation by the parents and sponsors. Inasmuch as the wording of the ritual suggests a complementary symbolism between these two rites and the deep theological implication of the preceding anointing with chrism, the symbols of robe and candle can be conveniently used to communicate the gospel teaching that the Christian is united to Christ who is the way, the truth, and the life. The clothing with the white garment reminds the community that the catechumens in the early Church, upon emerging from the baptismal water, were clothed in a white garment as a sign of their new birth and innocence.

The lighting of the child's candle from the paschal candle shows the close relationship between baptism and the paschal mystery of Christ's death and resurrection. Early Christian writers stressed baptism as an illumination by the divine light. The love that subsists among the three Persons of the Trinity and that is communicated to the child in baptism is like fire, heat, and warmth. It is this light, the fire of love, that is given to the child to help him or her grow and develop in the life of Christ that he or she shares through baptism.

At the conclusion of the new rite, the centrality of the Eucharist as the liturgical culmination of baptism is forcefully expressed as the celebrant summarizes for the community the ecclesial nature of baptism. Standing at the altar, he prays that the newly baptized may be filled with the Holy Spirit and may partake of the Lord's bread and cup in the community meal of the Church. He then invites the community to express its anticipation of the Eucharistic mysteries by saying the Lord's Prayer.

The new ritual provides a short blessing for the mother as she holds the child. The blessing of mothers after childbirth is thus incorporated into the rite of the sacrament itself. The celebration closes with a blessing for the father and for the assembly.

This is the first time that a distinctive rite for infant baptism has been drawn up for the Roman liturgy. For the past three hundred and fifty years, Roman Catholics have been using the rite contained in the 1614 ritual, a rite designed basically for the baptism of adults.

The introduction to the rite of baptism of children asserts clearly that when the parents are not yet prepared to profess the faith or to undertake the duty of bringing up their children as Christians, it is for the parish priest, bearing in mind the regulations that the conference of bishops may have established, to determine the time for the baptism of infants (no. 8, 4). A response of the Sacred Congregation for the Doctrine of the Faith, dated July 13, 1970, provided further information concerning the baptism of children born of non-Christian or non-practicing Christian parents.[5] The reply came as a response to a letter that the bishop of Dapango, Africa, sent to the Consilium, but for reasons of competence and importance, the letter was transmitted to the Sacred Congregation for the Doctrine of the Faith. The question was discussed by the cardinals of that Congregation, and their conclusions were approved by Pope Paul on June 19, 1970.

The response deals especially with children of non-Christians or "irregular Christians," the latter including those involved in invalid marriages, those legitimately married but who have ceased to practice the faith regularly, and those who seek baptism for their children for reasons of social convenience. Such parents must be

[5] *Notitiae* 7 (1971) 69–70.

clearly informed of their responsibilities. There must be sufficient assurance that the child will be educated as a Catholic. This assurance may be given by a member of the family, by a godparent, or by the support of the Christian community. If the pastor judges that these conditions are satisfied, the Church may proceed to baptize the infant, since children are baptized in the faith of the Church. If the conditions are not satisfied, the infant's name may be inscribed on the parish rolls in view of later baptism, or the pastor may keep in contact with the parents so that they may prepare themselves for the eventual baptism of their child.

INITIATION OF ADULTS

On January 6, 1972, a new order for the Christian initiation of adults was published by the Sacred Congregation for Divine Worship.[6] This order replaces the *Ordo Baptismi adultorum* in the Roman Ritual; this rite was revised in 1962 according to the stages of the catechumenate. The general introduction to Christian initiation, contained in the 1969 order of baptism of children, is not repeated in the new order of baptism of adults, but there is a lengthy introduction of sixty-seven sections giving the basic theological foundations and directives for the celebration. Although the rite for the baptism of children appeared in 1969, the clear intent was to have an integral ritual for Christian initiation, similar to the one title in the old Roman Ritual, with sections for adult initiation, baptism without confirmation or Eucharist for small children, confirmation without baptism for those already baptized in infancy, and a rite for the reception of baptized Christians into full communion with the Catholic Church.

As the order points out, catechesis is the primary element in Christian initiation. Celebration of the liturgical rites without in-depth catechesis is an abuse of the sacrament. Catechesis implies not only instruction in Christian doctrine but also and above all the full response of the faithful person in the context of a faithful community to God's gift of his life to his people.

Like the other rites prepared since the Second Vatican Council, the revised order of Christian initiation basically represents a restoration of past forms rather than a creative response to contem-

[6] *Notitiae* 8 (1972) 68–95.

porary pastoral needs. With the revised model in hand, national hierarchies will have to prepare their own rite of Christian initiation, taking into account pastoral needs and cultural variations. The liturgical rites of the catechumenate were developed in antiquity, in a culture vastly different from any that prevail in the world today. Some of those elements have been revised or replaced precisely in view of their appropriateness or lack of appropriateness for certain cultures and their initiatory rites, especially in so-called mission countries; a number of the rites of the catechumenate, however, appear somewhat artificial as expressions of the various stages in Christian conversion and as manifestations of the supportive faith-response of the Christian community into which adults are being initiated. The experience of Christian initiation presupposes the existence of Christian communities in which people effectively share and celebrate their faith. It also presupposes an understanding and implementation of ongoing catechesis on all levels of the Christian community. Hence the meaning of a Christian parish and its various educational and formational structures must be rethought before most national hierarchies will be in a position to devise their own rituals for a realistic catechumenate.

Although the actual rites of initiation begin with admission to the catechumenate, the order speaks of a "precatechumenate." This stage corresponds to an interest in, and an attraction to, Christian faith, which is always God's gift but which at this stage is frequently mediated into the life of the prospective convert through experience of the life of the Christian community. People in this stage have traditionally been called "inquirers" or "sympathizers." During this period the Christian community, through its various ministers, proclaims the faith and offers friendship and support to those who manifest an interest in Christianity.

Although no special liturgical rites are provided for at this stage, episcopal conferences are free to develop a simple ceremony for the reception of sympathizers or potential initiates. Those who formulated the new order of adult initiation were rightly hesitant to set up a rite for this period. On the one hand, inquirers or sympathizers are generally assumed not to have reached the stage of initial conversion; they are being evangelized. On the other hand, those who have sought admission to the catechumenate are assumed to have

Christian faith. The great pastoral concern is to demonstrate that they should not be sacramentally initiated until they have undergone a more or less lengthy period of formation and preparation and response to the gift of faith.

When those who are genuinely interested in Christianity are ready to profess publicly their "first faith" and "initial conversion," they apply for admission to the catechumenate. They choose or are given sponsors who are mature Christians, preferably from the same social and cultural background as the candidates. It is the responsibility of the sponsor to provide guidance and support throughout the whole process of conversion and initiation. The ritual for admission to the catechumenate is designed to express the dispositions of the converts and their association with the Christian community. It includes a formula of adherence to the Church, a signing of the forehead and the senses, and the imposition of hands. It may also include the conferral of a Christian name, and in those areas where pagan cults are prevalent, there may be a preliminary renunciation and exorcism.

The length of the catechumenate is unspecified, since it naturally depends on various circumstances, such as the educational resources of the local church and the level of faith-development in the catechumen. During the catechumenate, the candidates should receive systematic formation, including instruction, accommodated to the seasons of the liturgical year, and celebrations of the Word. There may also be minor exorcisms, anointings, and blessings. They are encouraged to participate in the Mass for the liturgy of the Word, but ideally they should not assist at the Eucharistic action. They are also to be encouraged by word and example to realize in their own lives the Christian ideals of prayer, discipline, and ministry.

The first stage of the catechumenate is called the period of "election." The candidates are examined concerning their development in the faith and conversion. They are chosen, then, as candidates for baptism. In Rome the candidates were traditionally called *electi;* elsewhere they were known as *competentes* — those searching for God with the Church. In the East they were called *illuminandi* — those to be illumined or enlightened by the grace of baptism.

This final stage of preparation for the sacraments of Christian initiation, the period of purification and enlightenment, normally takes place during Lent. As Tertullian once remarked, any day is a good day for baptism, but Easter is the best, since it is the most solemn commemoration of the mystery of the death and resurrection of Christ into which all are baptized.[7] The rites during this final period include scrutinies, the formal communication of the creed and the Lord's Prayer, and the choice of a Christian name, when this is desirable. When it seems advisable, the various episcopal conferences may specify other times during the year for adult initiation, but these periods of election should be more or less equivalent in length to the season of Lent. In the case of adult initiation, it is certainly desirable, if possible, to provide for groups of *electi* so that they may support and encourage one another and also be supported by the local community.

The actual rite of election, which normally takes place on the first Sunday of Lent, includes a presentation and formal examination of the candidates, together with their sponsors, and interrogation concerning their desire for full initiation, inscription of their names, a declaration of their election, and intercessory prayers. The scrutinies of the *electi* that take place during the time of purification and illumination consist not so much of examinations of the candidates' knowledge of doctrine and morality but rather of exorcisms and blessings, with imposition of hands, so that the candidates may be more and more opened to the strengthening grace of God and may be healed in their weakness. The new Roman Missal provides three traditional Mass formulas for the celebration of these scrutinies on the third, fourth, and fifth Sundays of Lent.

The "traditions" consist of the communication of cultic texts to the candidates. The order provides for the tradition of the creed and the Lord's Prayer, the first to be given during the week after the first scrutiny, the second during the week of the third scrutiny. These rites were customary during the patristic period and the early Middle Ages, and derive from a period when the Church observed the "discipline of the secret." Outside of that context, the ritual does not seem to make the same sense. Hence the conference of bishops may decide to structure these traditions as transitional rites preceding the stage of election. The order of initiation provides for

[7] See *De baptismo* 19.

biblical readings to accompany these traditions and prescribes that a homily be given on the text that is being given to the candidates.

Immediate preparation for the celebration of the sacrament of Christian initiation takes place, if possible, at a session on Holy Saturday that includes some or all of the following: a reading of the gospel, followed by a brief homily; the recitation of the creed by the candidates (the *redditio symboli*); the *Ephphetha* rite; the choice of a Christian name; and the anointing with the oil of catechumens, in places where this rite is retained. It does seem reasonable to antici-pate as much of the Easter Vigil service as is liturgically proper so that the night service will not be unduly prolonged.

In the course of the Easter Vigil, the candidates are baptized, con-firmed, and receive their first communion. When the principal celebrant is not a bishop, the priest who baptizes also confirms.

The final stage of Christian initiation is what is called mystagogy. It normally coincides with the Easter season. It is a period when the new initiates deepen their Christian faith through celebrations of the liturgy and through relationships with other members of the Christian community. It is a time when the new Christians are urged to assume a full life of witness and service in the community of faith. The term *mystagogia* means "introduction to the mysteries" and refers to the practice prevalent in the patristic period of explain-ing the meaning of the sacramental rituals to the newly initiated Christians during the octave of Easter by means of mystagogic homilies. Because of the "discipline of the secret," these rites had not been explained previously. The new order of Christian initiation does not provide any distinctive rites for the period of mystagogy, but it does prescribe that a special Eucharist be celebrated for the in-itiates on the Sundays after Easter. The readings for the A cycle of the new lectionary are suggested as being especially appropriate for these celebrations.

The new order of Christian initiation provides a simple rite for the initiation of an adult where it is decided that not all the stages of preparation and probation are needed. There is also a rite for Chris-tian initiation in danger of death, a chapter on the preparation for the confirmation and first Eucharist of those adults who were bap-tized as children but never received adequate catechesis, and a rite for the initiation of children who have reached "catechetical age."

An appendix to the new order contains a revised "Rite for the Reception of Baptized Christians into Full Communion with the Catholic Church." The use of this new rite has been a great improvement in Roman Catholic practice with regard to the reception of such persons into the Catholic Church. In former times the reception generally began with a rather sterile instruction concentrating on those teachings that sharply divided Roman Catholics from non-Catholics, such as papal infallibility, indulgences, mariology, and the canon law of marriage. It included an abjuration of heresy and error, most of which was probably neither professed nor understood by most of those seeking admission to the Catholic Church, and it concluded with conditional baptism, conditional absolution after confession, and reception of the Eucharist. The experience was generally very private and individualistic, with little or no realization or expression that a local faith-community should always be involved in genuine Christian initiation.

Since the promulgation of the ecumenical directory on May 14, 1967,[8] the provisions for the reception of baptized Christians into full communion with the Catholic Church gradually changed. An abjuration of heresy was not required of Christians baptized in other churches. In many parishes the catechetical instruction became more balanced and an "order of truths" was established, in keeping with the Second Vatican Council's Decree on Ecumenism. Furthermore, routine celebration of conditional baptism was not generally practiced.

If faithfully followed, the new rite should correct any continuing abuses in regard to the reception of baptized Christians. The new norms call for a clear distinction between catechumens and candidates for reception into full communion; however, they insist that "the baptized Christian is to receive both doctrinal and spiritual preparation, according to pastoral requirements in individual cases, for his reception. . . . He should grow in his spiritual adherence to the Church, where he will find the fullness of his baptism" (no. 5). Certainly this implies not only an involvement of a local community in the rite of reception but also a commitment of the community to support and challenge the faith of the one newly received.

The prescriptions of the 1967 ecumenical directory are repeated

[8] *AAS* 59 (1967) 574–92.

concerning conditional baptism. The validly baptized must not be baptized again "unless there is prudent doubt of the fact, or of the validity, of a baptism already administered" (no. 14).

It is the right of the bishop to receive baptized Christians into full communion by the celebration of confirmation, but those priests, ordinarily pastors, to whom the bishop entrusts the reception of converts have the faculty of confirming the candidate during the rite, unless the person has already been validly confirmed.

Normally the rite of reception, in the context of the Eucharist, takes place between the homily and the prayer of the faithful. On Sundays and solemnities, the Mass text is that for the day; on other days the Mass for Christian unity or initiation is used. If the rite cannot take place at Mass, it is celebrated in the context of a liturgy of the Word.

The actual rite of reception is very simple. Following the homily, the person is called forward with the sponsor to profess the Catholic faith in the presence of the community. He/she recites the Nicene Creed with the community and then, at the invitation of the celebrant, proclaims that he/she believes and professes all that the Catholic Church believes and teaches to be revealed by God. A brief statement of admission to the community is made by the celebrant, and then the person is confirmed, if he/she has not already been confirmed validly. In the case of Eastern Christians who enter into the fullness of Catholic communion, nothing more than a simple profession of Catholic faith is required. If the community is not too large, all the members are invited to welcome the person individually after the prayer of the faithful. Since this is a sign of welcome to the person, there would seem to be no reason why the sign of peace exchanged among all the members of the community should be omitted at the regular time during the Eucharist. It has been suggested that the rubric was inserted at this point because of the lingering desire on the part of the liturgical revisers to place the sign of peace at the beginning of the Eucharistic liturgy, a reform that was not made in the revised order of the Mass.

If the person needs to be baptized conditionally, the rite is celebrated privately. Depending on his/her personal disposition, he/she may celebrate the sacrament of reconciliation previously and receive sacramental absolution. The emphasis in the new rite is certainly on communion with the Church in the body and blood of Jesus Christ. Hence the real sacramental context for the rite of reception into full communion is the celebration of the Eucharist by the local community.

As a result of reflection on the experience of implementing the new rites of Christian initiation, the Sacred Congregation for Divine Worship issued a second *editio typica* of the order of baptism for children by a decree dated August 29, 1973.[9] The significant changes in the text reinforced the idea that baptism frees one from original sin and the power of darkness. Apparently it was felt that the remission of sin was not sufficiently stressed in the original text.

CONFIRMATION

The motu proprio *Sacram liturgiam,* issued in 1964, authorized the celebration of confirmation during Mass, after the homily,[10] but no major changes occurred in the rite until the apostolic constitution *Divinae consortium naturae* was issued on August 15, 1971.[11] (It might be noted here that an apostolic constitution is always issued if the essential words of a sacramental form are to be changed or if there is a major liturgical book to be issued.) In this constitution the Holy Father announced that a new rite for the sacrament of confirmation was to be issued shortly and would become obligatory on January 1, 1973. A decree of the Sacred Congregation for Divine Worship promulgated the text of the new order on August 22, 1971.[12]

The order prescribes that the sacrament of confirmation should take place in the context of a festive, communal celebration. Ordinarily it should be celebrated at Mass in order to express the place of the sacrament within the whole process of Christian initiation. If by chance those to be confirmed are children who have not yet received their first communion, they should not be confirmed within the Mass but rather at a liturgy of the Word. In every instance, however, the candidates are to renew their baptismal commitment just before they are confirmed.

[9] *Notitiae* 9 (1973) 268–72.
[10] AAS 56 (1964) 141–42.
[11] AAS 63 (1971) 657–64.
[12] *Notitiae* 7 (1971) 332–46.

The sacramental form of the sacrament was changed in the new order. In his apostolic constitution, Pope Paul VI declared that "the sacrament of confirmation is conferred through the anointing with chrism on the forehead, which is done by the laying on of the hand, and through the words: *"Accipe signaculum Doni Spiritus Sancti."* The actual order itself made no mention of the older rubric that directed the minister of the sacrament to place his hand on the candidate's head as he did the anointing. Since there was some confusion on the issue, the Pontifical Commission for the Interpretation of the Conciliar Texts issued a response on June 9, 1972,[13] which asserted that the act of anointing the forehead sufficiently manifested the laying on of the hand. Pope Paul had noted in his apostolic constitution that the general extension of hands over those to be confirmed, which is done with a prescribed prayer before the anointing, does not pertain to the essence of the sacrament, but it should be held in high esteem because it contributes to the full perfection of the same rite and to a clearer understanding of the sacrament.

The phrase *signaculum Doni Spiritus Sancti* appears in the rite of anointing in the East in the fourth and fifth centuries. The words were accepted by the Church of Constantinople and have been used by the Churches of the Byzantine rite down to the present time. The provisional ICEL translation of the text was as follows: "N., receive the seal of the Holy Spirit, the Gift of the Father." That has been changed so that the definitive form as approved by the Holy Father now reads: "Be sealed with the Gift of the Holy Spirit."

To understand the change made in the English translation of the revised sacramental form of confirmation, it should be noted that in a circular letter sent from the Sacred Congregation for Divine Worship to the various episcopal conferences on October 25, 1973, Cardinal Villot informed the bishops that the Holy Father had reserved to himself the power to approve all vernacular translations of the sacramental forms.[14] Such a reservation to the Roman pontiff derogated from the Constitution on the Sacred Liturgy, which maintained that translations from the Latin for use in the liturgy must be approved by the competent territorial ecclesiastical author-

[13] *Notitiae* 8 (1972) 281.
[14] *AAS* 66 (1974) 98–99.

ity.[15] Along the same lines and with the approval of Pope Paul VI, the Congregation for the Doctrine of the Faith on January 25, 1974, issued a declaration stating that while the liturgical restoration introduced some changes in the forms of the sacramental rites, these new words should be translated into the vernacular in such a way that the original sense may be expressed according to the character proper to the various languages; the translation should render faithfully the original meaning of the Latin text.[16]

The bishop is the ordinary minister of confirmation, but he may delegate other priests in certain instances. The order prescribes that these priests should hold an office in the diocese. In some dioceses the very questionable practice has developed whereby the bishop delegates abbots to confirm, presumably because they may wear mitres and hence look like bishops, rather than because they have a genuine office in the diocese that brings them into a real pastoral relationship with those to be confirmed. It would seem that in the absence of the bishop, the vicar general or the pastor of those to be confirmed should be given delegated authority.

Those priests who, in virtue of an office they lawfully hold, baptize an adult or child old enough for catechesis may confirm those who have been baptized; those who admit a validly baptized adult into full communion with the Church may also confirm. In the case where special need arises, as for example when there are many people to be confirmed at one time, the bishop may invite priests to assist in confirming. They join the bishop in the first general imposition of hands, but they do not say the prayer with the bishop. They do, however, follow the same procedure as the bishop for the actual anointing. It should be noted here that the general introductions to both the order of baptism for children and the order of Christian initiation for adults emphasize the integrity of sacramental initiation. Since the priest regularly baptizes, he should also confirm the newly baptized. That is the underlying reason why it is wholly proper that priests should join the bishop in the celebration of confirmation.

In the new rite, the gesture of striking the candidate's cheek has been suppressed and replaced by a sign of peace. Ordinarily there should be a sponsor for each person being confirmed. The sponsor

---

[15] *Sacrosanctum Concilium*, no. 36: AAS 56 (1964) 109–10.
[16] AAS 66 (1974) 661.

need not be of the same sex as the one being confirmed. The sponsor accompanies the candidate and during the anointing places his or her hand on the shoulder of the one being confirmed. If possible, the baptismal sponsor should also be the sponsor at confirmation. This directive abrogates canon 796 of the Code of Canon Law, which prohibited such an arrangement.

Although the new order for confirmation and Pope Paul's apostolic constitution have clarified certain issues, there remains considerable vagueness in a number of areas, including the theological interpretation of the sacrament, the best age for the confirmation of those born and reared in the Church, and the pastoral programs of preparation for confirmation.

In the area of theology, there is general agreement that confirmation further perfects the initiation begun at baptism, that it is the sacrament in which the Holy Spirit is conferred in a special way, and that the sacrament effects what the Holy Spirit does. But beyond these areas of agreement, there would seem to be four possible theological approaches to the sacrament: (1) confirmation properly marks the entry into Christian maturity or adulthood; (2) confirmation is the beginning, not the culmination, of growth into Christian maturity; (3) confirmation completes the initiation into full membership in the Christian community, independent of the person's age or maturity; (4) the original order of the sacraments of Christian initiation (baptism, confirmation, Eucharist) should always be regarded as normative and hence restored.

Each of these theological views has implications for the age at which confirmation is celebrated. Concerning age, the new order of confirmation makes the following provision: "With regard to children, in the Latin Church the administration of confirmation is generally postponed until about the seventh year. For pastoral reasons, however, especially to strengthen the faithful in complete obedience to Christ the Lord and in loyal testimony to him, episcopal conferences may choose an age which seems more appropriate, so that the sacrament is given at a more mature age after appropriate formation" (no. 11). If the first theological viewpoint cited above is adopted, it is likely that a person will be confirmed between the ages of eighteen and twenty-five. The age is determined by the time at which the candidate reaches Christian adulthood, not physical adulthood, and has made a deep personal commitment of faith.

The second theological viewpoint cited above relates confirmation to the continuing process of growth. During adolescence a person begins to take up positions concerning principles, values, and goals. Confirmation then gives expression to a Christian commitment regarding life and is at the same time a strengthening sacrament enabling one to confront the turmoil and struggle that is a normal part of adolescence. Hence confirmation is celebrated at about the age of fifteen or sixteen. There are also those who suggest the beginning of adolescence as a proper age, since the first formal catechesis of the youngster has been completed and he/she is about to make a transition from childhood to adolescence.

The third theological viewpoint has no implications for an appropriate age. If confirmation simply furthers the initiation process begun at baptism, it may be celebrated at any age.

The fourth theological viewpoint calls for confirmation before first communion, the order practiced in the early Church. Hence confirmation could take place any time from infancy on up to the day of first communion.

There are doctrinal and pastoral advantages in each approach to the sacrament. Whatever practical decisions are made about the age at which the sacrament is celebrated, it would seem that a certain amount of flexibility is desirable to adjust to the different levels of development of persons, even within the same age group. At any rate, it should be noted that the new order of Christian initiation of adults is clear in stating that in the case of adults (and really all those of an age at which they can be catechized), confirmation and Eucharist should follow baptism immediately. The positions on this matter taken in the order for adult initiation and the order for confirmation seem to be inconsistent, if not contradictory.

Chapter 5

SACRAMENTS:
PENANCE AND ANOINTING OF THE SICK

PENANCE

A new *Ordo Paenitentiae* was issued on December 2, 1973, by the Sacred Congregation for Divine Worship and made public on February 7, 1974. The Latin version went into effect immediately.[1] The publication was the result of long and difficult work carried out by experts and bishops from the Consilium, and then by the Sacred Congregation for Divine Worship, collaborating with other dicasteries of the Holy See that have an interest in the area. The first study group for the revision of the rite of penance was brought together in December 1966 under the auspices of the Consilium. During the initial stage of research, carried out from 1966 until 1970, an in-depth study was made of the doctrinal, historical, and liturgical aspects of penance as well as of the pastoral situations that must be confronted today.

The first draft of the new order was held up until the Congregation for the Doctrine of the Faith issued a series of pastoral norms on general absolution on June 16, 1972.[2] Basically those norms call attention to an instruction of the Sacred Penitentiary issued on March 25, 1944,[3] which enumerated cases in which general absolution

[1] *AAS* 66 (1974) 172–73.
[2] *AAS* 64 (1972) 510–14.
[3] *AAS* 36 (1944) 155.

could be given without previous confession of serious sins by individual penitents. This earlier instruction was issued during the Second World War, and it envisioned general absolution above all for soldiers going to the front lines of battle and for civilians threatened by bomb attacks. However, it also provided for general absolution, apart from danger of death, where there was serious necessity proportionate to the obligation of previous confession of serious sins, namely, when on account of the large number of penitents there are not enough confessors on hand to hear the confessions of each one properly within a reasonable time, with the result that the penitents, through no fault of their own, would be forced to go without the grace of the sacrament of penance and Holy Eucharist for a long time. The 1944 instruction directed that, where possible, the priest confronted with such necessity was to have previous recourse to the bishop; where recourse was not possible, he was to inform the bishop as soon as possible of the necessity and of the general absolution given.

The 1972 instruction of the Sacred Congregation for the Doctrine of the Faith indicates the possibility of general absolution without previous individual confession. Although it does insist strongly on the Tridentine obligation of individual confession of serious sins, it does give the impression that general absolution might well be given with some regularity: "Those who receive pardon for grave sins by a common absolution should go to individual confession before they receive this kind of absolution again, unless they are impeded by a just cause. They are strictly bound, unless this is morally impossible, to go to confession within a year" (no. 34).

As commentators made clear, various practical questions remained unresolved by the 1972 instruction of the Congregation for the Doctrine of the Faith. For example, what are the various circumstances that constitute moral impossibility of confessing sins? However, on the foundation of that instruction, which raised as many questions as it may have solved, the work of formulating a new order of penance went into its second phase.

A new study group was established in June 1972. The group presented a text to the consultors of the Congregation for Divine Worship on November 8 to 10, 1972, and to the members of the Congregation at their plenary session on November 22, 1972. The text was then corrected according to the Congregation's indications and was submitted again to the judgment of the members and consultors of the Congregation for Divine Worship as well as to the other Roman Congregations having an interest in the sacrament of penance. About three hundred suggestions were given to the study group, which made numerous corrections. The reworked text was finally discussed at a general session of the consultors that took place on March 1 to 3, 1973. After it had received the approval of the Holy Father, the new order was promulgated by the Congregation for Divine Worship.

In order to stress the existence of various forms of penitential celebrations that are not concluded with sacramental absolution as well as those that do conclude with absolution, the new publication has been called *Ordo Paenitentiae.* The term "reconciliation" is frequently used throughout the text to stress the divine initiative that makes it possible for people with penitent hearts to be united with the Church and with God.

The order consists of an introduction, four chapters, and three appendices. Theological and pastoral in tone, the introduction considers the mystery of reconciliation in the history of salvation; reconciliation of penitents in the life of the Church; the offices and ministries of reconciliation; the celebration of the sacrament of penance; penitential celebrations; and adaptation of the rites by episcopal conferences, bishops, and priests.

The first chapter contains the rite for the reconciliation of individual penitents. It presents a structure that is significantly new, while respecting what preceded. The new elements — the invitation to make an act of faith in God, a reading from Scripture, manifestation of sorrow, praise for the mercy of God, and dismissal of the penitent — certainly enrich the liturgy of penance even when celebrated individually. The proclamation of God's Word is especially important. Although it is optional, it should not be omitted, because it is meant as an invitation to conversion, as light to the individual conscience, and as a manifestation of the love of God, who brings forgiveness to each one of his people.

The new rite provides for the imposition of hands, or at least the right hand, during the formula of absolution. Hence the new order reintroduces the classical gesture of the ancient penitential liturgy;

this gesture fell into disuse with the progressive substitution of private penance for public penance. The Roman Ritual of 1614 reintroduced this gesture, but by prescribing for the first time the screen between the penitent and the priest, the ritual rendered the use of the gesture practically impossible. The new order has reinstated the gesture to indicate the gift of the Holy Spirit through the remission of sins and the manifestation of that reconciliation with God and the Church that the new formula proclaims and effects.

The second chapter contains the rite of reconciliation of more than one penitent with individual confession and absolution. The liturgical movement and the Second Vatican Council emphasized the communal dimension of the liturgical life of the Church. Various studies and polls criticized the celebration of the sacrament of penance according to the former rite because of its excessive ritual and psychological individualism. As a result, communal celebrations of penance, similar to what is proposed in chapter two of the new order, became popular over the past ten years. They consist of an initial gathering of the community and a liturgy of the Word, followed by a general confession and penitential prayers, individual confession and absolution within a certain period of time, and a final gathering in which the whole community celebrates its joy and peace over reconciliation with the Church and with God.

The rite proposed in the second chapter of the new order of penance follows along the same lines. The rite begins with a chant, a greeting, a brief address to the congregation, and a collect. The service of God's Word, including a homily, follows. There is then an examination of conscience; general confession, as in the first penitential rite of the order of Mass; prayer in litanic form with the Lord's Prayer; private confession and absolution; thanksgiving, blessing, and dismissal.

In some ways this is a well-constructed service, but there are a number of serious pastoral and practical problems raised. First of all, it is difficult to combine effectively in one celebration elements that are primarily public and those that are primarily private. Furthermore, it is often difficult to get people in any large numbers to come to a non-Eucharistic service these days. If large numbers do come, there is need for a relatively large number of priests for the individual confessions. If priests are not available, the celebration is unreasonably protracted. And if there are many priests hearing confessions, it is usually very difficult to provide the proper kind of sacred space in which to celebrate personal reconciliation.

Even with the retention of private confession, a public communal absolution would have been in line with the general expression of repentance, a common prayer for forgiveness and reconciliation, and even a general confession such as that contained in the penitential rite of the order of Mass. However, it has been pointed out that if there were a public communal absolution, it would be possible for people to leave the service without absolution at all. That danger could surely be eliminated by a brief instruction of the community. These difficulties could have been avoided if the 1972 pastoral norms had provided for communal absolution. Obviously the Holy See felt that the time had not come for a general sacramental absolution with the exception of the arrangements given in Part III of the new order of penance.

F. Sottocornola, secretary of the study group appointed in June 1972 to provide a text of the order of penance for the Congregation for Divine Worship, wrote a commentary on the new project in *Notitiae*.[4] He maintained that the theology of the sacrament of penance was still undergoing review by the theologians and that it was not the right of the Congregation for Divine Worship to anticipate their findings. There is also the problem of the validity of absolution of unconfessed serious sins, but it is said that the objections to such a procedure are not insurmountable.[5] There is the question of the advisability of giving absolution without previous individual confession, but this is a pastoral matter that alone cannot determine theological orthodoxy. It is significant, however, that much of the legislation concerning the celebration of the sacrament of penance in the past was dictated by pastoral concern. The unresolved question today is to what degree pastoral concern should determine theology and to what degree theology should determine pastoral practice.[6] Because of these various difficulties, the service of recon-

---

[4] Vol. 10 (1974) 63–79.

[5] See J.-M.-R. Tillard, "Pénitence et eucharistie," *La Maison-Dieu*, no. 90 (1967) 103–31.

[6] See J. D. Crichton, *The Ministry of Reconciliation* (London: Geoffrey Chapman, 1974) 53–54.

ciliation outlined in the second chapter of the order is pastorally less effective than it might have been.

The third chapter of the order contains the rite of reconciliation of more than one penitent with general confession and absolution. Since this rite does provide for general absolution, it is this chapter that has raised serious questions and caused considerable controversy since the new order was promulgated. The introduction to the order states that "individual, integral confession and absolution remain the only ordinary way for the faithful to reconcile themselves with God and the Church, unless physical or moral impossibility excuses from this kind of confession" (no. 31). If private confession is the ordinary manner of reconciliation, there must be extraordinary modes also. The document affirms that it is within the Church's competence to limit the manner in which reconciliation is celebrated, but it may also extend the manner when circumstances so require. Such circumstances are mentioned in the order and may be listed as follows:

1. When there is a large number of people and an insufficient number of confessors, so that people could not confess within a reasonable time and without their fault would be deprived of the grace of the sacrament and would have to go without holy communion for some time.

2. This can happen in missionary areas but also in other places as well.

3. There may be other gatherings of people where the same need can be demonstrated.

Reconciliation by general confession and absolution is conditioned by true repentance for sins committed, a firm purpose of amendment, the reparation of injury to others, and the intention to confess privately in due time.[7] Clearly all the requirements of the sacrament of penance remain except that of auricular confession on the given occasion. The penitent forgiven by general absolution must confess privately before receiving general absolution a second time, unless unable to do so for some just cause. It should be noted that in this regard the terms of the order are not restrictive; furthermore, the text does not state that it is a *divine* precept that obliges one to confess to a priest at least all grave sins, not previously con-

[7] The Rite of Penance, no. 33.

fessed privately, once a year. The footnote, however, that appears at the end of number 34 does refer to the pastoral norms issued by the Sacred Congregation for the Doctrine of the Faith in June 1972. Those norms did state that auricular confession is of divine precept, but the interpretation of that expression is still a matter of theological debate.

Since the new order of penance went into effect, various bishops have implemented the third chapter of the document. The decision on the fact whether the conditions required for general absolution have been realized in any given case is reserved to the bishop of the diocese, in agreement with other members of the episcopal conference.[8] In his pastoral letter for Lent in 1976, Bishop Eric Grasar of the diocese of Shrewsbury in England announced that general absolution would be given at station Masses that he and his auxiliary, Bishop John Brewer, would be attending in the various diocesan deaneries.[9] "In one general act of repentance," he wrote, "the bishops will grant all who are present and so desire the forgiveness of all their sins. They can then return immediately to holy communion."

In his letter Bishop Grasar noted that those who wish to receive general absolution must have the necessary dispositions, including a readiness to confess integrally, when possible, grave personal sins of which they are conscious. Unlike those who object that a liberal use of general absolution will mean that penitents will not go to confession subsequently, the Bishop emphasized that his initiative was designed to make the return of alienated members to the Church easier because of the strength received through general absolution and the Eucharist.

In Switzerland the third rite has been widely used.[10] Its use in the United States, however, has been the subject of a widely publicized controversy. Bishop Carroll Dozier of Memphis, Tennessee, gave general absolution at a Day of Reconciliation service held in the Mid-South Coliseum in Memphis and attended by about twelve thousand persons. The celebration took place on the first Sunday of

---

[8] *Ibid.*, no. 32.

[9] *The Tablet* (March 6, 1976), vol. 230, no. 7079, pp. 243–44.

[10] Eoin de Bhaldraithe, "General Absolution in Switzerland," *Doctrine and Life*, vol. 27, no. 5 (June 1977) 3–18.

Advent, 1976. The event was carefully prepared for throughout the diocese and was highly publicized in both the secular and religious press. Those responsible for the celebration found it pastorally very successful; in fact, there was a significant increase in the number of individual confessions throughout the diocese following the celebration.

Bishop Dozier's pastoral initiative, however, evoked a rather negative response from the Sacred Congregation for the Doctrine of the Faith on January 14, 1977. The letter expressed appreciation for the pastoral zeal that prompted Bishop Dozier to reach out to "religiously inactive Catholics," but it maintained that "the celebration of the Sacrament of Penance with general absolution as the focal point of a pastoral ministry of evangelization or reconciliation does not accord with the Pastoral Norms." The letter stressed that the pastoral norms were developed to assist pastors in confronting those existing situations in the life of the Church that are attended by extraordinary circumstances; "they are not intended to provide a basis for convoking large gatherings of faithful for the purpose of imparting general absolution, in the absence of such extraordinary circumstances." In a response to the letter from the Congregation, Bishop Dozier denied that he had convoked the celebration of reconciliation for the sole purpose of granting general absolution; he pointed to the extensive educational program that was conducted on reconciliation as elementary and constitutive of the gospel of salvation. "The call to reconciliation was misunderstood," he said, "if it was taken as being a call to the sacrament of reconciliation."[11]

The fact that large numbers of people are alienated from the Church, and specifically from the sacrament of penance, would in itself seem to be an extraordinary circumstance. Normally rituals and celebrations are expressive of meanings and values that already exist, but they can also be constitutive of values that do not yet exist. As Bishop Grasar pointed out, some people may need the celebration of reconciliation and absolution along with the strength of the Eucharist before they have sufficient courage to confess their sins individually in the sacrament of penance. This is what happened in Memphis. Apparently it has also happened in Switzerland.[12]

---

[11] "General Absolution," *The Tablet*, vol. 231, no. 7132 (March 19, 1977) 292.
[12] Bhaldraithe, *art. cit.*

In February 1977, controversy was again stirred up in Canada by the decision of Archbishop Joseph-Aurele Plourde of Ottawa to conduct a series of nine Lenten services of community reconciliation and general absolution in his archdiocese. This followed a detailed letter to all his priests, in which he agreed to celebrate general absolution rituals personally in parishes that wanted them. In his letter the Archbishop said that general absolution should be given as a "try" and that "instead of replacing individual confession, collective absolution . . . should strengthen it, make it more beneficial. Otherwise I fear that interest in individual penance will continue to decrease, the new [rites of penance] will remain wishful thinking and penitents will continue to go spiritually hungry."[13]

A number of bishops in the United States implemented the rite of community reconciliation and general absolution during the Lenten season of 1978. Obviously, the Sacred Congregation for the Doctrine of the Faith and various bishops throughout the world are not in agreement in their interpretation of the norms for general absolution, nor do they seem to have the same sense of what is pastorally effective and responsible in the Church today.

Another area that has involved much discussion and disagreement since the Second Vatican Council has been the problem of admitting children to first communion prior to first confession. In the decade following the close of the Second Vatican Council, the findings of developmental psychologists and the experiences of pastors, confessors, catechists, parents and children, as well as the research of theologians, led to the rather generalized practice in various countries of delaying first confession until after first communion, usually by two or three years. Within this context of testing an approach to the sequence of communion and confession that seems to have existed in the Church up until the Fourth Lateran Council in 1215, the General Catechetical Directory and its addendum on "The First Reception of the Sacraments of Penance and Eucharist" were issued by the Sacred Congregation for the Clergy on April 11, 1971.[14] The addendum recalled the first basic principle with which the Sacred Congregation of the Sacraments had concluded its decree on the age for admission to first communion, *Quam singulari*, issued on August

[13] *The Tablet*, vol. 231, no. 7134 (April 2, 1977) 339.
[14] AAS 64 (1972) 97–176.

8, 1910: "The age of discretion, both for first confession and first communion, is the time when a child begins to reason, that is approximately the age of seven years. From that time on the obligation of satisfying the precept of both confession and communion begins."[15] In citing this principle, the addendum significantly changed the meaning of the decree. Immediately before citing the principle, it said: "The suitable age for the first reception of these sacraments is deemed to be that which in the documents of the Church is called the age of discretion." However, *Quam singulari* did not say that the age of seven is *suitable* for first confession; rather, it said that children are to have access to confession from that appropriate age. *Quam singulari* ensured the possibility of confession from that age, but said nothing about the suitability or value of confessing at that age.

After defending early confession, the addendum asserted that the practice of putting confession ahead of first communion should be retained. Bishops were further instructed not to depart from the practice without first consulting the Holy See, and they were told not to allow pastors or educators or religious institutes to begin or to continue to abandon the traditional practice. However, in regions where new practices had already been introduced, the conferences of bishops were free to submit their experiments to the Holy See for a new examination. If they wanted to continue their experiments for a longer time, they were not to do so unless they had first communicated with the Holy See.

At the International Catechetical Congress held in Rome in September 1971, the addendum was strongly criticized by many participants. Cardinal John Wright, prefect of the Sacred Congregation for the Clergy, which had issued the addendum, maintained that the directory itself did not have the force of law but offered guidance to national hierarchies; he described his Congregation as a service department, not a legislative body. His remarks certainly did not clarify the binding force of the addendum.

In November 1972, the United States National Conference of Catholic Bishops voted to petition the Holy See for a two-year extension of the "experiment" to administer first communion to children before first confession. In a sense, the petition confused the issue,

---

[15] *AAS* 2 (1910) 577–83.

because the emphasis among catechists had not been on administering communion *before* confession, but rather on *delaying* confession until children were better able to understand and celebrate the sacrament.

On May 24, 1973, a declaration issued jointly by the Congregation for the Discipline of the Sacraments and the Congregation for the Clergy mandated the termination of further experimentation with the practice at the end of the 1972–73 scholastic year.[16] From a practical point of view, the declaration seemed unreasonable because of its late publication and its call for immediate implementation. It did not take into account the fact that implementation of the declaration implied radical changes in catechetical programs and materials, changes that would require considerable reflection and planning. As a result, various dioceses issued their own guidelines and asserted their own pastoral prerogatives. Many liturgists and religious educators were unconvinced of the validity of the argumentation used in the declaration.

The authority cited for imposing a return to the former practice of first confession before first communion was the decree *Quam singulari* of 1910. The goal of that decree, however, was the implementation of the decree of the Fourth Lateran Council requiring annual confession and communion during the Easter season and the declaration that the decree applied even to children, once they reached the age of reason. The primary concern of Pius X, who approved the decree *Quam singulari*, was that children must not be kept from receiving communion; he was not concerned primarily with their obligations but rather with their basic rights as baptized Christians. While assuming the existing discipline of confession before communion, he had not made a judgment about the propriety of such a practice. To cite his document as support for the decision of May 24, 1973, was irresponsible on the part of the Congregation for the Discipline of the Sacraments and the Congregation for the Clergy.

Theologians and canonists have regularly understood the decree of the Fourth Lateran Council as prescribing communion at least once a year, but only those who are conscious of having committed serious sin have the responsibility of going to confession prior to

---

[16] *AAS* 65 (1973) 410.

communion. The prescription of the Fourth Lateran Council was carried over into the Code of Canon Law,[17] but it should be noted that in speaking of the obligation of annual confession, the new order of penance in number 34 specifies that *grave* sins must be confessed annually; this is in keeping with the unanimous teaching of canonists and theologians. Experts in child psychology as well as many religious educators have maintained that most children of six or seven cannot commit serious sin. They may be conscious of doing wrong, but they do not grasp the meaning of sin as the violation of a personal relationship between themselves and God. This is not to deny their need for the experience of reconciliation within their own families and communities. Certainly confession should not be routinely imposed on children, without any concern for their own consciences, as a prerequisite for receiving communion, a right that is theirs as baptized Christians as soon as they are able to distinguish the Eucharist from ordinary bread.

In spite of these arguments, the Sacred Congregation for the Clergy and the Sacred Congregation for the Sacraments and Divine Worship issued a further formal response to a doubt concerning the legitimacy of receiving first communion before the reception of penance. The date of the response was May 20, 1977.[18] Signed by both Cardinal James Knox and Cardinal John Wright, the text simply but firmly asserted that first communion cannot be received, as a general rule, before the reception of the sacrament of penance in those parishes where such a practice was in effect for the last few years.

This response angered many experts in religious education. Some suggested a way to alleviate the tension between the Sacred Congregations and those involved in pastoral practice at the grass-roots level. They pointed out that the sacrament of baptism has been adapted to the condition of infants and children, and that a willingness to adapt the Eucharist to the condition of children is reflected in the Directory for Masses with Children and in the Eucharistic prayers for children. Since the new order of penance is clearly intended for adults, they asked whether a similar adaptation of this sacrament should not be made for children.

[17] Canon 906.
[18] *AAS* 69 (1977) 427.

The difficulty in preparing children for the sacrament of reconciliation lies not so much with the ritual of absolution as with the rite of individual auricular confession, which requires a sense of sin as a violation of one's relationship with God, a sense of responsibility, and sufficient control of language to enable one to express one's own identity. A child of six or seven does not possess the psychological and moral development necessary to make a meaningful auricular confession as it is required of adults.

Manuals of theology have regularly maintained that penitents may receive absolution without auricular confession if they are unable to articulate their sins; a simple sign of sorrow is required. This often happens in the case of patients in hospitals and of those who are mentally retarded. Young children would seem to be in a comparable situation. They regularly communicate their sorrow and desire for forgiveness to parents, teachers, and friends nonverbally by means of simple gestures, or if they do verbalize their feelings, they use very simple language. The difficulty or inability that young children have in confessing their sins in an adult manner would seem to be sufficient reason to excuse them from the requirement that they confess their sins as adults; absolution should be given to them, provided there is some manifestation of sorrow.

Confessors would be within the tradition and law of the Church if they granted individual absolution to young children within a penitential celebration. The children could be invited to reflect communally on their daily lives and to participate in a simple communal litany of sorrow for any wrongs they may have done. Each child would approach the priest, acknowledge that he/she has done wrong, and ask for forgiveness. The priest would then give individual absolution as an expression of God's forgiveness, give the child a sign of peace, and invite the child to share that peace with others in the community as an expression of reconciliation with God and his Church.

ANOINTING OF THE SICK

The apostolic constitution *Sacram unctionem infirmorum*, which revised the form and rites of the sacrament of the anointing of the sick, was issued on November 30, 1972.[19] This constitution was

19 *AAS* 65 (1973) 5-9.

followed by a decree of the Sacred Congregation for Divine Worship, *Infirmis cum ecclesia*, which was issued on December 7, 1972, and which promulgated the new order.[20]

On March 4, 1965, the Sacred Congregation of Rites had issued a decree authorizing ordinaries of places to allow priests to carry the oil of the sick with them while traveling.[21] Abrogating the restriction of canon 946 of the Code of Canon Law, the decree was intended to make the sacrament of extreme unction more readily available to the dying. On February 14, 1966, the Sacred Congregation of Rites issued a decree simplifying the ritual for the distribution of holy communion to patients in hospitals.[22] Although the decree did make the distribution of the sacrament more expeditious, its overall benefit was questionable, since in practice it tended to promote efficiency at the expense of a prayer experience celebrated by the priest and each patient. The decree allowed the priest to recite the prayers before and after communion a single time rather than repeating them for each patient.

There was certainly a great need for a thorough reform of the Church's ministry to the sick and dying. As the Constitution on the Sacred Liturgy noted, the sacrament of "extreme unction" should more correctly be called the "anointing of the sick."[23] In practice, before its revision, the sacrament of anointing was ordinarily administered to people in grave danger of death because of intrinsic reasons. Consequently, people receiving the sacrament were often not able to participate actively in the celebration. Then, too, the sacrament was often administered with haste, in situations scarcely conducive to liturgical celebrations, and often without the participation of family and friends. There was hardly any effective proclamation of God's Word to illuminate the ritual action.

The sacrament could not be repeated unless there was an improvement in the sick person's condition, followed by a regression. Another difficulty was that the form of the sacrament adopted in the Latin West during the Middle Ages tended to emphasize the penitential aspect, to the neglect of the positive gift of life and grace.

[20] *AAS* 65 (1973) 275–76.

[21] *AAS* 57 (1965) 409.

[22] *AAS* 58 (1966) 525–26.

[23] *Sacrosanctum Concilium*, no. 73: *AAS* 56 (1964) 118–19.

The revised formula gives a much more positive thrust to the sacrament. It stresses that the grace of the sacrament is the work of the Holy Spirit and asserts that the sacrament of the anointing is a remedy for both body and soul. The sacrament is penitential in the sense that it serves as a substitute for the sacrament of reconciliation if the latter cannot be effectively administered, but its principal effect is the grace of comfort and strength leading to salvation.

Instead of the traditional anointing of the various senses, there is ordinarily one anointing, normally on the forehead. If it is thought desirable, an additional anointing may be given on some part of the body affected by illness or disease, but the formula is recited only once.

The oil for the anointing is still consecrated by the bishop in the concelebrated Eucharist on Holy Thursday morning, but if necessary, oil may be consecrated by the priest celebrating the sacrament. The revised formula for consecrating the oil is eucharistic in the sense that the celebrant thanks God for his blessings through the use of oil in the economy of human salvation. The general thrust of the formula, then, is similar to that used in blessing the baptismal water to be used during the Easter season.

The revised rite also provides for a Scripture reading, a homily, a formula for common prayer with petitions for the recipient of the sacrament, for all those who are sick, and for those who minister to their needs. The general presumption is that the recipient is in a condition to participate consciously in the celebration, which should, if possible, take place in a community setting.

In the new order, there are considerable disciplinary modifications concerning the conditions required for celebrating the sacrament. In judging the seriousness of the illness, one need not be scrupulous; a prudent judgment suffices. The sacrament may be repeated if the sick person recovers after anointing or if, during the same illness, the danger becomes more serious. The sick person may be anointed before surgery if the surgery is to take place because of a dangerous condition. An elderly person in weakened health may be anointed even if not dangerously ill. However, the order does not allow for indiscriminate anointing of all who are sick, but only of those who are seriously ill. Children who are seriously ill and who have sufficient understanding to grasp the basic meaning of the sacrament and to be comforted by it may be anointed. Although the new order makes no specific mention of the mentally ill, those whose mental illness is serious and who would be comforted by the sacrament may be anointed. This follows from the assertion in the order that "it is part of the plan laid down by God's providence that we should struggle against all sickness and carefully seek the blessings of good health, so that we can fulfill our role in human society and in the Church" (no. 3).

If a priest is called to a person who has already died, he should pray that God will forgive the person's sins, but he should not administer the anointing of the sick. If there is doubt that the person is actually dead, the priest may administer the sacrament conditionally. The priest is the only proper minister of the anointing of the sick.

In addition to the ordinary rite for anointing an individual, along with a shortened form in emergency situations, the new order also provides for communal celebrations for the anointing of a number of people with participation by a sizeable congregation, and for the celebration of anointing of the sick at Mass, following the gospel and homily. Communal celebrations can give effective expression to the Church's concern and prayer for the sick. Such celebrations have become common in hospitals, nursing homes, and homes for the aged. They have also taken place in parish churches, with the parish community joining in the celebration. Such celebrations have not only manifested the support and concern of the parish for its sick and aged members, but they have also been occasions for initiating the participants into the Christian meaning of illness and suffering, and the Church's sacramental ministry to the sick.

The other sacramental rites for the sick and dying have also been revised, and provision has been made for developing these rites, as well as the rite of anointing, in accord with cultural conditions.

Chapter 6

SACRAMENTS:
MARRIAGE AND ORDERS

MARRIAGE

Various changes in the discipline regarding the sacrament of marriage have been issued since the Second Vatican Council, but most of these have been only indirectly concerned with the liturgical celebration of the sacrament. The instruction of the Sacred Congregation for the Doctrine of the Faith, *Matrimonii sacramentum*, issued on March 18, 1966, provided that the limitation formerly prohibiting the celebration of Mass in conjunction with mixed marriages could be lifted by the ordinary.[1] The apostolic letter *Matrimonia mixta*, which Pope Paul VI issued motu proprio on March 31, 1970, provided for the participation of a representative of another church at marriages celebrated in the Catholic Church.[2]

The revised order for celebrating marriage was promulgated by the Sacred Congregation of Rites on March 19, 1969.[3] The order contains four chapters: a rite for celebrating marriage during Mass; a rite for celebrating marriage outside of Mass; a rite for celebrating marriage between a Catholic and an unbaptized person; and texts for use in the marriage rite and in the wedding Mass.

The introduction to the new order stresses that Christian married

[1] *AAS* 58 (1966) 235–39; esp. IV, 238.
[2] *AAS* 62 (1970) 257–63.
[3] *Notitiae* 5 (1969) 203.

couples signify and share in the mystery of the unity and creative love of Christ and his Church. Reference is made to the Pauline teaching that married persons have their own proper gift from God. The text goes on to speak of the undivided love of marriage partners and to praise children as the great good of this state. The text states that the other purposes of marriage are not of less account than the procreation of children, which is a delicate way of handling the old controversy concerning the order of the ends of marriage. However, the introduction to the order is not so delicate, and in fact seems to be insensitive, as it inadvertently deals with the world's population problem. It speaks of God's creative love, which, through the married couples, "will constantly enrich and enlarge his own family" (no. 4).

Provision is made for the celebration of marriage within the Mass if one party is a baptized Christian but not Catholic. If one of the parties is unbaptized, celebration apart from Mass is indicated. The introduction reminds pastors that marriage is an excellent occasion for ministering the love and compassion of Christ to their people — an attitude so different from the arrogance and juridicism sometimes experienced by couples preparing for the sacrament. Pastors are also reminded not to favor wealthy people, but, unfortunately, honors due civil authorities in accord with general liturgical law may be retained (no. 10).

The ancient prohibition against "solemnizing marriage in forbidden times" is eliminated, but the celebrant is to advise the couple of the special character of the season. The Tridentine teaching[4] that expressed an earnest desire that local ceremonies and customs be retained in the Roman Catholic liturgy — a teaching repeated in the Constitution on the Sacred Liturgy — is repeated in the introduction to the new order of marriage. Conferences of bishops have the faculty to prepare marriage rites suitable to their people, but they must be approved by the Apostolic See. The consent of the couple and the blessing of those newly married must be retained in every rite.

Where the custom of celebrating marriage in the home prevails, the rites should be carried out in a Christian spirit. In English-speaking countries, civil and non-Catholic marriages are occasion-

---

[4] Session 24 (1563).

ally celebrated in the home. This would seem to be a wholly reasonable practice, because marriage is in many ways domestic.[5] But when Catholics have asked for permission to celebrate marriage at home, it has often been denied.

In accord with the introduction to the new order, episcopal conferences might be encouraged to allow the celebration of the sacrament in homes when such a celebration would respond to the needs of the people and be for their good. Those in authority do not always err by allowing people to do what they want to do. But it should be pointed out that the celebration of marriage should not be an occasion to cater to the natural selfishness and sometimes sentimental tastes of those being married. Since marriage is a sacrament, it involves the Church, which has a stake in every Catholic life. The Church has the responsibility, then, to see that all of the sacraments, including marriage, are celebrations of faith and not saccharine interludes that are superficial and sentimental.

SACRED ORDERS

The revision of the rites for the conferral of orders has been carried out in many steps. The Constitution on the Sacred Liturgy[6] decreed that the addresses given by the bishop at the beginning of each ordination or consecration could be in the vernacular. The same article also stipulated that in the consecration of a bishop, the laying on of hands may be done by all the bishops present. A decision of the Sacred Congregation of Rites, dated July 17, 1965, specified which parts of the then current ordination rites could be recited in the vernacular.[7]

The restoration of the diaconate as a permanent and independent order in the Western Church, which had been decided on by the Second Vatican Council,[8] was carried out by Pope Paul VI in a motu proprio, *Sacrum diaconatus ordinem*, dated June 18, 1967.[9] The document was issued only three days after the Pope had made public

[5] See Jean-Paul Audet, *Structures of Christian Priesthood: A Study of Home, Marriage, and Celibacy in the Pastoral Service of the Church* (New York: Macmillan, 1968) 3–74.

[6] *Sacrosanctum Concilium*, no. 76: AAS 56 (1964) 119.

[7] *Notitiae* 1 (1965) 277–79.

[8] *Lumen gentium*, no. 29: AAS 57 (1965) 36.

[9] AAS 59 (1967) 697–704.

his encyclical upholding the Latin tradition of priestly celibacy. In
his motu proprio he maintained that the diaconate must no longer
be considered as "a pure and simple step of ascent to the priesthood."
This document asserted that two types of deacons would exist: single
men, for whom the minimum age for ordination is twenty-five, and
married men, who must have their wives' consent in writing and for
whom the minimum age is thirty-five. The deacon's duties include
assisting at the liturgy, distributing holy communion, preaching,
administering baptism, officiating at marriages, and presiding at
funerals; reading the Bible to the faithful and teaching and ex-
horting them; presiding in the absence of a priest at religious services; conducting liturgies of the Word, especially when there is no
priest; doing charitable and social work on behalf of the hierarchy;
administering scattered Christian communities in the name of the
bishop and parish priest; and encouraging and helping the lay
apostolate. The deacon is not empowered to celebrate Mass or to
hear confessions. A number of replies have been issued subsequent to
this document in order to clarify the role of deacons in the celebration of marriage.[10]

It is up to the national bishops' conferences to decide whether to
restore the diaconate in their territories as a permanent and distinct
degree of the sacrament of orders, and their decisions must be approved by the Holy See. Permanent deacons are to be given sound

[10] March 26, 1968: AAS 60 (1968) 363. This response from the Pontifical Commission for the Interpretation of the Decrees of the Second Vatican Council affirmed that
deacons who do not intend to remain deacons permanently but to go on to the priesthood have the same functions as permanent deacons.

April 4, 1969: AAS 61 (1969) 348. This response declared that it is not necessary that
a priest be unavailable in order that a deacon assist validly at a marriage.

July 19, 1970: AAS 62 (1970) 571. This response declared that a deacon, regularly
assigned to a parish, can be equated with an assistant pastor (according to the mind of
canon 1096, §1), and can be given general delegation to assist at marriages (according
to the norm of canon 1095, §2).

When asked whether and to what extent, in accord with canon 1147, §1, C.I.C., the
dogmatic constitution Lumen gentium, no. 29, and the apostolic letter Sacrum
diaconatus ordinem, no. 22, a deacon can impart blessings, both constitutive and in-
vocative, as well as administer sacramentals, the Commission for the Interpretation of
the Decrees of the Second Vatican Council replied on November 13, 1974, that a
deacon can impart only those blessings and administer those sacramentals that are expressly allowed him by the law (AAS 66 [1974] 667).

theological and pastoral formation, which should extend throughout their lives. They are to be properly supervised in their ministry.

Prospective candidates for the permanent diaconate should have a competence in three areas: ministry of the Word (preaching), ministry of liturgy, and ministry of charity (including administration). The Dogmatic Constitution on Divine Revelation of the Second Vatican Council defined ministry of the Word as "pastoral preaching, catechetics, and all other Christian instruction, among which the liturgical homily should have an exceptional place."[11] The preaching ministry of the deacon is closely associated with his liturgical role; in fact, the ministry of the Word, in its most important aspect, is a liturgical aspect. If teaching and preaching are part of the deacon's office, candidates should be reasonably intelligent men.

The deacon is clearly one of the ordinary ministers of baptism and an official witness at marriages. A report of the Catholic Theological Society of America, commissioned by the bishops of the United States, recommended that the deacon be empowered to administer the sacrament of the anointing of the sick and that he be given faculties to administer the sacrament of penance in the context of his ministry to the sick and the dying.[12] No action has been taken on these recommendations.

The diaconate has traditionally been associated with the ministry of charity. Although it has been thought of regularly as a ministry to the poor, it should be viewed in a wider context as a ministry of the Church's temporalities. It is undoubtedly in this area that creative development must take place, since the area of temporalities has changed remarkably in the recent past. First of all, the traditional ministry of charity toward the poor has been both institutionalized and professionalized. Many of the social works of the Church have been taken over by government agencies. Administration of the Church's temporalities has come to encompass complex planning, social welfare, insurance, and rehabilitation of the destitute. Then, too, the Christian understanding of responsibility in the area of temporalities has matured significantly. It would seem that permanent

[11] *Dei verbum*, no. 24: *AAS* 58 (1966) 828–29.
[12] "A Report on the Restoration of the Office of Deacon as a Lifetime State," February 23, 1971, par. 36.

deacons should be well informed about social issues and structures that facilitate a response to such issues. They should be in a position to form the Christian social consciences of Church members, to develop leadership, and to provide creative solutions to social problems.

Since it is a sin against God and his Church to put spiritual power in the hands of the inept, those who are ordained to the permanent diaconate should have talent for public service, talent for prayer, zeal for preaching, teaching, and public worship, and good common sense. Surely those who are looking for the benefit of status derived from clerical culture should not be admitted to the order.

On June 18, 1968, Pope Paul VI, in his apostolic constitution *Pontificalis Romani*, announced a major revision of the rites of ordination to the diaconate, priesthood, and episcopate.[13] The new rites were promulgated on August 15, 1968.[14] Deacons and priests should ordinarily be ordained in the local church or diocese where they will minister. If the ordination must take place in another diocese, the presentation of the candidates may fittingly be made by a priest representing the particular dioceses where they will serve. It is especially important that a bishop be ordained in his own church rather than in another diocese if he is named from outside the local clergy. The rite states clearly that the local church presents the priest for ordination to the episcopate; the priests who accompany the bishop-elect represent the local presbyterium. The bishop-elect should be seen to be presented by representatives of his church, and he should be admitted to the college of bishops by all the bishops who are present. The consecrating bishops do not come forward merely for the imposition of hands; they participate throughout. It is desirable that they concelebrate the Eucharist.

In each ordination there is an instruction after the gospel and the initial presentation of the candidates. Given by the ordaining bishop, this instruction is addressed both to the candidates and the people. It takes the place of the homily, but it is desirable to relate the instruction to the scriptural readings that have just been proclaimed, and it should be concerned with the ministry of bishops, priests, or deacons, according to the occasion.

---

[13] *Notitiae* 4 (1968) 209–19.
[14] *Ephemerides Liturgicae* 83 (1969) 4.

The order provides a model instruction for each of the ordination rites, but it should not be read verbatim, as was generally done in the case of the ordination instructions of the older Roman Pontifical. When a bishop is ordained, it is fitting that he speak to the people briefly before the final blessing and dismissal, especially if he has just been ordained to minister to the people present.

In each of the ordination rites, provision is made for the expression of formal assent by the people to the choice of the candidate. This is done by having them say "Thanks be to God" or by some other sign such as applause. Since it replaces the consultation of the people found in the older Roman Pontifical, its intent should be explained to the people so that they may understand their role in the selection of their bishops and other ministers.

The various rites indicate the proper time for singing. If the music is simply meant to accompany a rite, it should not be prolonged after the rite has been completed. In other words, these rites are not meant to be occasions for concerts. The sung texts, such as the *Veni, Creator Spiritus* and the *Te Deum*, may be replaced by other appropriate songs.

Since ordinations are celebrated in the context of the Eucharist, the Mass is usually concelebrated. When a bishop is ordained, it is desirable that all the bishops present concelebrate the Eucharist together with the new bishop and his presbyterium. If all the priests of the diocese cannot concelebrate with the new bishop, at least a representative number of them should. The principal ordaining bishop may take the second place during the Eucharist, with the newly ordained diocesan bishop being the principal celebrant. The latter also takes the bishop's seat, so that he truly appears to be the head of the local church made up of priests, ministers, and people. This rule would not be applicable in the ordination of titular bishops and when a diocesan bishop is not ordained in his own diocese.

When priests or deacons are ordained, it is proper that the members of the local presbyterium concelebrate with the bishop. Newly ordained priests take the first place next to the bishop; concelebration becomes a clear sign of their incorporation into the presbyteral order. In the ordination of deacons, concelebration by priests is a sign that the diaconal ministry is to be exercised in conjunction with the bishop and his priests.

In the new order the traditional ritual offering of candles and, in the case of episcopal ordination, the offering of bread and wine have been changed; the offering of gifts is done by representatives of the local community. In the ordination of priests, the bread and wine used in the rite by which the signs of the office are given to the ordinands should be the bread and wine used for the Eucharistic sacrifice that follows.

The new rite for the ordination of deacons is used for the ordination of both permanent deacons and those who are later to be ordained priests. The text of the consecratory prayer has been changed, so that it is not interpreted as applying simply to deacons who later become priests. In his apostolic constitution of June 18, 1968, Pope Paul VI stressed that with regard to deacons, in addition to the content of his apostolic letter *Sacrum diaconatus ordinem*, issued motu proprio on June 18, 1967, the teaching of *Lumen gentium* should be especially recalled: "At a lower level of the hierarchy are deacons, upon whom hands are imposed 'not unto the priesthood, but unto a ministry of service.' For strengthened by sacramental grace, in communion with the bishop and his group of priests, they serve the People of God in the ministry of the liturgy, of the word, and of charity" (no. 29). The ancient concept of the deacon as a *minister episcopi* has been formally broadened to stress the deacon's relationship to the *presbyterium*.

On August 15, 1972, the revision of the minor orders was announced, and two documents were issued motu proprio on that day. The first, *Ministeria quaedam*, concerned the reform of the discipline of first tonsure, minor orders, and subdiaconate in the Latin Church.[15] The orders of porter and exorcist have been suppressed. The acolyte takes on the functions of the subdeacon, but national episcopal conferences are free to retain the name "subdeacon" for the one in that office, if they so choose.

Strictly speaking, Pope Paul suppressed the minor orders altogether. We are to speak of "ministries" rather than "orders" when referring to the functions of lectors and acolytes; and these ministries are conferred by installation rather than by ordination. The ministries are conferred on lay persons and do not imply that one has been admitted to the clerical state. Tonsure has been sup-

---

[15] *AAS* 64 (1972) 529–34.

pressed; admission to the clerical state takes place at the ordination to the diaconate. As noted, the order of subdiaconate has also been abolished.

The acolyte is above all a minister in liturgical celebrations, with the task of assisting the deacon or priest. He prepares the altar and the sacred vessels. He is by office a special minister of the Eucharist and is to function in that capacity according to the guidelines established in the instruction *Immensae caritatis*, issued on January 29, 1973. As a special minister of the Eucharist, he is qualified to give communion outside of Mass both to himself and to others in the absence of an ordinary minister of communion or if the ordinary minister is impeded. Hence the acolyte may bring communion to the sick. Where priests and deacons are few in number, the acolyte may minister communion to the faithful when Mass cannot be celebrated. Out of necessity and for sound pastoral reasons, he may expose the Blessed Sacrament but not give benediction.

The primary function of the reader or lector is to proclaim the Word of God in the liturgical assembly. Reading the Scriptures is a ministerial rather than a presidential function; hence the lector should exercise the role of reading the lessons before the gospel even though ministers of a higher rank may be present. When there is no one present to execute the psalm, the reader recites the responsorial psalm; in the absence of a cantor or deacon, he sings or proclaims the intentions of the general intercessions. He may also function as the leader of song. In general, however, the reader's functions should be limited to those that are specifically his or for which he is properly prepared. It is better to involve others in the liturgical celebration than to have one person assume all the ministerial roles.

Ordinaries may also permit lectors to exercise the ministry of preaching for a reasonable cause and in particular cases. This is suggested by analogy with canon 1342, §1 of the Code of Canon Law, which says that tonsured clerics and those in minor orders may preach for a reasonable cause and in particular cases, but tonsure and minor orders are now replaced by ministries. Such permission should not be given to the prejudice of the ministry of the Word by deacons, priests, and bishops; moreover, it should be given to lectors only if they are competent.

As a permanently instituted minister, the lector may help in preparing others who read occasionally in the liturgical celebrations. Certainly the new institution of lectors does not mean that other competent readers who are not permanently instituted should henceforth be excluded.

The ministries of acolyte and lector are envisioned as permanent ministries in themselves and not simply as transitional steps on the way to ordination to orders. They are conferred by the bishop and, in clerical religious institutes, by the major superior. Installation in the ministries of reader and acolyte is reserved to men, "in accordance with the venerable tradition of the Church" (no. VII). Women may certainly read Scripture in liturgical celebrations and may exercise by temporary appointment one of the most important functions of acolyte, namely, distribution of the Eucharist, but they may not aspire to permanent installation in these ministries. Exclusion of women from these ministries is certainly an ancient tradition, but many have questioned the venerable character of that tradition. The document does not cite any doctrinal or theological reasons for the exclusion of women from installation in these ministries; there would seem to be no solid doctrinal or theological reasons why they are so excluded. The basis for the tradition is cultural and sociological. It needs to be rethought in light of the Church's proclamation of a gospel of basic equality among all of God's people. Equality, of course, does not mean the obliteration of distinct roles.

In order that one may be admitted to the ministries of reader and acolyte, it is required that a handwritten petition be given by the aspirant to the ordinary who has the right to accept the petition. It would seem very desirable for the communities in which the ministries are to be exercised in a permanent way to have some role in the selection of candidates, but provision for this was not made in the apostolic letter.

Candidates for ordination as deacons and priests are to receive the ministries of reader and acolyte, unless they have already done so, and are to exercise them for a suitable time, in order to be better disposed for the future service of the Word and the altar. Dispensations from receiving these ministries on the part of such candidates are reserved to the Holy See.

It is left to the judgment of episcopal conferences to decide whether additional ministries, such as that of cantor or catechetical director, should be instituted for their regions. They may petition the Holy See if they think there is a need. However, the multiplication of permanently instituted ministries might result unfortunately in an excessive institutionalization of the Church and the presumption that only those so installed can minister effectively. This could possibly work to the detriment of the Church's free response to the great variety of gifts that God has given to his people.

The second apostolic letter, *Ad pascendum,* issued motu proprio on August 15, 1972, contained various norms for the exercise of the order of deacon.[16]

On December 3, 1972, the Sacred Congregation for Divine Worship issued a decree, *Ministeriorum disciplina,* which promulgated the new rites for the institution of readers and acolytes, for the admission to candidacy for ordination as deacons and priests, and for the commitment to celibacy on the part of those to be ordained deacons.[17] The rite for admission to candidacy is a public expression of intention on the part of the candidate and of acceptance by the Church. Professed members of clerical religious congregations who seek the presbyterate are not bound to this rite. The competent superior for this acceptance is the ordinary (the bishop and, in clerical institutes, the major superior). The candidates are asked to indicate their purpose in preparing for ordination; the ordinary receives the declaration on behalf of the Church. It is necessary that those who aspire to the diaconate leading to the presbyterate will have completed at least their twentieth year and will have begun their course of theological studies. Because of its nature, the rite of admission is never to be joined to an ordination or to the institution of readers or acolytes. It is celebrated either during Mass or during a liturgy of the Word.

A new rite, inserted into diaconal ordination, was prepared by which unmarried candidates for the diaconate, whether or not they later are ordained priests, publicly commit themselves to permanent celibacy. This rite is binding even on members of religious communities who have already publicly professed a vow of chastity. The repetition of such a commitment before ordination to the diaconate would surely seem to be questionable in the case of religious.

[16] *AAS* 64 (1972) 534–40.
[17] *Notitiae* 9 (1973) 17.

As part of the interrogation of all candidates for the diaconate, a new question has been added: "Are you resolved to maintain and deepen a spirit of prayer appropriate to your way of life and, in keeping with what is required of you, to celebrate faithfully the liturgy of the hours for the Church and for the whole world?" The obligation of the public prayer of the Church, the liturgy of the hours, is not absolute for permanent deacons, but it is certainly regarded as appropriate.

Stimulated by the women's liberation movement and by their quest for equal rights in the world, various theologians have raised the question of the ordination of women to the priesthood in recent years. Following a study undertaken by the Sacred Congregation for the Doctrine of the Faith at the direction of Pope Paul VI, a Declaration on the Question of the Admission of Women to the Ministerial Priesthood in the Roman Catholic Church was approved by Pope Paul VI on October 15, 1976.[18] It was released to the press in Rome and simultaneously at bishops' secretariats around the world on January 27, 1977. The declaration said that the "Church, in fidelity to the example of the Lord, does not consider herself authorized to admit women to priestly ordination" (no. 4). The declaration, however, omitted discussion of the ordination of women to the diaconate. A Vatican commentary released at the same time explained that this omission was by express design.

The declaration rejected the view that Jesus did not ordain women because it would have violated the customs of his time. Jesus "deliberately and courageously broke" with the prevailing attitudes of his society toward women, but he did not do so in calling the twelve apostles (no. 10). The fact that the Church restricts ordination to men is not based on any inferiority of women. But, it said, while men and women are equal, they do not have the same identity. The commentary stated that the exclusion of women from the ministerial priesthood is not an injustice to them, since ordination is not necessary to human fulfillment and is not, moreover, a right for either men or women. The commentary also noted that it is "precisely because the priest is a sign of Christ the savior that he must be a man and not a woman."

The questions raised by the declaration and the Vatican commen-

18 *AAS* 69 (1977) 98–116.

tary are issues of far-reaching, ultimately universal interest and importance. Sometimes heated debate and in-depth study of the issue have continued since the declaration was issued. Bolstered by a report of the Pontifical Biblical Commission,[19] which concluded that "it does not seem that the New Testament by itself alone will permit us to settle in a clear way and once and for all the problem of the possible accession of women to the presbyterate," various theologians, especially women, have questioned the foundations on which the declaration's conclusions rest. They have maintained that the "traditional" Church teaching on the matter of women's role in the Church has not been a matter of creative reflection on the effect of sexual identity on ministerial functioning but rather a matter of almost total benign neglect. Since the question has surfaced in recent times, there has been an amazingly rapid development of support for the opinion that there is no intrinsic reason standing in the way of the ordination of women to full ministerial activities.

Since it seems quite unlikely that the Church's official position on the ordination of women will change in the near future, attention has, to some extent, shifted away from the question of ordination to the priesthood and has begun to concentrate on other forms of ministry that should be open to women in the Church. Efforts are being made to open the lay ministries of lector and acolyte to women. The development of pastoral teams comprising faithful of both sexes is being promoted, and efforts are being expended so that women are given equal access to serve as extraordinary ministers of the Eucharist. Finally, efforts are being made to bring about changes in four specific areas of Church law:

1. Qualified lay women and men should be commissioned to preach the Word of God.

2. Women should be given the same access to tribunal functions as has been given to lay men.

3. All administrative positions in the Church not requiring the power of orders should be open to lay women and men.

4. Other instances of discrimination against women should be corrected, for example, in the area of papal enclosure.[20]

[19] *Origins*, vol. 6, no. 6 (July 1, 1976).

[20] "Consensus Statement from the Symposium on Women and Church Law," *Sexism and Church Law*, ed. James Coriden (New York: Paulist Press, 1977) 157.

Chapter 7

SACRAMENTS:
EUCHARIST (CELEBRATION)

Numerous new decrees and rites relating to the Eucharist have been issued in the past fifteen years. For the sake of clarity, it might be useful to comment first on those that pertain above all to the celebration of the Eucharist and then to comment on those that pertain to the distribution of communion and to the worship of the Eucharist. The distribution of communion and worship of the Eucharist must always, of course, be related to the celebration of the Eucharist and must be looked upon either as means of participating in the Mass or as extensions of the Eucharistic celebration.

CELEBRATION OF THE EUCHARIST

Apart from the various documents related to the reform of the Roman Missal, a number of documents affected the rubrics of the Mass itself. The first general instruction on the liturgy, *Inter Oecumenici Concilii*, of September 26, 1964, introduced a number of minor rubrical changes that went into effect on March 7, 1965.[1] These modifications were followed by a new *Ordo Missae: Ritus servandus in celebratione Missae et de defectibus in celebratione Missae occurrentibus*, issued on January 27, 1965.[2] On February 15,

[1] *AAS* 56 (1964) 877–900.
[2] Rome: Typis Polyglottis Vaticanis, 1965, 69 pp.

1965, the rubrical changes to be made in the Roman Missal because of the new order were officially promulgated.[3]

The new *Ordo Missae* included a General Instruction providing a codification of revised rubrics for celebrating Mass; an order of Mass with a congregation, incorporating the traditional prefaces of the Roman Missal as well as the new prefaces published in the summer of 1968; an order of Mass without a congregation; and an appendix containing alternate formulas for the penitential rite, acclamations, and Gregorian musical settings. The texts were obviously the result of compromise.

One of the principal objections raised to the new order of Mass has been the complicated entrance rite. Many liturgists favored placing the penitential rite at the end of the liturgy of the Word, together with the prayer of the faithful. They maintained that it is the proclamation of the Word of God that makes it possible for persons to be penitent. Although a penitential heart is one that is open and receptive to the Word and life of the Lord, the initiative for such conversion always resides with the Lord. The new order unfortunately situated the penitential act after the entrance song, where it is given a semi-Pelagian thrust, implying that people inaugurate their own conversion. In the first form of the penitential rite, the *Kyrie* has been retained, but it tends to dangle loosely, since it is not integrated with what precedes and what follows. The *Gloria* has also been retained at its usual place, with the result that the collect is separated so much from the entrance song as to lose its traditional function.

The decision to maintain the creed in its traditional position between the homily and the prayer of the faithful is also looked upon by many liturgists as a structural flaw in the new order. The homily is meant to mediate the Word of the Lord to the assembled community and to stir up a response of faith and trust, which is reflected in the prayer of the faithful. But when the creed is interjected between the homily and the prayer of the faithful, as happens regularly on Sundays and solemnities, it fractures the unity of the rite. The anaphora itself is the primary proclamation of the community's faith within a Eucharistic celebration; the creed fulfills that role most properly in the baptismal liturgy. If the creed is to be retained in the Eucharist, it would seem that the best place for it

[3] "Rubricae in Missali Romano emendandae," *Notitiae* 1 (1965) 215–19.

would be at the end of the offertory rites, where it marks the unity of faith within the community. It was so placed in the East, where it was first introduced into the Eucharistic liturgy.

Many liturgists also object to the offertory prayers, which they feel complicate what should be a very simple preparation of the gifts. They also object to the retention of the *Orate, fratres* and its response, on the grounds that it usurps the role of the prayer over the gifts. Perhaps the *Orate, fratres* should have been retained without the response, as an invitation to pray silently before the celebrant's prayer over the gifts.

In contrast to the *Ordo Missae*, the General Instruction of the Roman Missal (*Institutio generalis*) is a very impressive document. Cast within a broad theological framework, it provides regulations that are flexible and intelligible, while setting out directives that facilitate pastorally effective celebrations.

A new rite for concelebration was first published by the decree *Ecclesiae semper*, of March 7, 1965, in conjunction with the new rite for communion under both kinds.[4] The restoration of concelebration was done very hastily, after a period of experimentation with a new rite in a select number of communities. Experience since then has shown the limitations of the rite and has raised various theological and canonical problems. Up until 1965, concelebration had existed in the Roman Church only in a vestigial form. By the time the Sacred Congregation of Rites and the Consilium issued the instruction *Eucharisticum mysterium* on May 25, 1967, the practice of concelebration was already widely practiced and so generally accepted that the Congregation regarded it as quite normal, not only permitted but certainly favored and recommended. Although still permitted, the private Mass was considered exceptional.[5] In a declaration on concelebration, *In celebratione Missae*, issued on August 7, 1972, the Sacred Congregation for Divine Worship took a step further by stating that concelebration is "the most important form of Eucharistic celebration in communities."[6] Such a statement is surely a radical reversal of canon 803 of the 1917 Code of Canon

---

[4] *Ritus servandus in concelebratione Missae et Ritus Communionis sub utraque specie* (Rome: Typis Polyglottis Vaticanis, 1965) 104 pp.

[5] No. 47: *AAS* 59 (1967) 565–66.

[6] *AAS* 64 (1972) 327–32.

Law, which states that it is not permissible for several priests to con-celebrate.

Although there has been abundant theological literature on con-celebration, critical reflection and evaluation of the restored prac-tice have been sparse. It is above all on the ritual level that the rite needs to be reviewed.

Concelebration is simply defined as the simultaneous participa-tion of several ministers or priests in one liturgical function. In a sense, the definition is a tautology, since every liturgical celebration is a "simultaneous participation," even though historically the term "concelebration" has been used only of bishops, priests, and deacons. In every celebration of the Eucharist, all those present share and participate in the celebration, each in his or her own way. But there are certain characteristics that are applicable only to those liturgies that are properly termed "concelebrations." As Hendrik Manders has written, "Most authors, both old and recent, seem to agree that a genuine concelebration of the Eucharist presupposes the following conditions: a principal celebrant, a group or 'college' of priests functioning as such which, under the hierarchical guidance of the principal celebrant, celebrates the Eucharist together with him and does so in the midst of the participating community."[7]

In the West, interest in concelebration grew following the Second World War because of a renewed appreciation of the social dimen-sion of the liturgy and also because of its practical value on the occa-sions when many priests gathered for meetings. One suspects that in many areas the rite has become popular primarily because of con-venience. Added solemnity is also another reason. It does make it possible for a number of priests to celebrate Mass without having several altars and the other necessary appointments. Likewise, it does make an occasion more solemn, much in the same fashion as when extra altar boys used to be placed in the sanctuary on special feasts. But neither convenience nor added solemnity was the primary motive in restoring the rite.

The execution of the ritual often leaves much to be desired. Fre-quently the concelebrants recite the required section of the Eucha-ristic prayer in a ragged fashion. Often they seem to be competing

---

[7] "Concelebration," *The Church and the Liturgy*, Concilium 2 (New York: Paulist Press, 1964) 144.

with one another in volume and show little regard for cadence or the techniques of choral reading. The rite calls for the epiclesis, institution narrative, and memorial prayer to be prayed together by all the concelebrants, but only the principal celebrant is to be heard. Only one gesture is required of the concelebrants, that of the imposition of hands during the epiclesis. The gesture during the text of institution is optional.

There would seem to be several assumptions underlying the rite as it usually takes place. One is the feeling that a priest must celebrate Mass every day, a feeling that has been fostered by the medieval teaching on the fruits of the Mass and by the practice of taking Mass stipends. Another is the exaggerated stress placed on the priest in Western sacramental theology and the abnormal stress given to the consecration as a specific moment identified with the words of institution. Another is the tendency to ververbalize, a practice derived from the Gallican liturgy rather than from Rome. Although various instructions from the Holy See have been very firm and clear on all these issues, the theological underpinnings for such disciplinary statements have not been adequately developed; in fact, the theological ground for such statements has usually gone unexamined. As a consequence, concelebration often appears to be little more than a synchronization of several Masses celebrated by a number of priests. This is frequently the case from the time of the preface to the communion rite, since the role of the principal celebrant is often overshadowed by the dominance of the concelebrants.

Another issue that needs to be critiqued is the practice whereby each concelebrant takes a stipend for the Mass. The rite simply perpetuates the traditional teaching and practice concerning stipends and concelebrations.[8] No reason is given why the stipend may be accepted, and the only conditions placed on its acceptance are those that already exist in the general canons on stipends.[9]

The new rite of concelebration, however, has affected a traditional theory that canonical commentators had established as a basis for the practice of accepting stipends at a concelebrated Mass. They cited the principle *tot sacrificia quot sacerdotes* and applied it to concelebration. They reasoned that since each priest celebrated a

---

[8] No. 10.

[9] Code of Canon Law, canons 824–44.

Mass, he could therefore take a stipend. But the general decree promulgating the new rite destroys the validity of this argument. It insists that in a concelebrated Mass many priests confect and offer the one sacrifice in one sacramental act, and together they partake of that sacrifice. Hence there are not as many sacrifices as there are priests; there is one Mass being celebrated at a concelebrated Eucharist. The *tot . . . quot* theory cannot, therefore, be the basis for the acceptance of a stipend by each of the concelebrants. We have, then, a questionable practice in search of a theological foundation.[10]

Although the unity of the Church as communion and the unity of the Eucharistic assembly are theological values stressed in reflections on concelebration, these values are not clearly symbolized in the present rite. Concelebration was reintroduced in the Roman Church at a time when efforts were being made to declericalize the liturgy and to affirm the basic consecration of all Christians through baptism. Instead of affirming the basic unity of the Church as a communion, the new rite seems to symbolize the divisions within the Church that result from priestly ordination. In other words, concelebration as presently practiced seems to emphasize the unity of the ministerial priesthood or the equality of ministerial priests as distinguished from the laity, and it appears to do this to the detriment of the symbolic value of the unity of the Church. Such a ritual seems to be more a gesture of self-affirmation on the part of the priests concelebrating than an affirmation of their unitive role in the community. The ritual then becomes a primatial rather than a ministerial symbol.

Furthermore, the ritual is not an effective symbol of the unity of the Eucharistic assembly. A committee presidency at the Eucharist introduces confusion with regard to leadership, at least on the symbolic level. If each priest must have a part in order to feel that he is really a priest, then the ritual manifests an individualistic rather than a communal attitude. Certainly in secular life we do not set up a committee chairmanship at a convention or a formal banquet, with each member of the committee delivering a part of the presi-

[10] See Harmon D. Skillin, *Concelebration: A Historical Synopsis and Canonical Commentary*, The Catholic University of America Canon Law Studies, no. 450, pp. 116–18; Karl Rahner and Angelus Häussling, *The Celebration of the Eucharist* (New York: Herder and Herder, 1968) 88–125.

dential address or with all of them reciting it chorally. If consistency were maintained in the present rite of concelebration, then all the deacons would divide the gospel reading among themselves and the other ministers present would distribute among themselves the duties proper to their ministries.

It would seem that the present rite of concelebration is not effectively symbolizing the theological meaning it is meant to express. One of the first new rituals to be formulated after the promulgation of the Constitution on the Sacred Liturgy, the rite needs to be reformed in the light of experience and theological reflection.

The Sacred Congregation for Divine Worship issued a declaration concerning concelebration on August 7, 1972.[11] The document asserted that capitulars and members of religious institutes who are obliged to celebrate for the pastoral good of the faithful may on the same day concelebrate the conventual or community Mass. It also noted that those who concelebrate at the principal Mass on the occasion of a pastoral visitation or a special gathering of priests, such as a convention or pilgrimage, may again celebrate the Eucharist for the benefit of the faithful. However, the declaration maintained that the priests who celebrate for the pastoral good of the faithful and concelebrate a second Mass are not allowed by any title to accept a stipend for the concelebrated Mass.

The question of Mass stipends has been treated a number of times in recent documents emanating from the Holy See. On November 29, 1971, the Papal Secretariat of State issued a notification to the effect that all decisions concerning reduction, condonation, and commutation of Mass stipends had been temporarily reserved to the Holy Father.[12] The intention was to review and establish equitable regulations for the practice of accepting Mass stipends.

With the apostolic letter *Firma in traditione*, issued on June 13, 1974, Pope Paul VI granted certain faculties concerning stipends to the Congregations of the Roman curia, local ordinaries, and bishops.[13] On July 1, 1974, papal reservation concerning Mass stipends ceased and the Congregations of the Roman curia were empowered to resume their competence in the matter, but they were

[11] *AAS* 64 (1972) 561–63.

[12] *AAS* 63 (1971) 841.

[13] *AAS* 66 (1974) 308–11.

obliged to accommodate their practice to carefully defined regulations. In addition to the faculties given to the congregations and to local ordinaries, a number of new faculties were granted to bishops. Although special care has been taken by the Holy See to regulate the practice of accepting Mass stipends, the custom is still open to various abuses and needs to be critiqued in the light of recent developments in the theology of the Eucharist.

On September 25, 1965, Cardinal Larraona, prefect of the Sacred Congregation of Rites, sent a letter to Cardinal Ciriaci, prefect of the Sacred Congregation of the Council, concerning the texts to be used when the Mass of a Sunday or holy day of obligation is anticipated on the vigil.[14] At the vigil celebration, the liturgical texts proper to the Sunday or the feast are to be used. Also, the homily and the prayer of the faithful are not to be omitted.

As already noted, the second general instruction, *Tres abhinc annos*, of May 4, 1967, made more revisions in the celebration of the Eucharist. These were officially listed in a decree of the Sacred Congregation of Rites, *Per instructionem*, of May 18, 1967.[15]

The use of the new Eucharistic prayers and prefaces was discussed at the first Synod of Bishops in 1967,[16] and a letter on the subject was subsequently sent by Cardinal Gut, the president of the Consilium, to the presidents of the episcopal conferences.[17] The three new anaphoras and eight new prefaces were officially promulgated by the Sacred Congregation of Rites on May 23, 1968, and their use was authorized from August 15, 1968.[18] In a declaration dated November 6, 1968, the Consilium provided for a uniform text in the consecration of the Mass to be used in the four approved Eucharistic prayers.[19]

Despite their hybrid structure, resulting from a combination of the Roman and Antiochene traditions, and despite their limited reflection of contemporary theological perspectives, the three new canons promulgated in 1968 are a marked improvement over the

---

[14] *Notitiae* 2 (1966) 14.

[15] *Notitiae* 3 (1967) 196–211.

[16] *Notitiae* 3 (1967) 353–70.

[17] *Notitiae* 4 (1968) 146–55.

[18] *Notitiae* 4 (1968) 156–79.

[19] *Notitiae* 4 (1968) 356.

traditional Roman canon. They were composed as an organic unity and progress smoothly through the essential constitutive elements of an anaphora, from praise and thanksgiving to memorial and epiclesis, to intercession and doxology. They are not marked by a disproportionate stress on the renewal of the oblation by the Church, which is the dominant perspective of the Roman canon. The commemoration of the saints is integrated into the prayers, stressing communion within the whole Church rather than intercession. Since the role of the Holy Spirit is much more satisfactorily developed, these canons are more explicitly trinitarian than the Roman canon. The inclusion of acclamations after the text of institution provides for extended participation in the Eucharistic prayer by the whole community.

The rubrics accompanying the texts are also a considerable improvement over the older rubrics in the Roman canon. The celebrant's posture is not indicated in detail, nor is he instructed to pronounce any of the words *secreto*. The account of the Lord's institution of the Eucharist is given as a proclamation in the midst of the community. The priest, then, is no longer isolated from the assembly over which he has been presiding, and the text of institution itself is integrated appropriately within a framework of praise, thanksgiving, and remembrance.

Use of the new canons has shown that they might well be more effective in a revised translation. In some circles there is strong opposition to the use of what is thought to be sexist language, especially in the fourth Eucharistic prayer. In other circles there is a feeling that the English translations are so devoid of poetry that the element of mystery has been obliterated. Perhaps the basic issue is the need to develop other formulations of the Eucharistic prayer that are truly reflective of the diverse cultures throughout the world but are nonetheless faithful to the rich tradition reflected in the traditional liturgical texts.

On April 27, 1973, the Sacred Congregation for Divine Worship sent a letter, *Eucharisticae participationem,*[20] to the episcopal conferences throughout the world. It dealt with the text of the Eucharistic prayers and prohibited the use of any other than the four approved texts unless specifically authorized by the Holy See.

[20] *Notitiae* 9 (1973) 193–208.

The basic reasons given for not using unauthorized texts were the possible weakening of Eucharistic and ecclesial communion and the consequent challenge to both Church unity and legitimate authority. Moreover, there is the serious danger that such prayers will be poorly prepared and deficient in the essential elements of an anaphora. The letter also invited celebrants to express creativity in those parts of the liturgy where it is legitimate. The text mentioned the broad faculty to choose Mass formularies and readings; the possibility of varying the introductions and invitations during the celebration; the possibility of adapting the homily to the needs and background of each assembly; and the creativity that is possible within the prayer of the faithful. The circular letter also affirmed the legitimacy of adapting the brief introductions to prayer texts, the advisability of accommodating the penitential rite to particular circumstances, and the possibility of introducing the Lord's Prayer in such a way that it relates to the communion rite of the Mass.

As a whole, then, the circular letter attempted to combine a rigorous posture concerning unauthorized Eucharistic prayers with an affirmative stance concerning development and diversity within the total celebration.

The third general instruction on the liturgy, *Liturgicae instaurationes*, of September 5, 1970, made no significant changes in the rites of the Mass. A reply by the Commission for the Interpretation of the Decrees of the Second Vatican Council, dated January 11, 1971, clarified the role of lay persons in giving a homily at Mass.[21] It simply affirmed that those who are neither priests nor deacons but who simply participate in the sacred liturgy as lay persons may not give the homily.

A decree of the Sacred Congregation for Divine Worship, *Cum de nomine Episcopi*, dated October 10, 1972, revised the rules for naming the local bishop in the Eucharistic prayer and authorized mentioning the names of other bishops who assist in the diocese or territory.[22] Since the office of auxiliary bishop is theologically ambiguous and since there are numerous auxiliary bishops in some large dioceses, the latter authorization would seem to be questionable. Mentioning them all by name tends to clutter the canon and to

[21] *AAS* 63 (1971) 329–30.
[22] *AAS* 64 (1972) 692–94.

draw excessive attention to the episcopal leadership in the community.

The directives concerning the use of vestments at Mass were simplified by the instruction *Tres abhinc annos*, dated May 4, 1967.[23] Permission was granted to omit the maniple at all times and to wear the chasuble for the *Asperges* before Sunday Mass, for the blessing and imposition of ashes on Ash Wednesday, and for the absolution following the funeral Mass. The instruction stipulated that all concelebrants should wear vestments, but permission was granted to omit the chasuble for a good reason.

Since May 1, 1971, the Sacred Congregation for Divine Worship has issued various rescripts granting permission for the use of a specially designed chasuble commonly called "the chasuble without alb."[24] The rescripts maintain that with regard to color, the only requirement for the vestment is that the stole, worn on top of the garment, be of the color appropriate to the Mass. The document also stressed that the approbation of such a vestment should not arrest the research efforts of artists and designers concerning the form, material, and color of fabrics worn during liturgical celebrations.

In recent years queries have been submitted to the Sacred Congregation for Divine Worship asking whether it is lawful to celebrate Mass without sacred vestments or with only a stole worn over the cassock or civilian dress. The inquiries have been prompted by practical reasons, especially in cases of traveling, camping, and celebrations outside of churches. The response given by Archbishop Bugnini was strictly in conformity with what had previously been laid down in liturgical documents since the Second Vatican Council.[25] His primary concern, however, was that dignity and a certain solemnity surround every celebration of the sacred liturgy.

An instruction, *Actio pastoralis Ecclesiae*, was issued on May 15, 1969, by the Sacred Congregation for Divine Worship on the celebration of the Eucharist for particular groups.[26] The instruction was a great disappointment to many liturgists and those involved in pastoral ministry. Among the positive values to be experienced in so-

---

[23] *AAS* 59 (1967) 442–48.
[24] *Notitiae* 9 (1973) 96–98.
[25] *Notitiae* 10 (1974) 306–7.
[26] *AAS* 61 (1969) 806–11.

called "home Masses" are simplicity of structure, spontaneity in prayer, and a vital experience of the Eucharist as a sacred meal. The instruction prescribed that in domestic liturgies celebrants must wear full vesture, communion is to be given only under one species, and that if a meal is served on the same occasion, it must not be served on the same table on which the Eucharist was celebrated. The presumption behind such regulations seems to be that one cannot symbolize the sacred in contemporary forms. Experience with home liturgies in other world religions would seem to indicate that the sacred can be effectively mediated in an informal yet dignified way within a domestic context.

On November 1, 1973, the Sacred Congregation for Divine Worship issued a Directory for Masses with Children.[27] Although the document dealt directly with liturgies for preschool and grade-school children, it proposed norms that have pastoral implications for the celebration of the Eucharist generally. The document distinguished between Masses celebrated with a primarily adult assembly at which there are some children in attendance and Masses celebrated with an assembly of children at which there are some adults in attendance. It provided that with permission of the bishop some of the adaptations made for the latter celebrations may be made for the former.

The directory insisted first of all on active participation of the assembly, not just because liturgy of its nature requires the participation of the community but also because it helps to avoid boredom. In liturgies where children predominate, the goal is not celebrations for youngsters but celebrations involving the youngsters; hence they should participate in the preparation of the space for the celebration and should serve as readers and in executing the music; they should respond to the homily, take part in the prayer of the faithful, in the offering of the gifts, and in other forms of participation customary in each area. In assemblies where children predominate, they should assume a major role, whereas in communities where adults predominate, adults should take on the important roles. In no celebration should any person be relegated to the role of mere spectator.

As the directory implies, very young children should not be

[27] *AAS* 66 (1974) 30–46.

brought to Mass, but should be entrusted to a nursery attendant during the celebration. Not only are they usually bored during liturgical celebrations, but they also tend to distract those who do want to celebrate. The directory suggests that they be brought into the assembly, at least on occasion, for a special blessing at the end of the celebration.

The directory envisions various possibilities for Masses with adults at which school children also participate. Special monitions may be directed to the children at the beginning and end of the Mass and also during part of the homily. If it is convenient, a proper homily may be given by a qualified minister to the children in a special place, provided they join the rest of the community for the Eucharistic liturgy. If it is well prepared, a homily for children might also be quite profitable for adults. As a group, children may also sing one or other of the songs, and they may take part in the offering of the gifts. However, children should not normally serve as lectors or cantors in primarily adult assemblies, nor should they always be the acolytes in such congregations.

While insisting on the importance of music in celebration, the directory encourages both congregational singing and instrumental music. It also authorizes the use of recorded music, according to norms established by the episcopal conferences. In keeping with the nature of the liturgy as a ritual action and in accord with the psychology of children, who communicate and express themselves often more effectively through gestures than through words, the directory encourages participation through bodily postures. Ritual dance would be included here. The directory also recommends the use of visual media and asserts the importance of silence in every celebration, even those with children.

Although the directory provides for adaptation of various parts of the order of Mass with children, it certainly does not envision the development of a distinct rite. The goal of the directory is to facilitate the progressive initiation of youngsters into the normal celebration of the Eucharist. It insists that the texts of the acclamations and responses, the Lord's Prayer, and the trinitarian formula of blessing at the end of Mass should never be changed. The entrance rite, however, may be greatly simplified; the number of readings may be reduced to one, but the gospel must never be omitted. Since the directory allows for a dialogue homily and permits someone other than a priest or deacon to give the homily, the current legislation grants more rights to children in regard to the homily than to adults. The Apostles' Creed may be substituted for the Nicene Creed. Considerable freedom is also granted in the choice and adaptation of collects from the Roman Missal. The celebrant is urged to give a final monition before the blessing and dismissal so that he may summarize the theme of the celebration and suggest a concrete application in the lives of the children.

On November 1, 1974, the Congregation for Divine Worship forwarded to all conferences of bishops projects for five additional Eucharistic anaphoras.[28] Three of them were designed for celebrations for children and two for celebrations of reconciliation. The individual conferences were invited to select, for use in their respective regions, one of the proposed texts for children and one for reconciliation. The rather questionable decision to restrict the choice in each case to one text was probably motivated by a desire to have a limited number of officially approved canons, out of fear that some celebrants might feel free to use unauthorized texts once the number of authorized texts increased in number.

The introduction to the texts for children indicated that the use of such Eucharistic prayers must be limited to Masses celebrated with children. The first text was designed to provide greater simplicity, the second to facilitate more participation, and the third to provide greater variety. Certainly for pastoral reasons permission should have been granted to all episcopal conferences to utilize all three texts. In preparing vernacular versions, the bishops were encouraged to provide translations that were free and creative while preserving the prescribed structure and basic content.

Experience with the texts has shown that they are rather lengthy for children, whose attention span is quite limited. Also, it would have been preferable to have texts containing more concrete images rather than so many abstract formulations. The most welcome innovation has been the introduction of repeated acclamations throughout the anaphoras. Of special interest is the provision in the three texts for an acclamation after the anamnesis instead of after the narrative of institution. The introduction to the texts explained

[28] *Notitiae* 11 (1975) 4–12.

that this was done so that the children would understand the connection between the command of Christ to make a memorial, which concludes the narrative, and the memorial formulated by the celebrant in the anamnesis. This structure would also have been preferable in the anaphoras of the new Roman Missal.

The introduction also asserts that in view of the psychology of children, it seems better to refrain from concelebration when Mass is celebrated with children. While emphasizing the prerogative of ordained priests, the rite of concelebration would tend to inhibit full participation on the part of children.

The two texts proposed for celebrations of reconciliation were drawn up for use during the Holy Year (1975) at celebrations expressing the intentions of the year and then, after the Holy Year, at Masses having the mystery of reconciliation as a special theme. The texts are well structured and provide a rich pastiche of Old and New Testament themes on penance and reconciliation.

Permission to use the canons for Masses with children and those for Masses of reconciliation was originally given for a three-year period. On December 10, 1977, however, the Sacred Congregation for Sacraments and Divine Worship sent a letter to episcopal conferences notifying them that the Holy Father had given them the faculty to use these Eucharistic prayers for another three years, that is, up to the end of 1980.[29]

[29] *Notitiae* 13 (1977) 555–56.

Chapter 8

SACRAMENTS:
EUCHARIST (COMMUNION AND WORSHIP)

As already noted, a new rite for communion under both kinds was issued by the decree *Ecclesiae semper*, of March 7, 1965, along with the new rite for concelebration.[1] The basic rules for communion under both kinds were modified somewhat on a number of occasions since the publication of the new rite, especially by the instruction *Sacramentali communione*, issued by the Sacred Congregation for Divine Worship on June 29, 1970.[2] The subject was also treated in the instruction *Eucharisticum mysterium*, issued by the Sacred Congregation of Rites on May 25, 1967,[3] and in the General Instruction of the new edition of the Roman Missal.[4]

In number 240, the General Instruction of the Roman Missal summarizes well the theological motivation behind the reintroduction of communion under both kinds: "The sign of communion is more complete when given under both kinds, since the sign of the eucharistic meal appears more clearly. The intention of Christ that the new and eternal covenant be ratified in his blood is better expressed, as is the relation of the eucharistic banquet to the heavenly banquet."

[1] *AAS* 57 (1965) 410–12.
[2] *AAS* 62 (1970) 664–67.
[3] *AAS* 59 (1967) 558–59.
[4] Nos. 67, 240–51.

In one sense, the reintroduction of the practice of communion under both kinds may be looked upon as a departure from a long-standing custom in the Roman rite, but in another sense it is simply the restoration of a tradition followed everywhere in the Church until the twelfth century and still observed faithfully by Orthodox Catholics and Christians of other rites. The most obvious reason for restoring communion under both kinds to wider use is fidelity to the injunction of the Lord: "Unless you eat the flesh of the Son of Man and drink his blood, you shall not have life in you. He who eats my flesh and drinks my blood has life everlasting and I will raise him up on the last day. For my flesh is food indeed and my blood is drink indeed. He who eats my flesh and drinks my blood abides in me and I in him" (Jn. 6:54-57).

The words of Jesus are not addressed to select groups in the Church such as priests or religious or lay persons in certain circumstances; they are addressed to all Christians. Fidelity to the injunction of the Lord would seem to demand that the present discipline be changed so as to allow all Christians to exercise their right and responsibility to share in the cup whenever and wherever the Eucharist is celebrated.

The rite presently in force provides for four different methods of communicating from the cup: the communicant may drink from the cup directly; the minister of communion may dip a part of the host in the chalice before giving it to the communicant (intinction); the communicant may receive the precious blood through a tube; the minister of communion, using a spoon, may distribute some of the precious blood to the communicant.

The first method would seem to be the most natural way to communicate, in keeping with the human way of drinking. Experience has already shown that with proper planning, hundreds of people can reverently receive communion from the cup without delaying the celebration unduly. The second method (intinction) is hard to reconcile with the Lord's command that we should *drink*. It also precludes the possibility of receiving the Eucharistic bread in one's hands. Furthermore, the method is awkward when substantial bread that really looks like bread is used in the celebration. The third method, involving as it does the purification of tubes, is both clumsy and inefficient. The fourth method is not only clumsy but is also foreign to the common experience of children and adults who are not used to being fed with a spoon. With proper catechesis, careful planning, and a dignified execution of the ritual, communion can be offered from the cup not only to the benefit of those who communicate but also to the enrichment of the Church's symbolic life and ministry.

On April 25, 1964, the Sacred Congregation of Rites issued a decree, *Quo actuosius*, that changed the formula to be used in distributing holy communion from the longer statement, "Corpus Domini nostri Iesu Christi custodiat animam tuam in vitam aeternam. Amen," to the words "Corpus Christi." The communicant has been instructed to affirm belief in the Eucharistic presence by responding "Amen."[5]

On May 29, 1969, the Sacred Congregation for Divine Worship sent an instruction, *Memoriale Domini*, to the presidents of episcopal conferences.[6] While insisting on maintaining the traditional manner of giving communion, it allowed the conferences of bishops to present their reasons for placing the consecrated bread in the hand of the communicant. In spite of earlier widespread opposition to any modification in the manner of receiving communion, opinion has changed remarkably, so that communion in the hand has become an option in numerous countries throughout the world. The introduction of the change is conditioned by a two-thirds majority vote by the episcopal conference before the decision can be presented to the Holy See for confirmation.

A reaffirmation of the Church's faith in the Eucharist was expressed by Pope Paul VI in his encyclical *Mysterium fidei*, which he issued on September 3, 1965.[7] In the history of the Church, various conceptual and imaginative frameworks have been used to interpret the Christian faith. Eucharistic theology has been an area where diverse explanations of the Christian faith have regularly been found and different aspects have received contrasting emphases. The real presence, the relation of sacrifice and meal, the sacramental character of the Eucharist, and the role of the priest and the community in the celebration are all questions that have received a

[5] *AAS* 56 (1964) 337–38.
[6] *AAS* 61 (1969) 541–45.
[7] *AAS* 67 (1965) 753–74.

variety of theological answers over the centuries. In his encyclical, Pope Paul discussed a number of these issues. He singled out three areas that caused him concern: sacrifice, sacrament, and Eucharistic piety.

Pope Paul maintained that the communal Mass should not be so emphasized that Masses celebrated privately are thereby disparaged. He said nothing about whether concelebration is preferable, or about whether a priest ought always celebrate rather than participate in the Eucharist by receiving communion. To have said that would have meant a rejection of the ecclesiastical legislation that does not oblige a priest to celebrate Mass daily. What he said was that those who concelebrate or those who participate must not do this from a conviction that Masses celebrated privately are always undesirable. This part of the encyclical must be read in conjunction with article 27 of the Constitution on the Sacred Liturgy:

> It is to be stressed that whenever rites, according to their specific nature, make provision for communal celebration involving the presence and active participation of the faithful, this way of celebrating them is to be preferred, as far as possible, to a celebration that is individual and quasi-private.
>
> This rule applies with special force to the celebration of Mass and the administration of the sacraments, even though every Mass has of itself a public and social nature.[8]

Responding to theological attempts to reinterpret the real presence of Christ in the Eucharist, Pope Paul stressed the necessity of continuity in Christian theology. Throughout history, Eucharistic theology has been strongly influenced by developments in christology and ecclesiology and by the relationship between liturgy and popular devotion. Recent years have witnessed a greater involvement of the Christian assembly in the celebration of the Eucharist and an increasing frequency of receiving holy communion within the Mass itself. These important developments have resulted in a shift of emphasis away from adoration of the real presence of Christ in the sacred species outside of Mass to an appreciation of the full implications of the meaning of the Eucharist in the Christian life as a whole.

This shift of practical belief is reflected in contemporary theology,

[8] *AAS* 56 (1964) 107.

which tends to concentrate on the broader significance of Christ's presence in the Church and in the sacraments rather than on the more specific question of how Christ may be said to be truly present, body and blood, soul and divinity, under the form of bread and wine. Under the influence of phenomenology and existential philosophy, people are asking new questions about Christ's presence. New theological questions naturally stimulate new developments in theology itself. However, fresh concerns do not of themselves imply a denial of traditional formulations such as transubstantiation, which was itself a particular answer to a question raised at a particular time, but rather they often indicate the need to develop new categories in which to interpret a particular Christian doctrine such as the mystery of Christ's presence to his people.

Certainly the word "transubstantiation" did not originate with the Council of Trent; it seems likely that the word was used as early as the twelfth century. Nevertheless, the term was canonized by Trent, which dealt with the subject in four principles contained in chapter 4 and canon 2 of its thirteenth session (October 11, 1551). Letters, diaries, and draft decrees written by the Fathers and theologians at the Council indicate that the dogma of transubstantiation was thought out and expressed in Aristotelian categories, but the strictly Aristotelian content of these categories was not included in what the dogma expressed.

The Council of Trent first of all maintained that in the doctrine of transubstantiation the Church was simply expressing its faith in a reality that existed long before any attempts to explain the faith were made. It then asserted that the substance of bread and wine do not persist in the Eucharist. This means that the entire fundamental being of bread and wine ceases to be. The Council then went on to say that the substance of bread and wine is converted into the substance of the body and blood of Christ, a change "most fittingly" expressed by the term "transubstantiation." Only the species of bread and wine remain. In other words, although the "entire fundamental being" of bread and wine is changed, the "empirical being" of bread and wine remains. Hence, from a chemical point of view, the bread and wine remain bread and wine; from an ontological point of view, they become the body and blood of Christ.

Theological attempts to reinterpret the real presence were more or less dormant in Catholic circles from the Council of Trent down to the end of World War II, when a fresh controversy developed between the defenders of a physical interpretation and the defenders of an ontological interpretation of the change. In its Constitution on the Sacred Liturgy, the Second Vatican Council stressed the multiple presences of Christ in the liturgy — his presence in the sacrifice of the Mass, not only in the person of the minister but especially in the Eucharistic species; his presence in the other sacraments; his presence in his word; and his presence when the Church prays and sings.[9] The Council's teaching produced considerable tension in the Catholic community. To resolve these tensions, Pope Paul taught in his encyclical that it is not

> allowable to discuss the mystery of transubstantiation without mentioning what the Council of Trent states about the marvelous conversion of the whole substance of the bread into the body and of the whole substance of the wine into the blood of Christ, speaking rather only of what is called "transignification" and "transfinalization," or finally to propose and act on the opinion according to which, in the consecrated Hosts which remain after the celebration of the sacrifice of the Mass, Christ is no longer present.[10]

The term "transignification" is used to denote a change that occurs not in the order of being but in the religious value that the Eucharist expresses. The theory maintains that reality can be considered either from a physical point of view or from an anthropological point of view. What changes in the Eucharist, then, according to this theory, is our conception of the reality; bread and wine remain objectively unchanged, but their significance for God and his people is changed.

The theory of "transfinalization" is somewhat similar. It maintains that every created reality has a finality given by God, who is the creator and guardian of all being. In the Eucharist, God gives a fundamentally unchanged reality a new religious finality.

The problem with both theories lies, not in their explicit denial of objective real presence, but in their inadequate formulation of what takes place in the Eucharistic celebration. In a sense, one may accept both theories. This is indicated by Pope Paul in his qualification

---

[9] *Sacrosanctum Concilium*, no. 7: AAS 56 (1964) 100–101.
[10] AAS 57 (1965) 755.

that one cannot speak "only" of these theories. If one accepts these theories in conjunction with the teaching of Trent, they are acceptable, since the conversion of bread and wine into the body and blood of Christ implies not only a substantial conversion but a new significance or new value and a new finality.

Pope Paul ends his encyclical with an appeal to the unity themes of the Eucharist. He reflects a broad understanding of the Eucharist in which Christ, in his life, death and resurrection, is seen as the sacrament of the Father, and the Church itself is seen as the sacrament of Christ in the world. This means that the primary and fundamental presence of Christ lies in the communion of the faithful effected by the Spirit, and the Eucharist is the creative celebration of that presence in a bodily, historical, and concrete manner.

On May 25, 1967, the feast of Corpus Christi, the Sacred Congregation of Rites issued an instruction on worship of the Eucharist, *Eucharisticum mysterium*.[11] The text was prepared by the Consilium for the Implementation of the Constitution on the Sacred Liturgy and was signed by Cardinal Lercaro, president of the Consilium, as well as by Cardinal Larraona, prefect of the Congregation. A lengthy document, the instruction was primarily concerned with the catechesis of the people concerning the Eucharist, but there was also a concluding section on the cult of the Eucharist as a permanent sacrament. It dealt specifically with Eucharistic reservation, devotions, processions, exposition, and congresses.

An important assertion in the instruction was that care should be taken to enable the faithful to communicate with hosts consecrated during Mass so that even through signs communion may be seen more clearly to be participation in the sacrifice that is being celebrated. The document picked up the strong recommendation of the Constitution on the Sacred Liturgy that the faithful, after the priest's communion, should receive the Lord's body from the same sacrifice as a more perfect form of participation in the Mass.[12] The same teaching was reaffirmed in the General Instruction of the Roman Missal: "It is most desirable that the faithful should receive the body of the Lord in hosts consecrated at the same Mass. . . ."[13]

[11] *AAS* 59 (1967) 539–73.

[12] *Sacrosanctum Concilium*, no. 55: *AAS* 56 (1964) 115.

[13] No. 56 (h).

In many celebrations of the Eucharist, this directive is simply not implemented. Ministers and the other faithful are usually unaware of the incongruity of the common practice of receiving hosts reserved in the tabernacle since an earlier celebration. As long as people understand communion only as a personal encounter with Christ sacramentally present in the bread, it will not seem important to receive communion from the altar rather than from the tabernacle; but if communion is understood above all as the privileged moment of sharing in the Eucharistic celebration and as a symbol of participating in a celebration together with others who share the same bread, then it will appear inconsistent to reserve large quantities of hosts in the tabernacle for the distribution of communion at Mass.

An instruction, *Immensae caritatis,* on facilitating sacramental communion in particular circumstances was issued by the Sacred Congregation for the Discipline of the Sacraments on January 29, 1973.[14] It extended the times when communion could be received twice a day. In this regard, it followed up on the decree *Cum hac nostra aetate,* issued on February 14, 1966, by the Sacred Congregation of Rites.[15] The latter document had simplified the rite of communion in hospitals. While providing for efficiency in the administration of the sacrament, it tended to isolate the sacramental rite more and more from the sacramental word.

In many areas Eucharistic piety underwent a considerable change between the end of the Second Vatican Council and the publication of *Immensae caritatis.* From a disciplinary point of view, the document relaxed previous restrictions that prohibited people from receiving communion at a second Mass on the same day, that prohibited priests from concelebrating at a second Mass, and that limited the opportunities for frequent communion for the sick and the elderly.

These changes were welcomed but were not as important as the underlying theological presumptions in the document. The instruction affirmed and promoted the sound liturgical principle that communion is for all the normal form of full, active participation in the celebration of the Eucharist; hence, no one so committed to the sacramental life of the Church as to join in a second celebration on

[14] *AAS* 67 (1973) 264–71.
[15] *AAS* 58 (1966) 525–26.

the same day should be prevented from full participation by either communicating or concelebrating, if he happens to be a priest. As the instruction points out, it is not a question of multiplying the number of times communion is received, somewhat as people used to multiply the number of Masses heard on a single day, being prompted by a quantitative understanding of grace; it is rather that people should be able to share fully in the Eucharist if and when their life of Christian commitment leads them to a Eucharistic celebration. Although the instruction lists such occasions when one might normally want to communicate more than once a day, it also authorizes the local ordinary to extend such permission on special occasions.

The instruction also provided for the institution of extraordinary ministers of the Eucharist. The most important benefit derived from their institution has been the opportunity for the sick and the aged to receive holy communion more frequently in their homes. It is usually impossible for parish priests to visit the sick and elderly on Sundays and feast days. The instruction makes it possible for these people to receive the Eucharist on such days and so to have a genuine share in the parish celebration of Mass.

Extraordinary ministers also help to minister the Eucharist within the celebration of Mass. In large parishes the ministry of communion often takes an inordinately long time. Although priests and deacons may assist, they usually are not present for the whole celebration but appear only for communion. It certainly is a better practice to have extraordinary ministers who participate in the celebration of the Eucharist than priests and deacons who do not. Furthermore, the regular use of extraordinary ministers should make it possible to have communion under both kinds for all participants, not only at simple celebrations but also on Sundays and feasts. In many places there is at present the anomalous situation in which communion is given under both kinds during the week but not at more solemn celebrations.

Although brief, the instruction *Immensae caritatis* was theologically and pastorally more adequate than the encyclical *Mysterium fidei* in that it rightly emphasized the Eucharist as an eschatological meal and asserted the essential relationship between the Mass and communion, even when received outside of the Mass. The instruction formed the foundation for the section of the Roman Ritual entitled "De Sacra Communione et de Cultu Mysterii Eucharistici extra Missam," which was released by the Sacred Congregation for Divine Worship on October 18, 1973. The document was dated June 21, 1973.[16] Four chapters were included in the booklet: (1) communion outside of Mass; (2) communion and viaticum distributed by a special minister; (3) various forms of Eucharistic devotions — exposition, processions, congresses; (4) texts for use during distribution of communion and Eucharistic devotions. The document was basically a compilation of previous statements and released rites. Besides relying on the instruction *Immensae caritatis*, it also indicated a dependence on the 1967 instruction from the Congregation of Rites, *Eucharisticum mysterium*.

A declaration of the Sacred Congregation for the Doctrine of the Faith, issued on May 2, 1972, commented on the question of the fragments of hosts and the respect due them.[17] It insisted that particles should be either consumed or reserved in the tabernacle. Reverence should certainly be observed in this regard, but scrupulosity is to be avoided. The Eucharist has been left to the Church under the signs of bread and wine, both substances that are to be partaken of as food. Miniscule particles, even though chemically constituted from the same substances that make up bread, do not look like bread nor taste like bread; neither can they be eaten like bread. Likewise, droplets and stains, even though chemically constituted from the same substance that makes up wine, do not look like wine nor taste like wine; neither can they be drunk like wine. Hence, excessive preoccupation with purification rites, derived from the Middle Ages and concentrating on the physical presence of Christ under the Eucharistic signs rather than on his personal presence, is more a distraction to the community and a caricature of dignified ritual behavior than a manifestation of true reverence and devotion.

Three major documents on the subject of intercommunion have been issued since the Second Vatican Council. The first was a declaration, *Dans ces derniers temps*, issued by the Secretariat for Chris-

---

[16] *AAS* 65 (1973) 610.
[17] *Notitiae* 8 (1972) 227.

tian Unity on January 7, 1970.[18] It was followed by an instruction, *In quibus rerum,* published by the same Secretariat on June 1, 1972,[19] which in turn was clarified by a declaration from the Secretariat for Christian Unity on October 17, 1973.[20] The documents have insisted that two principles must be kept in mind when discussing the question of sacramental sharing. First, there is the intrinsic relationship between the mystery of the Church and the mystery of the Eucharist, between ecclesial and Eucharistic communion. Second, there is the transformation that the sacraments effect in those who celebrate and receive them. Although these two principles must be applied simultaneously, the Directory for the Application of the Decisions of the Second Vatican Council Concerning Ecumenical Matters, which was issued on May 14, 1967, maintained that "since the sacraments are both signs of unity and sources of grace, the Church can for adequate reasons allow access" to separated Christians.[21]

For a person to be admitted to the Eucharist, five conditions must be met simultaneously: (1) a person must manifest faith in the sacrament in conformity with the faith of the Catholic Church; this is a faith not merely in the real presence but also in the doctrine of the Eucharist as taught by the Catholic Church; (2) there must be a serious spiritual need for the strength of the Eucharist, that is, a "need for an increase in spiritual life and a need for a deeper involvement in the mystery of the Church and of its unity";[22] (3) for a prolonged period the individual is unable to receive the Eucharist in one of his or her own communities; (4) the non-Catholic Christian spontaneously asks for the sacrament; (5) the individual must have proper dispositions and lead a worthy Christian life.

The directory gives two examples, apart from the danger of death, when intercommunion would be permissible: people who are in prison and those who are suffering from persecution. But it does acknowledge that there are other cases of urgent necessity that are not confined to circumstances of suffering and danger. For example,

[18] *AAS* 62 (1970) 184–88.

[19] *AAS* 64 (1972) 518–25.

[20] *AAS* 65 (1973) 616–19.

[21] Part I, no. 55: *AAS* 59 (1967) 574–92.

[22] Instruction of June 1, 1972, 4 (b): *AAS* 64 (1972) 523.

Christians such as migrants might be scattered far from their own proper ministers and cannot receive communion except at great inconvenience and expense.

It is the responsibility of the local ordinary to examine these cases and to decide when the required conditions are met. The explanatory declaration issued on October 17, 1973, does assert that when particular cases present themselves fairly often in a certain region, episcopal conferences can issue guiding principles for ascertaining that all the conditions are verified in particular cases.[23]

The question of reciprocity arises only with those Churches that have preserved the substance of the Eucharist, orders, and apostolic succession. It follows, then, that a Catholic in similar circumstances cannot request the Eucharist except from a minister who has been validly ordained.[24]

The norms regulating the admission to the Eucharist in the Catholic Church are different for Eastern Christians. Through apostolic succession, the Eastern Churches have the true sacraments of priesthood and the Eucharist. Reasons for admitting intercommunion then are more extensive. In fact, the Second Vatican Council's Decree on Ecumenism declared that some worship in common with the Eastern Churches is not only possible but is to be encouraged.[25]

If they are properly disposed and make a request of their own accord, separated Eastern Christians may be given the sacraments of penance, the Eucharist, and the anointing of the sick. Moreover, Catholics may ask for the same sacraments from non-Catholic ministers in whose Church there are valid sacraments, as often as necessity or true spiritual benefit recommends such requests and access to a Catholic priest is physically or morally impossible.[26]

The question of intercommunion continues to raise serious difficulties; in some areas it has brought the ecumenical movement to a standstill. When Church unity and sacramental communion are defined in terms of each other, there is a closed-circuit view of

[23] No. 6: *AAS* 65 (1973) 617.

[24] Declaration from the Secretariat for Christian Unity, October 17, 1973, no. 9: *AAS* 65 (1973) 619.

[25] *Unitatis redintegratio*, no. 15: *AAS* 57 (1965) 102.

[26] *Orientalium Ecclesiarum*, no. 27: *AAS* 57 (1965) 84.

Church and sacraments. The advocates of the Roman Catholic policy resolve the problem by making signification and causality coincide, so that it is the existing unity of the Church that is first signified and then enhanced by sacramental causality. Those who would advocate a more open policy in the matter of intercommunion would solve the problem by seeking Church unity through the efficacious causality of the sacramental celebration. They stress the unity that is already present through baptism and deepened by sacramental celebration. They hope, then, that the sacramental union that is effected will become the cause of ecclesial union.[27]

The legislative texts discussed above constitute the principal texts issued since the Second Vatican Council concerning the revision of the rites for the sacraments and the norms for their renewed pastoral administration.

[27] See Franz Josef van Beeck, "Intercommunion: A Note on Norms," *One in Christ*, vol. 12, no. 2 (1976) 124–41.

Chapter 9

REVISION OF LITURGICAL BOOKS:
RITUAL, MISSAL, AND PONTIFICAL

The revision of liturgical rites necessitated the revision of liturgical books. From 1963 to the present, there have been substantial revisions of the Roman Ritual, the Roman Missal, and the Roman Pontifical. These revisions, however, were made in accordance with special norms for the preparation of liturgical texts and their translation into the vernacular.

Norms Concerning the Preparation and Editing of Liturgical Texts

On October 16, 1964, Cardinal Lercaro, the newly appointed president of the Consilium, wrote to the presidents of episcopal conferences stressing the need for unity of language in the new liturgical texts.[1]

The International Committee for English in the Liturgy (ICEL) was established on September 20, 1965, in response to that need.[2] A more detailed instruction on translations of liturgical texts was issued by the Consilium on January 25, 1969.[3] It was followed by a declaration from the Consilium in February 1969 on the translation

---

[1] *Notitiae* 1 (1965) 194–96.
[2] *Notitiae* 1 (1965) 308, 339–45.
[3] *Notitiae* 5 (1969) 3–12.

of interim liturgical texts.[4] The first section of the instruction dealt
with general principles of translation and the art of communication.
The text maintained that the audience for whom the translation is
intended must be considered and the manner of expression carefully
formulated. The second section examined particular problems in the
translation of biblical texts, parts to be sung or recited aloud, and
liturgical hymns. The final section on translation committees
treated the establishment, nature, and role of national and international committees for translation. The conclusion of the document noted that texts translated from another language are certainly
not sufficient for the celebration of a fully renewed liturgy. It
recognized the need to create entirely new texts, but it also noted
that "translation of texts transmitted through the tradition of the
Church is the best school and discipline for the creation of new texts
so 'that any new forms adopted should in some way grow organically from forms already existing' (Constitution on the Sacred
Liturgy, art. 23)."

On February 6, 1970, the Sacred Congregation for Divine Worship issued detailed norms concerning unity of translation of liturgical texts.[5] The document stated that henceforth unity of translation
would be required in the texts of the ordinary of the Mass, in those
prayers that require the direct participation of the people, such as
acclamations, responses, and dialogue, and in the psalms, hymns,
and prayers at lauds and vespers.

An undated declaration by the Sacred Congregation for Divine
Worship was issued in 1970.[6] It was sent to the presidents of
episcopal conferences and liturgical commissions on February 25,
1970, and concerned the copyright for liturgical translations and
provisions concerning the identification of the translators, who were
to remain anonymous. A response from the Sacred Congregation for
Divine Worship in May 1973 directed that liturgical books must be
published in their entirety, including papal constitutions and all
pertinent decrees of the Roman congregations, even though the
books are destined for popular use.[7]

[4] *Notitiae* 5 (1969) 68.
[5] *Notitiae* 6 (1970) 84–85.
[6] *Notitiae* 6 (1970) 153.
[7] *Notitiae* 9 (1973) 153–54.

On October 25, 1973, the Sacred Congregation for Divine Worship sent a circular letter to the presidents of episcopal conferences concerning the norms to be observed in translating liturgical books into contemporary languages.[8] The letter was sent by Cardinal Villot, the secretary of state, by special mandate of the Holy Father, and was also signed by Archbishop Bugnini, in the absence of a prefect for the Congregation for Divine Worship. Three significant points were made in the letter. First of all, the Holy Father reserved to himself the right to approve directly all translations of the sacramental forms into the vernacular. Secondly, the vernacular translations of the sacramental forms should not only be doctrinally correct but should be a faithful rendering of the Latin text. Thirdly, if the translations are being made into languages other than the major modern languages, the appropriate liturgical commissions should prepare the translations of the sacramental forms; they should be approved by the episcopal conferences, and then, with a full explanation of all the words, sent on to the Congregation for Divine Worship.

As already noted, on January 25, 1974, the Congregation for the Doctrine of the Faith issued a declaration again warning that it is necessary that the translation of the essential forms in the rites of the sacraments faithfully render the original meaning of the official Latin text.[9] The current legislation on the subject of the translation of liturgical texts was summarized in a letter sent by the Congregation for the Sacraments and Divine Worship to the bishops throughout the world on June 5, 1976.[10]

THE ROMAN RITUAL

The Roman Ritual contains the prayers to be recited and the directions to be followed in the celebration of the sacraments and sacramentals. Many sections of the new ritual have already been published. Comment has already been made on certain sections when discussing the revision of the sacraments. Three sections were published in the *editio typica* in 1969. The *Ordo Baptismi parvulorum* was first issued in 1969 but was revised in 1973. The *Ordo*

---

[8] *AAS* 66 (1974) 98–99.

[9] *Ibid.*

[10] *Notitiae* 12 (1976) 300–302.

celebrandi matrimoniorum and the *Ordo exsequiarum* were also issued in 1969. The latter text refers to the new funeral rites, authorized by the decree *Ritibus exsequiarum* of the Sacred Congregation for Divine Worship on August 15, 1969.[11]

The Constitution on the Sacred Liturgy stated that the rituals for Christian burial should express more clearly the paschal character of Christian death and should also conform where possible to various cultural traditions and be adapted to local circumstances. It also directed that there be a revision of the burial rites for infants. Hence, on August 15, 1969, the Sacred Congregation for Divine Worship issued the new order for funerals. The publication was preceded by an experimental rite of burial that was used in various dioceses under careful supervision since 1966. The results of that experiment were collated and evaluated; they influenced the shape of the finalized ritual.

The general thrust of the new order is union with Christ in his death and resurrection. In the sacrament of baptism a person is inaugurated into the paschal mystery of Christ. In death he/she joins the Lord and passes to new life shared by the saints. However, he/she must await the union of the body with the soul until the second coming of Jesus at the parousia.

The new order expresses genuine concern for the consolation of the family on the occasion of the death of a loved one. With the implementation of the new order, the pendulum has swung from the dread of death as a judgment on our sins to a joyous hope through the resurrection of Christ. But as often happens in cases of reform, the pendulum has at times swung too far. With the stress on hope and resurrection, we are tempted not to take seriously the reality of death and the grave. The new emphasis can fail to speak to the needs of the living, above all their need to disengage themselves from the dead and discover new life for themselves. The resurrection is the event on which we base our faith that there is life beyond the grave. But the resurrection is also one of the most difficult doctrines for contemporary men and women to embrace. Therefore, while we are faithful to the truth of the resurrection in the actual structure of the funeral rite, we may nevertheless fail to communicate with those

---

[11] *Notitiae* 5 (1969) 423–35.

who need some kind of message in their time of crisis — a message that gives them real hope for the deceased person and for themselves.

The ritual's concern for the family is important. If we accept the reality and meaning of death, we will be willing to give people a chance to mourn. Since many contemporary people seem to have difficulty accepting both the reality and meaning of death, there is a heavy pressure on people today to cheer up and get interested in other things immediately after a death in the family. This is reflected in the overemphasis on resurrection themes and neglect of the theme of actual death in the celebration of the wake service and funeral. If we have the proper ritual structure, we give people permission to mourn, but then part of the structure says that it is time to stop. This is what people have done through the ages — permitted mourning but set a limit so that people could come back to life again. The widow put on her black clothes and the son put on his black armband, but then a time came when they took them off and life began anew.

Our entire person is involved in the death of a loved one. Memories, emotions, hopes, thoughts — every part of us reacts when death enters into our lives. We need effective rituals to cope with the trauma. If the funeral rituals are well structured, they have the ability to reinvoke past emotion, to bind the individual to his own past experience, and to bring the members of the group together in a shared experience. A ritual is able to express and constructively channel the reactions of the mourners. The individual person should be able to find his or her own emotions, thoughts, doubts, and convictions resonating within the rituals. In addition, the community should find its deeply felt grief and desire to help the family ingrained in the ritual action. An effective funeral ritual provides a context within which the personal feelings of all the mourners can be expressed, and it offers each individual the occasion to support freely every other individual in a time of crisis.

The purpose of the wake, then, is to give relatives and friends of the deceased a chance to conclude the life of the departed person in their own minds. This involves recalling what the life of the deceased person meant. The wake can give people a chance to make their peace with the deceased and to resolve the guilt or conflicts not resolved before the death. The theme that should be stressed at the wake service, then, should be the reality of death. In this way the wake can serve as an effective preparation for the Mass of Christian burial and the actual burial service.

The general thrust of the funeral prayers and wake service in the new order is positive. Although they recognize the justice of God, they call upon his mercy in view of the promises made in and through the risen Christ. The ritual contains three possible plans to accommodate the different customs of burial throughout the world. It recognizes the necessity of ritualizing the stages of wake and burial. The first plan refers to the home, church, and cemetery as the three places for community prayer; the second plan has stations at the cemetery chapel and grave; and the third plan indicates just one station in the home of the deceased.

The pastoral notes in the order emphasize the diverse ministries in the celebrations. The priest presides over the liturgical services and celebrates the Eucharist; in his absence a deacon may celebrate all the rites except the Eucharist. In the absence of both a priest and deacon, lay persons may be deputed to carry out some of the roles. Since the celebration is to be shaped to meet the needs of the occasion, planning of the rites should involve the priest, the family, and the larger community so that choices of readings, psalms, songs, and prayers, as well as the fulfillment of specific functions such as lector, acolyte, pallbearers, and bearers of the gifts will witness to the faith dimension not only of the mourners but of the larger community as well.

At the place of vigil or wake, the priest or deacon, usually vested in a stole over his street clothes, leads those present in a scriptural service that includes a greeting, psalm, prayer, reading, homily, intercessions, the Lord's Prayer, and a final oration. Sometimes song is introduced and usually holy water is used. As already noted, the emphasis in the service should be on the sense of loss, mourning, and a preparation for the Eucharist that is to follow. The priest or deacon might well wear a violet stole on this occasion to signify more clearly the human emotion of the moment. The prayers manifest a particular concern for the family and the mourners. The suggested scriptural readings deal with human sorrow, tears, and loss. Except where the funeral Mass is celebrated on the evening before the burial, the wake service is the public celebration for many who may not be able to participate in the funeral Mass.

Where it is not customary for the priest to lead the casket in solemn procession from the home to the church, the priest greets the family and friends at the entrance of the church. A special rite of greeting has been formulated that recalls the water and robe of baptism. A white pall may be placed on the casket as a symbolic remembrance of the baptismal robe. The paschal candle, the symbol of the risen Lord, the light of the world, accompanies the body up the aisle and stands at the head of the casket during the Mass. In some instances white vestments are used, although black or violet ones are permitted.

If possible, members of the family and friends should fulfill the ministerial roles during the Mass. The priest should preach a genuine homily based on the readings rather than a panegyric. If incense is used at the offertory, the celebrant is urged to incense the paschal candle and the body along with the gifts; the acolyte should incense the priest and the people. This action is meant to express the unity in Christ of both the living and the dead through the Eucharist.

The final commendation follows the Mass. It is not meant to be an absolution as in the former ritual, since absolution from sin is effected through the Eucharist that has already been celebrated. The commendation is a final farewell, a tribute, and a remembrance before the burial.

It seems unfortunate that in many cemeteries the body is not taken to the grave but is left in a memorial chapel and is buried later. The actual burial is meant to be the transition point in the ritual when it becomes evident that those present must go on living without the deceased person, yet living in the light of resurrection.

The new order also provides a special rite for the burial of children. It makes a distinction between children who have died before the reception of baptism and those who have died after being baptized. The rite is complete with wake, church, and cemetery services, and provides special prayers and suggested readings. Since children are body persons rather than angels, their funerals need no longer be celebrated at liturgies whose text is the Mass of the Angels.

Two questions related to the order for Christian burial are the legitimacy of cremation and the burial of excommunicated Catholics. On May 8, 1963, the Sacred Congregation of the Holy Office issued an instruction on the cremation of corpses.[12] The text makes it clear that cremation is not something intrinsically evil nor of its nature incompatible with Christianity. In fact,

> The Church has always accepted the view that extraordinary circumstances may exist to justify cremation of the bodies of the faithful. In time of war or during an epidemic it may be necessary for the public good to dispose of corpses in this way. In some countries the shortage of ground for purposes of burial, especially in or near rapidly expanding cities, may become so acute, or the price of such land may become so exorbitant, or the distance to the nearest cemetery may eventually involve such serious inconvenience and unwarranted expense, that cremation may become a public necessity for many more people than it is today.[13]

Although it is still the express will of the Church that the practice of burying bodies of the faithful be kept when reasonably possible, pastors should presume that the reasons for choosing cremation fall within those recognized by the Church as not depriving the deceased of ecclesiastical burial. The introduction to the new order for funerals states that the rites that are normally held at the cemetery may in the case of cremation be held in the actual chapel or place of cremation.[14]

The privation of ecclesiastical burial has the nature of a penalty and hence is to be strictly interpreted. To be denied Christian burial by canon 1240 of the Code of Canon Law, two essential conditions must be fulfilled simultaneously: (1) A notorious crime in the canonical sense must have been committed. The crime, both as to the illegal act itself and as to the intention to violate the law, must be so clearly established before the people that there cannot be even the slightest doubt about either. (2) There must be the total absence of any sign of repentance given before death.

On September 20, 1973, the Sacred Congregation for the Doctrine of the Faith issued a decree concerning ecclesiastical burial.[15]

[12] *AAS* 56 (1964) 822–23.
[13] *Ibid.*
[14] No. 15.
[15] *AAS* 65 (1973) 500.

It noted that the Fathers of the Congregation, in a plenary session on November 14 to 15, 1972, had decreed as follows: Funeral rites should not be prohibited for manifest sinners if before their death they gave some signs of repentance and there is no public scandal of other faithful. The Holy Father approved this decree on November 17, 1972, and ordered it to be made a matter of public law.

Those who would be classified as ordinary excommunicates, that is, those who had no sentence passed on them, are not to be deprived of Christian burial simply because of their excommunication. This includes those who contracted marriage while bound by a previous union. Canon 1240 explicitly refers only to those who have been excommunicated by sentence, whether declaratory or condemnatory. Excommunication as such is not, therefore, a reason for denying anyone Christian burial. It would seem that the privation of Christian burial will be a rare occurrence.

On June 11, 1976, the Sacred Congregation for the Doctrine of the Faith issued a decree on the public celebration of Mass in a Catholic church for deceased non-Catholic Christians.[16] It sometimes happens that Catholic priests are asked to celebrate the Eucharist as a suffrage for deceased persons who were baptized in other Churches or ecclesial communities. The Code of Canon Law stipulates that Masses may not be celebrated for those who have lived out their last day outside full communion with the Catholic Church.[17] Since the religious and social conditions that recommended this discipline have changed today, the Congregation decreed that although the current discipline must be retained as a general norm, that norm can be derogated from whenever the following conditions are simultaneously verified: (1) public celebration of Masses is expressly requested by members of the family, by friends, or by subjects of the deceased out of a genuinely religious motive; (2) in the judgment of the ordinary, scandal on the part of the faithful is absent. In these cases public Mass may be celebrated, on condition, however, that the name of the deceased not be mentioned in the Eucharistic prayer, since such commemoration presupposes full communion with the Catholic Church.

[16] *AAS* 68 (1976) 621.
[17] See canon 1241 collated with canon 1240, §1, 1.

On February 2, 1970, the new *Ordo professionis religiosae*[18] was authorized by the decree *Professionis ritus,* issued by the Sacred Congregation for Divine Worship.[19] The new order, drawn up to implement article 80 of the Constitution on the Sacred Liturgy,[20] consists of two distinct formulations, one for men religious and one for women religious. Both formulations are divided into five chapters: (1) initiation, (2) temporary profession, (3) perpetual profession, (4) renewal of vows, and (5) biblical readings and prayer formulas. The order also contains an appendix with a model formula for the profession of vows and four Masses for profession: one for simple profession, two for perpetual profession (with a proper preface and formulas for a commemoration in the prayer of oblation), and one for the renewal of vows.

The new order is presented basically as a norm for the rite of religious profession and is to be followed by institutes unless special provision has been made otherwise by an indult. Nevertheless, since the rite of profession should express the spirit of the religious family, each institute has been instructed to adapt the rite so as to bring out its own unique character. The decree authorizing the use of the new order maintained that such adaptations were to be presented to the Apostolic See for confirmation by the Sacred Congregation for Divine Worship.

There are a number of changes in the rite of initiation or of entrance to the novitiate. The rite should not include investiture with the religious habit, since the habit is regarded as a symbol of religious dedication in the institute. Investiture with the habit should be part of the rite of profession. It is forbidden to perform the rite of initiation during Mass. Since the beginning of the novitiate implies a testing period and a very tentative commitment on the part of both the novice and the community, the rite should be very simple and direct, in the presence of the religious community only. It should be celebrated in the chapter hall or similar room, but not publicly.

The fundamental norm for the rite of simple temporary profession

[18] Rome: Typis Polyglottis Vaticanis, 1970, 128 pp.
[19] *Notitiae* 6 (1970) 113–26; 319–22.
[20] *AAS* 56 (1964) 120.

is based on the fact that while there is a religious commitment, there is not a definitive commitment; probation continues. The practice of making temporary religious vows was uncommon before the time of Ignatius of Loyola. Up until the sixteenth century, first profession was generally final profession. Serious unresolved theological questions concerning the meaning of temporary religious vows continue to be raised. The rite of temporary profession includes investiture with the religious habit or some form of symbol distinctive of the institute; it may properly be celebrated within Mass, ideally after the gospel, but it should not be celebrated with great solemnity. The rite may also be celebrated within a liturgy of the Word or within one of the hours of the office, such as lauds or vespers, where it would follow the reading and precede the canticle.

The rite of perpetual religious profession is an act of definitive religious dedication. The basic consecration of the Christian, of course, takes place at baptism. Perpetual religious profession implies the personal commitment of the individual to continue to search for God and to respond to his revelation all life long in the context of a particular religious institute and according to a specific religious rule. It is proper, then, that the rite be celebrated in the context of the Eucharist, which is the source and privileged place of Christian consecration. It should also be celebrated solemnly and publicly so that the larger ecclesial community may join in the act of worship that is expressive of its own basic consecration.

The profession itself takes place after the gospel. There are several reasons for this. Christian dedication is really a response to the initiative of God's word calling his people to conversion. Hence, this is the regular place in the renewed liturgy for the special dedication or commitment of persons, such as the ordination of deacons, priests, and bishops, the celebration of marriage, and also the sacraments of baptism and confirmation when they are celebrated at Mass. From a ritual point of view, the placement of the profession at this point is not so disruptive of the order of the Eucharistic celebration, since the rite is followed quite naturally by the presentation of the gifts of bread and wine by the newly professed. The introduction to the new order of religious profession states precisely that profession in the presence of the Blessed Sacrament, that is, before receiving communion, is not in harmony with a true understanding of the liturgy; hence, new religious communities may not adopt this practice. Those institutes that do follow the practice under a particular law are advised to discontinue it.

Perpetual profession should be so structured that it forms an integral celebration with the Eucharist. Those about to be professed should therefore be included in the entrance procession. The liturgy of the Word should develop the theme of religious commitment, but the homilist should refrain from presenting the call to a religious institute as an elitist vocation superior to other vocations in the Church. All people are called to holiness; the call to a religious institute is simply one manifestation of that universal call.

If the religious superior who is to receive the profession is a priest, he should be the principal celebrant of the Eucharist. In non-clerical communities the profession should be received by the superior of the religious institute, not by the priest who happens to be the principal celebrant of the Mass. Litany prayer should be offered for the professed and should also develop the mission of the Church and the needs of the world. In the case of temporary profession, according to the new order, the rite should conclude with the prayer of the faithful. The rite of perpetual profession may be concluded by the sign of peace given to the newly professed by the members of the community. If the sign of peace is given at this point, it is omitted before communion.

The new order carefully distinguishes between the renewal of vows prescribed by law and the devotional practice of renewing vows on such occasions as the annual community retreat or monthly days of renewal. The norm is very simple: devotional practices should not be carried out in public celebrations of the Eucharist. Renewal of vows prescribed by law, as, for example, when temporary vows have expired, or renewal of vows on the occasion of major anniversaries may take place within the celebration of the Eucharist, but the rite should be simple.

In large communities temporary and perpetual professions and renewal of vows have traditionally taken place at the same celebration of the Eucharist. This practice complicates the question of relative solemnization. The problem does not seem to have been envisaged by those who formulated the new order. Individual communities, then, should address the question seriously and try to come to a reasonable solution — which will probably be a compromise.

The new order also makes provision for promises in place of temporary vows. Many religious communities, especially those of women religious, have adopted the practice of making promises. The formulation of this rite, which may be celebrated at a liturgy of the Word, the office, or Mass, would seem to avoid the unresolved theological questions concerning the meaning of temporary vows.

The new orders for the sacraments of the initiation of Christian adults and the anointing of the sick and their pastoral care were published in 1972, and in 1973 the order for the sacrament of penance was issued. The ordinary rites for the sacraments of orders and confirmation are part of the Roman Pontifical. The ordinary rites for the Eucharist are outlined in the General Instruction of the Roman Missal. All these sacraments have been discussed in earlier sections of this commentary.

The April 1971 issue of *Notitiae*[21] carried a report by P.-M. Gy, director of the Institute of Liturgy at Paris, on the project for the revision of the blessings of the Roman Ritual. The revision of this section of the ritual has been difficult because of cultural differences in attitudes toward blessings. In traditional agrarian countries and rural sections of industrial countries, blessings are often deeply appreciated and frequently used; in highly secularized countries they tend to be ignored.

The report in *Notitiae* indicated that the new formularies for blessings will most likely be based on the traditional concept of blessing, for which the Eucharist is the norm and model. Hence they will consist primarily of a blessing of God for created things. It is to be hoped that this structure will not lend itself readily to any superstitious use. The new formularies would then manifest a sound appreciation of the goodness of the secular world and of human creativity itself. This has not always been evident in the blessings of the present ritual, which are often simple exorcisms.

It is likely that a number of the new blessings will be ministered by lay men and women as well as clerics. Since the Middle Ages,

[21] Vol. 8 (1971) 123–32.

most blessings in the ritual have been reserved to priests and deacons. A change in this policy would acknowledge that all baptized Christians share in the priestly ministry of Christ and so have a right to give certain blessings.

No matter how simple the blessing or the circumstance in which it is given, it is always the Church's liturgy that is being celebrated. Every blessing is an extension of the great Eucharistic blessing. Therefore the ritual action should always be accompanied by a proclamation of the Word of God, from whom all blessings come. No longer should any person or object be blessed simply with a sign of the cross.

The report indicated that there will be no attempt in the revised ritual to provide blessings for every occasion; rather, the ritual will contain model blessings for various occasions. It will be the responsibility of the national conferences of bishops to adapt these blessings and develop others to respond to national and local needs.

THE ROMAN PONTIFICAL

As was the case with the Roman Ritual, various sections of the revised Roman Pontifical have been issued at irregular intervals. The publication of a manual of pontifical celebrations to replace the old *Caeremoniale Episcoporum* is forthcoming, but it has not been finalized.

The first section of the new pontifical was published in 1968 and covered the ordination rites to the diaconate, the priesthood, and the episcopate. The order for these celebrations has already been discussed.

The second section was published in 1970 and provides the new rite for the consecration of virgins.[22] This text was authorized by a decree of the Sacred Congregation for Divine Worship, *Consecrationis virginis*, issued on May 31, 1970.[23] The custom of consecrating women to a life of virginity was common even in the early Church. It led to the development of a solemn ritual affirming the dedication of the person to a life of virginity and establishing her as a symbol of the Church as the Bride of Christ. Both nuns and lay women living

[22] *Ordo consecrationis virginum*, Rome, Typis Polyglottis Vaticanis, 1970, 68 pp.
[23] *Notitiae* 6 (1970) 313–16.

in secular environments were consecrated, although in recent centuries the consecration has regularly been reserved to nuns.

The new order allows the consecration to be received by both nuns and women living apart from religious institutes. In the case of nuns, it is required that they should always have been unmarried and never have lived in public or open violation of chastity, that they should have already made their perpetual profession as a religious, and that their religious community should have made use of the rite because of a long-established custom or by new permission of the competent authority.

In the case of women living in a secular environment, it is required that they should always have been unmarried and never have lived in public and open violation of chastity, that by their age, prudence, and universally approved character they should give assurance of perseverance in a life of chastity dedicated to the service of the Church and their brothers and sisters, and that they should be admitted to this consecration by the bishop who is the ordinary of the place. He also is to decide on the conditions under which these women are to undertake a life of perpetual chastity.

The use of the rite of consecration of virgins raises some difficult questions in the contemporary world. The words "virgin" and "virginity" carry a meaning in Christian theology that does not exactly correspond to their meaning in secular speech. Our secular culture is apt to define virginity simply in physical and negative terms: a virgin is a person who has never had full genital intercourse. Christian theology acknowledges the secular meaning but defines virginity above all in spiritual and positive terms. The fact of not having had full genital intercourse is the material of the virtue of virginity, but its formal cause is the firm resolution to abstain perpetually for the sake of dedicating oneself to God. In those who have preserved their virginity in order to consecrate it to God, the state of bodily integrity is not a matter for pride but a symbol of God's gift of his love and mercy. Thus, it follows that some people who are virgins in the secular sense may not be so in the theological sense, because the interior purpose is not present. Christian theology, which views the intention of the heart as the primary and essential element, recognizes that the gift of Christian virginity can be present in varying degrees and is capable of development. It can also be recovered through repentance by a person who has lost the material element.

The new order for the consecration of virgins disqualifies only those who have been married or who have lived publicly or openly in a way contrary to chastity. On the one hand, the advantage of this policy is that it puts the accent firmly on the spiritual and Christian meaning of virginity, that is, on the intention of the heart, and it makes the liturgical rite a public consecration of something that is present at the time of the celebration, namely, the person's intention for the present and the future. On the other hand, it is currently difficult to establish clearly what is meant by living publicly or openly in a way contrary to chastity, since many people today tend to live casually with one another and to have sexual relations, but they are apt to maintain that their lives and behavior patterns are private rather than public.

The difficulty of using the rite in enclosed communities has derived from the fact that it has been closely linked with solemn profession. It is also very questionable whether the rite, even in its revised form, expresses an adequate theology of Christian virginity. Surely any rite is undesirable that puts the accent on the wrong place, obscures the meaning of and the need for ongoing Christian conversion, places psychological burdens on those aspiring to life in a religious institute, sets up distinctions within a community or possibly leads people into idolatry and pride. The very term "consecration" seems to imply that one has already arrived at a state of perfect chastity and purity of heart. Frequently widows and now even divorcees are admitted to profession in religious institutes. The fact that they cannot receive the consecration might make them feel like second-class members of the community. Also, the fact that the rite may be used only in religious communities that have regularly celebrated the consecration of virgins or have recently received permission to do so may lead some communities to feel that they are more privileged than others. Aware of the difficulties inherent in the use of the rite, various communities that formerly celebrated the consecration of virgins have been reluctant to implement the new order.

The order for the blessing of abbots and abbesses[24] was authorized by the Sacred Congregation for Divine Worship on November 11, 1970, by the decree *Abbatem et abbatissam*.[25] The blessing, after canonical election, of an abbot or abbess of a monastery has been a traditional rite in the Church's liturgy, but in the course of centuries it took on different forms that clouded the essential meaning of the blessing. The revised order has eliminated these inappropriate rites and has sought to express more clearly the spiritual responsibilities of the head of a religious family.

A number of the inappropriate rites in the ritual for blessing an abbot were derived from the ritual for the consecration of a bishop. The conferral of the privilege of using pontificalia, in fact, made an abbot look like a bishop. The new order for the blessing of an abbot has retained the conferral of the pastoral staff. This is proper because the pastoral staff is an effective symbol of responsible leadership and authority, the responsibility above all to beget and develop spiritual life in the community. The conferral of the ring and the mitre are optional in the new order. It would seem advisable that newly elected abbots should not wear symbols that are primarily episcopal and that consequently confuse the abbatial and episcopal offices. Furthermore, in our day abbots who continue to exercise their office until death are rare indeed; they frequently resign within a few years after their blessing. Hence, in having a limited term of office they are no different from the superiors in other religious communities. It seems only proper, then, that the celebration of the blessing of an abbot should be quite simple and devoid of ostentation, in keeping with the basic frugality that should characterize monastic life.

The blessing of an abbess raises a serious theological and canonical question that needs to be addressed. If an abbess is given a special blessing by the Church—one similar to that given to abbots—and if she is entrusted with the rule and responsibility for the proclamation of the Word of God in the liturgy of the hours and for the spiritual leadership of her community, why is she not given

[24] *Ordo benedictionis abbatis et abbatissae*, Rome, Typis Polyglottis Vaticanis, 1971, 31 pp.

[25] *AAS* 63 (1971) 710–11.

true jurisdiction instead of only so-called dominative power in the Church? The question is related to the Holy See's regular insistence that the superior of a monastic community of men must always be a priest. Of its nature, a monastic community is not essentially clerical; there would seem to be no sound reason, then, why the major superior need be a priest to exercise true jurisdiction. The tradition of linking the power of jurisdiction with the power of orders is not only a questionable tradition but one that seems to lack a sound theological foundation.

The revised rite for the blessing of holy oils[26] was published in 1971. It had been authorized by the decree *Ritus Hebdomadae*, issued by the Sacred Congregation for Divine Worship on December 3, 1970.[27] Since the restored rites for Holy Week were inserted in the new Roman Missal, it seemed proper that the order for blessing the holy oils, which is part of the Roman Pontifical, should be revised. The new order notes that the Chrism Mass is one of the principal expressions of the bishop's priesthood and symbolizes the close unity of the priests with their bishop. During the Mass, which the bishop concelebrates with priests from various sections of the diocese, the bishop consecrates the chrism and blesses the oil of catechumens and the oil of the sick. The prayers of blessing allude to the Old Testament practice of anointing kings, priests, and prophets and relate these figures to Christ, who is the anointed of the Lord. The blessing of the oil of the sick takes place before the doxology of the canon; the blessing of the oil of catechumens and the consecration of the chrism take place after communion. For pastoral reasons, however, the entire rite of blessing may be celebrated after the liturgy of the Word. This would seem to be the better place for the rites, in keeping with the general practice of performing special blessings and dedications at this time in the Eucharistic liturgy.

As has already been noted, the new order for confirmation followed the publication of the apostolic constitution *Divinae consortium naturae*, of August 15, 1971, and the decree *Peculiare Spiritus Sancti donum*, issued on August 22, 1971. The rites for the

[26] *Ordo benedicendi oleum catechumenorum et infirmorum et conficiendi chrisma*, Rome, Typis Polyglottis Vaticanis, 1971, 20 pp.

[27] *Notitiae* 7 (1971) 89–92.

conferral of ministries, the reception of candidates for the priesthood and diaconate, and the promise of celibacy were authorized by
the decree *Ministeriorum disciplina*, issued on December 3, 1972.

By a decree issued on May 29, 1977, *Dedicationis ecclesiae*,[28] the
Sacred Congregation for Sacraments and Divine Worship promulgated a new order for the dedication of a church and altar. The
order consists of seven chapters and contains the most important
rites found in Book II of the 1961 Roman Pontifical: laying of the
foundation stone or beginning of the work; dedication of a church;
dedication of an altar; blessing of a church; blessing of an altar;
blessing of a chalice and paten. An appendix containing music for
the antiphons and other chants accompanies the order.

The primary criterion that guided the preparation of the new
order was that of simplification of the ceremonial development
undergone through the ages by the old rituals of dedication. Chapters two, three, and four, containing the rites for the dedication of a
church and altar, are the most important chapters in the document.
The new rituals for these occasions, replacing rites that date from
1294 and that were partially reformed in 1961, eliminate many
duplications in words and gestures, so that what used to be a very
long celebration is now lengthy but considerably shortened.

Bishops are the only ministers authorized to dedicate a new
church. They no longer perform exorcisms over the Gregorian
water, a mixture of water, ashes, salt, and wine used for sprinkling
the altar and walls of the church. The water itself is still blessed and
sprinkled. The bishop no longer traces the Greek and Latin alpha-
bets with the end of his pastoral staff on ashes placed on the floor in
the form of a cross. Gestures that formerly had to be repeated
several times are now executed only once; among these is the procession previously made six times around the exterior of the church.

The new liturgy of dedication takes place within the context of the
Eucharist. It includes a special inauguration of the presidential
chair, sprinkling of the walls with blessed water, dedication of the
lectern, baptistry, and confessionals, and a procession to the place of
Eucharistic reservation for the special blessing of the tabernacle.
The principal part of the new rite centers around the consecration of
the new altar.

[28] *Notitiae* 13 (1977) 364–65.

Chapter seven of the revised order for the dedication of a church and an altar is devoted to the blessing of a chalice and paten. The introduction to the chapter affirms that such vessels are indeed "sacred vessels," since they are intended solely and permanently for the celebration of the Eucharist. The intention of devoting such vessels entirely to the celebration of the Eucharist is made manifest before the community by a special blessing, preferably imparted during Mass. Although any bishop or priest may bless a chalice and paten, provided they have been made according to the norms laid down in the General Instruction of the Roman Missal,[29] it would seem that such a blessing is optional. As a matter of fact, the actual use of such objects in the liturgy would seem to be a sufficient blessing.

Reference should also be made to three documents on the simplification of pontifical rites. The motu proprio *Pontificalia insignia*, of June 21, 1968, announced a simplification of these rites.[30] They were listed in the instruction *Pontificales ritus*, issued on the same day by the Sacred Congregation of Rites.[31] The instruction *Ut sive sollicite*, issued by the Secretariat of State on March 31, 1969, gave additional rules concerning the roles of bishops and other prelates.[32]

THE NEW ROMAN MISSAL

Texts concerning the new missal may be divided into two categories: those pertaining to the lectionary and those pertaining to the *Missale Romanum*.

The Lectionary

The typical edition of the new lectionary was authorized by the Sacred Congregation for Divine Worship on May 25, 1969.[33] The episcopal conference of Germany had prepared a ferial lectionary that was approved *ad experimentum* by the Consilium.[34] Permission was also given to other episcopal conferences to use the same texts.[35] The French episcopal conference prepared its own arrangement of

---

[29] Nos. 290–95.
[30] *AAS* 60 (1968) 374–77.
[31] *AAS* 60 (1968) 406–14.
[32] *AAS* 61 (1969) 334–40.
[33] *Ordo lectionum Missae*, Rome, Typis Polyglottis Vaticanis, 1969, xxv + 434 pp.
[34] *Notitiae* 2 (1966) 6–7.
[35] *Notitiae* 2 (1966) 7, 168.

ferial readings and received the Consilium's approval for experimental use.[36] An undated statement concerning the approval of particular lectionaries was published in *Notitiae* in 1968.[37]

The decree *Ordinem lectionum*, issued by the Sacred Congregation for Divine Worship on May 25, 1969, prescribed that as of November 30, 1969, the readings on Sunday would be taken from series "B," and the second series of readings throughout the year would be used on weekdays.[38] This has established the cycle now followed in the liturgical year. A short instruction, *Decreto quo novus Ordo lectionum*, issued by the Sacred Congregation for Divine Worship on July 25, 1969, gave norms for the gradual introduction of the new lectionary and preparation of texts for the readings at Mass.[39]

The *Ordo lectionum Missae* consists of six parts:

1. Lessons for the temporal cycle. This part is divided into two sections, one for Sundays and feast days and the other for ferial days. For Sundays and feast days the lectionary follows a three-year cycle and proposes three lessons for each day (the first from the Old Testament, except for the Easter season, when readings from the Acts of the Apostles are used). For ferial days the lectionary proposes two lessons for each day. For Advent, the Christmas season, Lent, and the Easter season it follows a one-year cycle, but for the rest of the year it follows a two-year cycle for the first lesson, which is taken from either the Old or the New Testament.

2. Lessons for the proper of the saints according to the new universal calendar. These lessons are arranged according to the civil calendar. For solemnities three proper lessons are proposed; for other feasts and commemorations only two. The three lessons proposed for solemnities and feasts are regarded as mandatory.

3. Lessons for the common of the saints, including lessons for the common of the Blessed Virgin and for the dedication of a church. For each category a variety of lessons from both the Old and New Testaments is given. In each case provision is made for three possible readings.

---

[36] *Notitiae* 2 (1966) 168–71.

[37] Vol. 4 (1968) 41–88.

[38] *AAS* 61 (1969) 548–49.

[39] *Notitiae* 5 (1969) 238–39.

4. Lessons for ritual Masses. In this section lessons are proposed for the various rites of the catechumenate, baptism of adults and children, admission to communion in the Church of those persons already validly baptized, confirmation, first communion, ordination, marriage, religious profession, funerals and Masses for the dead.

5. Lessons used in Masses for various occasions. These lessons are divided into four groups according to the plan for intentions of the prayer of the faithful: the Church, civil society and government, various circumstances of public interest, and particular needs.

6. Lessons to be used in votive Masses. In this section lessons are proposed for Masses in honor of the Holy Trinity, the Triumph of the Holy Cross, the Holy Eucharist, the Sacred Heart, the Precious Blood, the Holy Name of Jesus, the Holy Spirit, and the Apostles.

The *Ordo lectionum Missae* is prefaced with a lengthy introduction outlining the principles used in structuring the lectionary, and a description of the arrangement of readings for the various seasons of the liturgical year. It is obvious that a very serious effort was made to provide a much richer proclamation of Scripture in the celebration of the liturgy, in accordance with the directive of article 15 of the Constitution on the Sacred Liturgy.[40] Before the texts were selected, a careful study was made of the various historical lectionaries of the Latin liturgies, of the Eastern rites, and of the Protestant and Anglican Churches. An effort was made to harmonize the Old Testament and gospel pericopes so that a common theme can be found running through the two readings. In selecting the second reading for those Masses with three readings, no attempt at harmonization was made. The pericopes constituting the second reading are more or less continuous texts taken from the epistles. Such an arbitrary arrangement surely presents a difficulty for preaching and catechesis. No satisfactory solution has been found to this problem. The rubrics permit the omission of the proclamation of the epistle reading, but such a practice would not be in keeping with the prescription of the Constitution on the Sacred Liturgy that a more representative selection of Scripture be proclaimed.[41]

[40] *AAS* 56 (1964) 104.
[41] *Sacrosanctum Concilium*, no. 35: *AAS* 56 (1964) 109.

The Roman Missal

The history of the revision of the Roman Missal is rather complicated. In addition to the actual texts of the Mass, there is also the *In-*
stitutio generalis, or General Instruction, of the Roman Missal,
which contains both theological principles and directives for the
celebration of Mass. Reference has already been made to some of the
documents discussing the rubrics of the Mass when we treated the
sacrament of the Eucharist.

On February 15, 1965, the Sacred Congregation of Rites sent to
the publishers of liturgical books a list of changes to be made in the
rubrics of the missal.[42] These changes were deemed necessary so that
the rubrics of the missal might be in accord with the instruction
Inter Oecumenici, issued on September 26, 1964, and the new *Ordo*
Missae, published on January 27, 1965.[43] The apostolic constitution
Missale Romanum was promulgated on April 3, 1969.[44] Its aim was
to help the faithful to participate in the celebration of the Eucharist
in an intelligent and dynamic way. It was followed by a decree of
the Sacred Congregation for Divine Worship issued on April 6,
1969, which stated that the use of the new missal would be obligatory as of November 30, 1969.[45]

The instruction *Constitutione apostolica Missale Romanum*,
issued by the Sacred Congregation for Divine Worship on October
20, 1969,[46] followed the publication of the declaration *Institutio*
generalis Missalis Romani.[47] These documents called for the inclusion of the General Instruction of the Roman Missal in all new missals, and for the gradual implementation of the apostolic constitution *Missale Romanum*. The bishops' conferences were directed to
draw up and approve vernacular texts of the missal. On November
10, 1969, the Sacred Congregation for Divine Worship issued norms
concerning an appendix to the Roman Missal.[48] A number of Latin
texts were to be included in the vernacular missals so that priests
who might not know the vernacular would be able to use Latin in

[42] "Rubricae in Missali Romano emendandae," *Notitiae* 1 (1965) 215–19.
[43] See *Notitiae* 1 (1965) 100–101.
[44] *AAS* 61 (1969) 217–22.
[45] *Notitiae* 5 (1969) 147.
[46] *Notitiae* 5 (1969) 418–23.
[47] *Notitiae* 5 (1969) 417–18.
[48] *Notitiae* 5 (1969) 442–57.

the celebration of the liturgy. These texts were also issued in a separate publication.[49]

The typical edition of the Roman Missal was authorized by the decree *Celebrationis Eucharisticae,* issued by the Sacred Congregation for Divine Worship on March 26, 1970.[50] Celebrants were free to use the text as soon as it was published. The *vacatio legis* for the use of the new Roman Missal was extended to November 28, 1971, by the notification *Instructione,* of June 14, 1971.[51] A number of changes in the text of the General Instruction of the Roman Missal became necessary as a result of the abolition of the subdiaconate on January 1, 1973. The modifications to be incorporated in subsequent editions of the missal were made public by the Sacred Congregation for Divine Worship on December 23, 1972.[52]

The new *Missale Romanum* is fundamentally a sacramentary in the tradition of the Gregorian and Gelasian sacramentaries. It contains the prayers to be used at the Eucharist but does not contain a lectionary. It differs from the traditional sacramentaries in that it includes entrance and communion texts; there are no offertory verses. Its backbone is the liturgical year as set out in the revised Roman calendar; the proper of seasons is organized around the important feasts and seasons of Advent, Christmas, Lent and Paschaltide, ending with Pentecost. Since there are certain new features in the missal, a brief description of its content might be helpful.

The Proper of the Seasons

Advent: As before, there are four Sundays of Advent; they retain their former entrance and communion texts, but now have new collects or opening prayers. For use on weekdays there are six new Mass formularies, made up of an opening prayer, prayer over the gifts, and prayer after communion. These texts are to be used until the sixteenth of December. From the seventeenth until the twenty-third of December, there is a Mass formula for each day.

Christmas: The texts for the celebration of Christmas begin with a formula to be used at evening Mass on Christmas Eve. For Christ-

[49] *Missale parvum e Missali Romano et Lectionario excerptum ad usum sacerdotis itinerantis,* Rome, Typis Polyglottis Vaticanis, 1971, 176 pp.

[50] *AAS* 62 (1970) 554.

[51] *Notitiae* 7 (1971) 215–17.

[52] *Notitiae* 9 (1973) 34–38.

mas Day there are texts for midnight, dawn, and day Masses. The rest of the period is provided with texts for the feast of the Holy Family, the Solemnity of Mary, the Mother of God, and three ferial Masses for the twenty-ninth, thirtieth, and thirty-first of December. There is a Mass formula for the second Sunday after Christmas and formularies for Epiphany and the Baptism of the Lord. Six texts to be used before and after Epiphany are provided for the days from the second of January to the Saturday before the Baptism of the Lord.

Lent: There is a Mass formula for every day, as in the Tridentine missal, but a proper preface for each Sunday of Lent has been added.

Holy Week: The liturgy of Holy Week extends from Palm Sunday to Easter Sunday.

Eastertide: Mass formularies are provided for the ferias in Easter week and for the seven Sundays of the season. The Ascension comes after the sixth Sunday; Pentecost, which is provided with a Mass text for the Mass on Saturday evening and one for the Mass of the day, concludes the Easter season and the proper of the seasons.

Sundays of the Year

In the *Missale Romanum*, thirty-four Mass formularies for the ordinary Sundays of the year are provided. Alternatives for the communion verse are given, the second generally taken from the text of the gospel and to be used when the gospel text appears in the Mass for the day.

Solemnities of the Lord

Included here are the Mass formularies for the feasts of the Holy Trinity, the Body and Blood of Christ, the Sacred Heart, and the Kingship of Christ.

The Order of Mass

In the *Missale Romanum*, the order of the Mass appears about halfway through the book. Texts are provided for the celebration of Mass both with and without a congregation. There are fifty-one prefaces; thirty-one additional prefaces are given in their proper places in the course of the missal. The four Eucharistic prayers come after the prefaces; the rite of communion follows. In the typical edition, an appendix comes next, giving the alternative greetings at Mass, the alternative penitential rites, alternative beginnings and conclusions of prefaces that may be used in drawing up vernacular editions, the alternative acclamations after the consecration, and the solemn blessings and prayers over the people, which may be used before the blessing at any Mass during the year.

Proper of Saints

This extends from the first of January to the thirty-first of December, rather than from November to December as in the Tridentine missal. Each solemnity and feast has a proper Mass formulary, and almost every memorial has at least a proper opening prayer.

Commons

This section of the missal has been completely reorganized. It comprises the following: dedication of a church (considered a feast of the Lord), the Blessed Virgin, martyrs, pastors, doctors, virgins, men and women saints (six Mass formularies), religious (two Mass formularies), those renowned for their works of mercy, teachers, and holy women. The last group of formularies might well serve as models in the construction of texts appropriate for local calendars.

Ritual Masses

Since all the sacraments and most important ecclesial acts may now be celebrated within the context of the Mass, a new section of ritual Masses had to be inserted in the missal to provide for this situation. There are formularies for the various stages of Christian initiation, the catechumenate, baptism, and confirmation. There are texts for the celebration of ordination, for the administration of Viaticum, for weddings (three formulas), wedding anniversaries (three formulas), for the consecration of virgins, and for the renewal of religious vows.

Masses and Prayers for Various Occasions

The Tridentine missal had a collection of such formulas and prayers, but in the new missal it has been considerably expanded and makes provision for a greater variety of occasions. It is intended to provide for the diversity of needs in the modern Church and world. There are three sections, covering what are basically public needs in the Church and civil affairs; a fourth section gives formulas for more personal needs and would most likely be used for small group celebrations.

Votive Masses

The General Instruction of the Roman Missal (no. 329) asserts that these formulas are to serve the devotion of the people; hence, they are not meant to express primarily the devotion of the priest. The texts provided are for the Holy Trinity, the mystery of the Holy Cross, the Eucharist, the Name of Jesus, the Precious Blood, the Sacred Heart, the Holy Spirit, the Blessed Virgin Mary, the Angels, St. Joseph, the Apostles, St. Peter and St. Paul, one Apostle, and All Saints. This section of the missal is smaller than it was in the Tridentine missal, since the curious formulas in honor of the Holy Winding Sheet and the Holy Lance and Nails have disappeared.

Masses for the Dead

This section of the missal has been structured in accordance with article 81 of the Constitution on the Sacred Liturgy, which maintained that funeral rites should express the paschal character of Christian death and should correspond to the circumstances and traditions found in various regions. Formulas are provided for a pope, bishops, priests, for young persons, for those who have died suddenly, for those who have died after a long illness, for a child, and even for an unbaptized child.

Appendix

An appendix to the missal provides formulas for blessing water, typical general intercessions, preparation before Mass and thanksgiving after Mass, the plainsong for various texts of the liturgy, and three indices: an alphabetical index of all the celebrations (i.e., solemnities, feasts, etc.), an index of the various prefaces, and a general index of the whole book.

The new Roman Missal surely represents a greatly enriched collection of liturgical texts compared to earlier editions of the missal. In general it is an excellent work of restoration. Responsible use of the texts over the past few years has pointed up the need for further creative manifestations of the Roman Catholic liturgical tradition and greater sensitivity to contemporary experience.

It seems appropriate at this point to comment briefly on the restored Holy Week services. The revised rites were published in Latin as part of the new *Missale Romanum.* The readings for the Holy Week services, together with the accompanying chants, surely represent an improvement over those that were formerly used. Apart from the changes in Scripture readings and prayers, which have been either changed or altered for all the services, there were few really drastic changes in these services, except for the Easter Vigil.

The ritual for Palm Sunday provides for a simplified form of processional liturgy at the Mass at which palms are blessed. After the entrance antiphon or a suitable hymn, either in a separate place or in the church itself, the palms, which have previously been distributed to the people, are blessed with one of two prayers, both of which are slightly changed forms of the prayers contained in the Tridentine missal. Then there is a procession to the church or into the sanctuary, accompanied by chants chosen from the traditional repertory.

There have been few changes in the Holy Thursday liturgy other than the revised readings, responses, and orations. All of these stress the doctrine of the Eucharist as a sacred banquet with sacrificial and eschatological implications. At the direction of the local bishop, all the faithful may communicate under both kinds, a practice certainly in keeping with the words of Jesus proclaimed at the Last Supper, "Take this, all of you, and drink from it."

Apart from the modified readings, there have been few changes in the Good Friday liturgy. The text of the solemn prayers has been slightly changed, and a tenth petition for all needs has been added. Two forms for the veneration of the cross have been provided. In recent years many have questioned the retention of the reproaches in the Good Friday liturgy. People of the Jewish faith have long resented the Christian use of the reproaches, convinced that they imply a hostile and insulting view of the Jewish people and convey the notion of collective Jewish responsibility for the crucifixion of Jesus. Many Christians share this evaluation. It should be pointed out that the use of the reproaches is optional; the basic question, then, is whether or not they should be suppressed. If and when use of the reproaches does in fact stimulate anti-Semitic sentiments, they should be suppressed, but the popular understanding of the reproaches has traditionally centered on the belief that Jesus' words from the cross refer to all humanity and not just to a special group. In a liturgical context, the worshipers who hear the reproaches on Good Friday do not simply encounter the history of the Jewish people; such worshipers encounter their own history. Liturgical texts must not be understood in a narrow, literal sense; they must be understood typologically. Thus, with proper catechesis promoting a correct understanding of the reproaches, the texts might well be used as an enrichment rather than as an impoverishment of the Good Friday liturgy.

Changes in the Easter Vigil are more significant. The structure has been simplified so as to constitute four distinct parts: the service of light, liturgy of the Word, baptismal liturgy, and Eucharistic liturgy. The light service takes place either outside the church or within, near the entrance. After a brief introduction to the celebration, the fire is lighted and blessed with a prayer that through Christ, the Light of the world, God may purify our minds by the Easter feast and bring us to the eternal celebration of light. The Easter candle is then lighted. Following the procession with the candle to the sanctuary, the *Exsultet* is sung. The function of the *Exsultet* is to bless the Easter candle.

The liturgy of the Word has been unified. The Old Testament readings used to be separated from the epistle and gospel by the baptismal liturgy and the preliminary rites of the Eucharistic liturgy, but now the sequence is as follows: Old Testament readings, each followed by an appropriate responsorial psalm and collect; *Gloria*; epistle; alleluia; gospel; homily. The new lectionary gives seven Old Testament readings; at least three of these are to be used, including the reading from Exodus 14.

The baptismal liturgy takes place after the homily. If there are baptisms, the celebration continues at the baptistry, if that is feasible; if not, in the sanctuary. The litany of the saints is sung, and the prayer for the consecration of baptismal water is recited. The candidates are then baptized and confirmed. When the rite has been completed, or if there is no baptism, immediately after the blessing of water, all stand with lighted candles and renew their baptismal profession of faith. The prayer of the faithful and the offertory rites then follow. Lauds of Easter Sunday are retained in the reformed liturgy, but not as part of the vigil service. The prayer after communion is followed immediately by the dismissal.

There is no doubt that the revised form of the vigil service is an improvement over the old rites, but experience has shown that the great majority of Roman Catholics do not take part in the Easter Vigil service; they continue to celebrate the Eucharist on Easter Sunday morning. It would seem desirable, then, that a simple rite be introduced at Easter Sunday Masses featuring a proclamation of the paschal mystery, blessing of water, and the renewal of baptismal promises. The simple renewal of baptismal promises that takes place in many parishes after the Easter homily does not seem to be adequate from a pastoral and liturgical point of view. Such a renewal needs to be situated in the context of the Easter water and to be related to the Easter candle through the proclamation of the paschal mystery.

Chapter 10

THE LITURGY OF THE HOURS
AND OTHER LITURGICAL BOOKS

THE LITURGY OF THE HOURS

After the promulgation of the Constitution on the Sacred Liturgy, norms were issued for the simplification of the divine office and for its recitation in the vernacular.[1] Various petitions were sent to the Holy See by clerical religious bound to the choral recitation of the office for a recognition of their right to pray in their own language. They received a response in the form of an instruction of the Sacred Congregation of Rites, dated November 23, 1965.[2] The document maintained the requirement of article 101 of the Constitution on the Sacred Liturgy that Latin be used in the choral recitation of the office. It did make some minor concessions with regard to the use of the vernacular in the office, but it actually sought to restrict the use of the vernacular by religious at Mass to the lessons, at least as a general rule, by prescribing the same norms for the Mass as for the office.

The objectionable provisions of that instruction were paralleled by those of an instruction of the Congregation of Seminaries entitled "Concerning the Liturgical Formation of Seminarians." This document never appeared in the *Acta Apostolicae Sedis* or in *Notitiae*. In article 15, the instruction maintained that while Latin should be the

---

[1] See *Sacram liturgiam*, no. 9: *AAS* 56 (1964) 144.
[2] *AAS* 57 (1965) 1010–13.

language of the Mass and office in the seminary, the vernacular might well be used in celebrations on some days (for example, once a week), in consideration of the fact that the seminarians will later be required to celebrate the liturgy in the vernacular once they are assigned to parishes. These two documents were basically expressions of an unreconstructed preconciliar mentality.

On August 15, 1966, Pope Paul VI sent an apostolic letter, *Sacrificium laudis,* to the superiors general of those clerical religious institutes bound by the obligation to recite the divine office in choir.[3] He reinforced their responsibility to celebrate the divine office in Latin and to preserve the Latin tradition in the Church.

The proposed text and order of the new liturgy of the hours were explained by the Consilium in an article published in early 1969.[4] But it was not until November 1, 1970, that Pope Paul VI issued the apostolic constitution *Laudis canticum,* promulgating the new breviary.[5] On April 11, 1971, by the decree *Horarum liturgia,* the Sacred Congregation for Divine Worship actually promulgated the typical edition of the liturgy of the hours.[6]

The revised Roman office manifests the same basic characteristics as the other revised rites of the Roman liturgy. It is conservative in that it is more a restoration than a creative reform. It contains the office of readings, morning prayer, daytime prayer, evening prayer, and night prayer. The office of readings replaces matins of the former office and consists of a hymn, three psalms, and a biblical and non-biblical reading. Its primary concern is to stimulate reflection on God's Word. Morning and evening prayer, the principal hinges on which the whole liturgy of the hours turns, each consist of two psalms and a canticle from the Old or New Testament, a reading, responsory, intercessions, and concluding prayer. Daytime prayer consists of a hymn, three psalms, a reading, verse, and prayer. Night prayer has one or two psalms, a reading, a canticle from the New Testament, concluding prayer, and at the conclusion a Marian antiphon.

There is much more variety and richness in the repertory of texts

---

[3] *Notitiae* 2 (1966) 252–55.
[4] *Notitiae* 5 (1969) 74–85.
[5] *AAS* 63 (1971) 527–35.
[6] *AAS* 63 (1971) 712.

employed in the new breviary. It has a flexible structure in that it provides for various modifications and for considerable options in the choice of texts. One of the most constructive aspects of the revised Roman office is the lectionary for scriptural readings; the two-year cycle provides for a rich and well-planned encounter with God's Word in the Bible.

The patristic lectionary contains a more representative and better choice of patristic readings than in the former breviary, but it seems very unfortunate that the scope of the lectionary was so narrowly conceived. A wider choice of readings from Christian classics of every age, including the present century, would have enriched the volumes. It would seem that the quality of the texts should have been the primary consideration in the choice of materials; it does not seem proper that certain Christian writers who in some aspects were heterodox but were nonetheless able to give a powerful expression to the Church's faith in other writings should have been excluded. A declaration concerning a patristic lectionary for optional use was published in *Notitiae* in 1971.[7] Episcopal conferences were authorized to prepare special series of patristic readings taken from the works of those renowned for their Catholic doctrine and the holiness of their lives. A declaration published in *Notitiae* in 1972 stated that readings were not to be selected from the writings of persons still living.[8]

Special norms were issued on November 11, 1971, concerning the interim use of the former breviary.[9] By a notification issued by the Sacred Congregation for Divine Worship on August 6, 1972, a lengthened office was authorized for use in religious institutes that maintained choral recitation.[10] An interim revised office for Holy Week was also made available on March 3, 1972.[11]

One of the major difficulties with the revised liturgy of the hours has been that the same formula was imposed for private recitation, the prayer of non-monastic religious communities, and parish celebrations. The Constitution on the Sacred Liturgy expressed the hope

[7] Vol. 7 (1971) 289.
[8] Vol. 8 (1972) 249–50.
[9] *Notitiae* 7 (1971) 379–83.
[10] *Notitiae* 8 (1972) 254–58.
[11] *Notitiae* 8 (1972) 96–99.

that the liturgy of the hours would be restored as the prayer of the whole Church; it was no longer meant to be the prayer simply of clerics and religious.[12] However, experience in using the revised form of the office has shown that it is not an ideal prayer form for ordinary congregations. Unless more popular forms for morning and evening prayer are developed, the hope of restoring the celebration of the hours to parishes seems quite illusory.

A relatively minor issue that has attracted the attention of both the Congregation for Divine Worship and the Congregation for Religious and Secular Institutes has been the development of a distinctively monastic office. On July 8, 1971, the Sacred Congregation for Divine Worship sent a letter to the three branches of the Benedictine family (O.S.B., O. Cist., O.C.S.O.), asking them to come to some kind of agreement concerning the basic elements each order could use as the starting point for shaping up the office. There was some very strong feeling on the part of the Holy See that there should be a common monastic breviary. This proposal met with widespread rejection on the part of the monastic superiors. The members of the three branches of the Benedictine family found it very difficult to collaborate on liturgical matters because of differences in approach to the content and style of monastic liturgy. They did agree to work on a general instruction on the monastic office that would set forth the basic principles on which the monastic office should be built. Instead of producing a common document, each branch has drawn up and received approval for its own proper document.

On February 10, 1977, the Sacred Congregation for Sacraments and Divine Worship confirmed the *Thesaurus liturgiae horarum monasticae*.[13] The fruit of years of experience and intensive work by the Benedictine Confederation, the official Latin text is meant to be a model and a help in the renewal of the divine office for the monks, nuns, and sisters attached to the Benedictine Confederation. The text contains the following items:

— a directory of the divine office, namely, the basic principles in the monastic tradition for the divine office, restored in the light of the principles of the *Liturgia horarum;*

---

[12] *Sacrosanctum Concilium*, nos. 84, 90, 100: *AAS* 56 (1964) 121, 122, 124.
[13] *Notitiae* 13 (1977) 157–58.

— the premises, namely, the practical norms and directives for the celebration of the Benedictine *Liturgia horarum;*

— four schemes of the psalter with antiphons, verses, short responses: (a) as laid down in the Rule of St. Benedict; (b) the entire psalter in the course of a week without repetition; (c) and (d) two arrangements of the psalter, with repetition of psalms, over a two-week period;

— the temporal and sanctoral cycles in accordance with the Benedictine calendar, with all the antiphons, responsories, etc., necessary for each section;

— the common of the saints.

The text was prepared under the guidance of the liturgical commission of the Confederation. It is based on the longstanding Benedictine tradition, but it is updated in accord with the best principles of recent liturgical studies. The general instruction on the liturgy of the hours issued by the Sacred Congregation for Divine Worship on February 2, 1971,[14] highlighted the spiritual values of celebrating the *Opus Dei.* These values were from the beginning and continue to be the special heritage of monastic communities.

OTHER LITURGICAL BOOKS

In addition to the ritual, the pontifical, the missal, and the liturgy of the hours, a number of other liturgical books have been published since the Second Vatican Council. Most of them have been concerned with sacred music. On December 14, 1964, a *Kyriale Simplex* was promulgated by the Sacred Congregation of Rites.[15] It contained simple Gregorian chants for use in the ordinary of the Mass. A collection of Gregorian chants for use at Mass and especially suited for concelebrated Mass was authorized by the decree *Edita instructione,* also issued by the Sacred Congregation of Rites on December 14, 1964.[16] The collection was actually published in 1965.[17]

---

[14] *Officium divinum ex decreto Sacrosancti Oecumenici Concilii Vaticani II instauratum auctoritate Pauli Pp. VI promulgatum, Instituto generalis de Liturgia Horarum,* Rome, Typis Polyglottis Vaticanis, 1971.

[15] *AAS* 57 (1965) 407.

[16] *AAS* 57 (1965) 408.

[17] *Cantus qui in Missali Romano desiderantur,* Rome, Typis Polyglottis Vaticanis, 1965, 34 pp.

On March 5, 1967, the Sacred Congregation of Rites issued the instruction *Musicam sacram*, which contained important norms for the use of music in the liturgy.[18] It described itself as a continuation and complement of the earlier instruction on implementing the liturgy constitution, *Inter Oecumenici*, which had been issued on September 26, 1964. The document gave evidence of strong differences of opinion among its compilers. The main emphasis was placed squarely on expounding the constitution's pastoral implications for music, but several paragraphs modified and at times contradicted the main part of the text of the instruction. Their goal seems to have been to maintain the musical *status quo*.

In its opening chapters the instruction reformulated basic principles in order to emphasize the pastoral thrust of liturgical celebrations. It stated that although the liturgy takes on a more noble form when it is celebrated in song, the most joyful and solemn form is that in which the whole assembly expresses its faith and piety in song. The document clarified the meaning of solemnity in stressing that it depends on preserving the "integrity of the liturgical service, that is, the execution of all parts in accordance with their true nature. A more ornate form of song and more magnificent ceremonial are sometimes desired, when they can be done properly. Yet it would be contrary to true solemnity if this increase in solemnity should lead to the omission, change, or improper performance of any element of the service."[19] "Improper" musical performances would include changes made in the form and nature of chants, giving to the choir chants that belong to the people, and delaying the progress of the liturgical celebration by excessive length. Another important clarification that the instruction made appeared in the emphasis on sung liturgy as the normative form from which all others derive.

Concerning the people's share in liturgical song, the instruction emphasized two points: (1) the people should sing; (2) the choir must not, either by its repertoire or performance, exclude or hinder the people from actively participating in the celebration. Their participation should, first of all, be conscious, that is, interior, so that they attend to what they say and hear, but it must also be external, manifesting interior participation in actions, speech, and song. During

---

[18] *Notitiae* 3 (1967) 87–108.
[19] *AAS* 54 (1964) 879.

the liturgical action, silence, which was so often in the past an excuse for evading popular participation, should be observed at the
proper times (no. 17).

The instruction inspired the publication of various statements on
the place of music in the liturgy by episcopal conferences throughout
the world. Of special note here is the statement published by the
United States Bishops' Committee on the Liturgy in November 1967
and revised in 1972.[20]

On September 3, 1967, by the decree *Sacrosancti Oecumenici
Concilii*, the publication of the *Graduale Simplex* was authorized.[21]
It was prepared by the Consilium and was designed to facilitate the
integral celebration of what used to be called the "high" Mass in
"small" churches (which in practice would mean most parish
churches), where the use of the chants of the *Graduale Romanum* is
not generally possible. The publication fulfilled the prescription of
article 117 of the Constitution on the Sacred Liturgy for an edition
of simple Gregorian chant melodies.[22]

In the Simple Gradual the number of strictly proper chants is reduced to a minimum. The principle of "commons" is applied to both
the temporal and sanctoral cycles; hence, only the most important
Sundays and major feasts are provided with proper chants. For the
rest there are seasonal texts: two for Advent, one for the time after
Epiphany; one for the pre-Lenten season; two for Lent; two for the
Easter season; and six for the Sundays after Pentecost. All of the
chants were taken from the traditional Gregorian repertory.

A major concern in preparing the volume was to restore the
chants of the Mass to their proper function and to promote participation by the congregation. An English translation of the texts was
prepared by ICEL, and several musical settings were published, but
they did not prove very successful. They were produced at a time
when the custom of singing four hymns at the Eucharist (entrance,
offertory, communion, and recessional) was deeply entrenched in
many parishes and religious communities. The project of producing
the Simple Gradual, however, did stimulate and inspire the creation

---

[20] *Music in Catholic Worship* (Washington, D.C.: United States Catholic Conference, 1972).

[21] *Notitiae* 3 (1967) 311.

[22] *AAS* 56 (1964) 129.

of new texts and musical settings that have proven to be more satisfactory.

On June 24, 1972, the Sacred Congregation for Divine Worship promulgated a new *Ordo cantus Missae*.[23] In the Constitution on the Sacred Liturgy, the Second Vatican Council declared that the treasury of Gregorian chant which tradition has transmitted down to our time should be preserved.[24] In order that this norm could be kept, the Sacred Congregation for Divine Worship compiled the *Ordo cantus Missae*, indicating certain points whereby the *Graduale Romanum* should be accommodated to the new state of the liturgy.

In 1974 the Abbey of Solesmes published the new *Graduale Romanum* in accordance with the plan indicated in the *Ordo cantus Missae*.[25] For those who wish to sing the Mass in Latin, all the necessary musical settings are given in full; the possibilities of choices offered in the *Ordo cantus Missae* for both the temporal season and the sanctoral cycle are retained. To avoid the monotony that can issue from the frequent use of the same pieces, sometimes a choice of texts is indicated. The often inferior, newly composed Gregorian melodies that had been introduced for modern saints have been replaced with better chants. The volume also includes the *Ordo exsequiarum*, the *Cantus in Ordine Missae occurrentes*, the litanies of the saints, the *Te Deum*, the *Veni Creator*, and the *Tantum ergo*. A section containing the proper of the Benedictine order has also been included.

Additional liturgical books still to be published include the martyrology, the *Antiphonale Romanum*, and the *Caeremoniale Episcoporum*.[26] The *Caeremoniale Episcoporum* has been published in manuscript form to permit examination by experts nominated by national liturgical commissions. The volume contains all the material in the liturgical books so far published that has a particular significance for episcopal celebrations. It has been adapted for the use of bishops, but the text has yet to be finalized.

[23] *AAS* 65 (1973) 274. Typical edition: *Missale Romanum ex decreto Sacrosancti Oecumenici Concilii Vaticani II instauratum auctoritate Pauli Pp. VI promulgatum, Ordo cantus Missae*, Rome, Typis Polyglottis Vaticanis, 1972.

[24] *Sacrosanctum Concilium*, no. 114: *AAS* 56 (1964) 128–29.

[25] *Graduale Sacrosanctae Romanae Ecclesiae*, ed. Abbey Saint-Pierre de Solesmes (F 72300 Sable sur Sarthe), 1974, 918 pp.

[26] See *Notitiae* 2 (1966) 172–80.

Chapter 11

THE LITURGICAL YEAR

One of the first postconciliar changes in the liturgical calendar was the transfer of certain holy days of obligation to the preceding Sunday. On October 18, 1968, the Congregation of Rites issued a declaration concerning the celebration of certain feast days in 1969.[1] A number of episcopal conferences had obtained from the Holy See the faculty to transfer the solemnities of the Epiphany, Ascension, and Corpus Christi to Sunday, thus removing the precept from the proper day. Various rubrical questions arose concerning the celebration of Mass and the divine office on such days. In its declaration the Congregation of Rites provided for the manner of celebration until the restoration of the breviary and missal.

By an apostolic letter, *Mysterii paschalis,* issued motu proprio by Pope Paul VI on February 14, 1969, the changes in the Roman calendar were officially promulgated.[2] In a consistory on April 28, 1969, the Pope described the purpose of the changes as follows:

> You will note that the liturgical year has not been radically changed. The goal in reworking it has been to see to it that the elements of each liturgical season focus more clearly on the paschal mystery of Christ as the center of all liturgical worship. The new calendar also ratifies, as far as possible, the celebration of saints' feast days, choosing saints whose life and example have importance for the universal Church;

[1] *Notitiae* 4 (1968) 279.
[2] *AAS* 61 (1969) 222–26.

other saints, less well known, are left to local veneration, in accordance with the true historical import of their lives and feast days. The aim of this approach is to show that holiness in the Church is relevant for all times and all places, and that all of the faithful, in every class of society, are summoned to seek after holiness, as the ecumenical council taught in its constitution *Lumen gentium*.[3]

The new calendar went into effect on January 1, 1970. The motu proprio of February 14, 1969, was enlarged upon by the decree *Anni liturgici*, issued by the Sacred Congregation of Rites on March 21, 1969.[4] It prescribed how the liturgical books were to be adapted to the new calendar on an interim basis. A further decree, *Decreto Sacrae Congregationis*, issued by the Sacred Congregation of Rites on June 29, 1969, prescribed the same norms for particular calendars.[5] A notification of May 17, 1970, stated that the interim calendar would be used throughout 1971.

The first steps in the reform of the calendar were taken by Pope Pius X on November 1, 1911, when he gave Sundays precedence over minor feasts.[6] In the following fifty years there was gradual pressure to ensure a more appropriate observance of Lent. Under Pius XII there was a decree of the Congregation of Rites on the simplification of the rubrics making it possible to choose the daily Lenten Mass in preference to that for the feast of a saint.[7] The new code of rubrics promulgated by decree of the Congregation of Rites on July 26, 1960,[8] upgraded the Lenten ferias, thus making it possible to celebrate the Mass of the day almost throughout the whole of Lent. The exceptions were the important feasts like that of St. Joseph and the Annunciation.

The Constitution on the Sacred Liturgy stated clearly that "the minds of the faithful must be directed primarily toward the feasts of the Lord by which the mysteries of salvation are celebrated in the course of the year. Therefore, the Proper of the Time must be given the preference which is its due over the feasts of the saints, so that

---

[3] *AAS* 61 (1969) 428–29.

[4] *Notitiae* 5 (1969) 163–86.

[5] *Notitiae* 5 (1969) 283.

[6] Apostolic constitution *Divino afflatu: AAS* 3 (1911) 633–51.

[7] March 23, 1955, *Decretum generale: AAS* 47 (1955) 218–19.

[8] *AAS* 52 (1960) 596–740.

the entire cycle of the mysteries of salvation may be suitably re-called."[9] The new Roman calendar made this possible. Sundays now have an almost unique position in the calendar. They may be super-seded only by feasts of the Lord, such as the feast of the Holy Fam-ily, the Baptism of the Lord, Holy Trinity, Christ the King, and other major solemnities. In effect, the only saints' feasts that can be celebrated on Sunday are the Birth of John the Baptist, the Apostles Peter and Paul, the Assumption of Our Lady, All Saints, and patronal feasts. In Advent, Lent, and the Easter season, Sundays have absolute priority.

The celebration of the paschal mystery on Sunday is closely linked with the liturgy of Holy Week. In this regard, the introduction to the calendar reiterates the teaching found in the Constitution on the Sacred Liturgy.[10] During the whole year the Church celebrates the saving life, death and resurrection of the Lord. These mysteries are celebrated in a special way during Holy Week and Easter, although it is the same paschal mystery that is sacramentalized every Sunday of the year. In order to affirm the unity of Christ's death and resur-rection, the name of the celebration has been changed from the *Sacrum Triduum* to the *Sacrum Triduum Paschale;* it begins with the evening Mass of the Lord's Supper on Holy Thursday, is centered on the Easter Vigil, and ends with Vespers on Easter Sunday. The three days form a unity in which the Church celebrates the whole paschal mystery.

In the years before the Second Vatican Council, there was some debate about when the liturgical year should begin, whether on the first Sunday of Advent or on Septuagesima Sunday. The introduc-tion to the calendar does not attend to the debate, but simply asserts that the paschal celebration of the Lord's death and resurrection is the culmination of the liturgical year.

Next in order of importance comes the celebration of Sunday, the original feast of the Church that was celebrated by the apostles and from which the annual celebration of Easter derives. Second in im-portance to the annual and weekly celebration of the paschal mystery is the time after Easter, which is the oldest known season of the Church's year. The season of fifty days is known to have been in

---

[9] *Sacrosanctum Concilium*, no. 108: *AAS* 56 (1964) 126.
[10] *Sacrosanctum Concilium*, no. 106: *AAS* 56 (1964) 126.

existence in the second century, long before the season of Lent was structured. It was regarded as a continuation of the paschal mystery. In the new calendar, the season consists of seven Sundays. What used to be known as Low Sunday is now the second Sunday of Easter, since the Easter octave ends with the Saturday after Easter. The Easter season ends on Pentecost Sunday, the fiftieth day after Easter. The octave of Pentecost has been suppressed.

As far as the calendar is concerned, Lent has been restored to its original observance; it is a preparation for the celebration of the paschal mystery. The primary features of this preparation are the catechumenate and works of penance and prayer. The season extends from Ash Wednesday to the evening Mass of Holy Thursday. The fifth Sunday of Lent is no longer called Passion Sunday; the sixth Sunday, traditionally called Palm Sunday, is now Passion Sunday. The last celebration of Lent is the consecration of the holy oils by the bishop at the morning Mass on Holy Thursday.

Through the celebration of the Lenten and Easter seasons, the main lines of the Church's year are clearly established; it is essentially a celebration of the saving work of Christ. Throughout the rest of the year the various aspects of that saving mystery are unfolded. Of special importance is the celebration of Christmas, which extends from the celebration of the Lord's birth beginning on the eve of the twenty-fourth of December and running to the Sunday after Epiphany, or after the sixth of January if the latter feast is kept on a Sunday. Christmas retains its octave. The mysteries highlighted in the infancy narratives in the gospels are observed; the season comes to an end with the Baptism of the Lord, marking the beginning of Christ's public ministry. The first of January is marked by the celebration of the oldest feast of Mary as the Mother of God.

The season of Advent has been somewhat ambiguous in its significance. The introduction to the calendar seeks to dispel that ambiguity by affirming that the season is meant to be a preparation for the first coming of Christ, celebrated at Christmas, and a preparation for the second coming of Christ at the end of time. The season is to be observed in a spirit of devotion and joyful expectancy; hence, the penitential aspect is suppressed. There are two parts to the season: the first extends from the first Sunday up to the seventeenth of December; the second part extends from the seventeenth of

December until the twenty-fourth of December. The latter days are concerned primarily with the coming of Christ in his human birth; the readings stress the roles of Mary, Joseph, and John the Baptist.

To the seasons already discussed must be added the time of the Sundays of the year, which are celebrations of the mystery of Christ in its fullness. There is a maximum of thirty-four such Sundays, the exact number in any year being determined by the date of the first Sunday in Advent.

The introduction to the calendar describes the Rogation and Ember Days as occasions when the Church prays for harvests, the work of human hands, and the various needs of the human community. They are also times for thanksgiving. Their celebration is to be adapted to cultural conditions, and the national conferences of bishops are to determine when they are to be celebrated and the forms that the celebrations should take. Mass formulas for such celebrations are provided in the new Roman Missal.

The new calendar of saints has proven to be more controversial than the temporal cycle. One of the most notable features of the calendar is the drastic reduction in the number of saints' days. In 1568 Pope Pius V ordered the promulgation of a reformed calendar in which the number of saints' days was reduced to about one hundred and fifty, but that number was more than doubled in the last four hundred years. Although a certain arbitrariness was probably inevitable in selecting the saints to be celebrated in the new calendar, the revisers hoped to make the calendar universal from a geographical and chronological point of view. The Constitution on the Sacred Liturgy had prescribed that only saints of universal importance should be proposed to the universal Church for obligatory commemoration.[11] Geographically, all five continents are now represented, but Eastern Europe is poorly represented; Italian and French saints are the most numerous. Chronologically, the selection covers the whole period of the Church's history, but there is a certain emphasis put on the early martyrs whose acts are authentic. Most of those with dubious legends have disappeared from the calendar.

There has been much shifting of dates in the new calendar, and in most cases the shift has restored the saints to their proper feast days.

---

[11] *Sacrosanctum Concilium*, no. 111: *AAS* 56 (1964) 127.

In some cases, however, the dates have been changed for questionable reasons. It is unfortunate that better account was not taken of the tradition of local churches. Although uniformity is generally desirable in the matter of liturgical calendars, local churches should have been given the right to honor their saints on the traditional day. Thus, certain changes in the sanctoral calendar have caused not only confusion but also some hostility, both of which could probably have been avoided.

Many aspects of the new calendar have proven satisfactory. The basic principles set forth in the introduction are generally sound, and the balance between the celebration of the temporal cycle and the celebration of saints' days is thought to be proper. History has shown, however, that the feasts of saints have a tendency to infiltrate the temporal cycle. Such intrusions will have to be resisted. Ecumenical discussions have raised a number of important questions concerning the possibility of a fixed date for Easter and a common calendar shared by various Churches, but solutions to these problems have been left to the future.

An instruction for particular calendars was issued on June 24, 1970.[12] Since many saints no longer appeared in the general calendar, it seemed appropriate that arrangements be made to provide for their veneration in the particular churches and in religious institutes. All previous indults on the matter were to be considered abrogated, and each ordinary was asked to forward to the Sacred Congregation for Divine Worship the list of liturgical privileges that had previously been granted so that proper revisions could be made where necessary and new local calendars established.

Because the revised calendar changed a number of the holy days of obligation previously established, it also became necessary to determine the days on which pastors and others were obliged to celebrate Mass for their people. The decree *Litteris apostolicis*, issued by the Sacred Congregation for the Clergy on July 25, 1970, prescribed that as of January 1, 1971, those obliged to celebrate Mass for the people must do so on all Sundays of the year and on all holy days of obligation celebrated as such in the place.[13] A further notification from the Sacred Congregation for Divine Worship on June 14, 1971,

[12] *Notitiae* 6 (1970) 348–70.
[13] *Notitiae* 6 (1970) 380.

extended the *vacatio legis* for the new calendar to January 1, 1972, and provided norms to be used in 1972 and 1973 until the new liturgical texts were published and translated in the vernacular.[14]

The Congregation for Sacraments and Divine Worship, in a decree dated October 7, 1977, transferred the feast of the Baptism of the Lord to the following Monday in places where the Epiphany of the Lord occurs on Sunday, the seventh or eighth of January. This was done in view of the doctrinal, pastoral, and ecumenical aspects of the feast of the Baptism of the Lord in the reformed Roman calendar; the feast, which is ordinarily assigned to the Sunday after Epiphany, would otherwise be omitted in those places where the Epiphany is transferred to the Sunday occurring on one of these days.[15]

---

[14] *AAS* 63 (1971) 712–15.
[15] *AAS* 69 (1977) 682.

Chapter 12

STRUCTURES ORIGINATING AND
IMPLEMENTING LITURGICAL REFORM

No attempt has been made in the preceding pages to comment on all the liturgical documents issued since the Second Vatican Council, but hopefully what has been said does provide a context in which the numerous documents may be situated. It is a basic hermeneutical principle that texts can be properly understood and interpreted only when they are situated in their proper context; but even when that is done, the hermeneutical task is complex, especially years after the documents have been formulated. Texts almost always reflect something of the intellectual framework of those who authored them, and they are usually nuanced by the ideological and sociological biases of the period in which they are written.

Although there is a major difference between the theological and juridical methodology used in interpreting texts, it is not legitimate for the canonist to abstract completely from theology, since legislative documents regularly have significant theological underpinnings. Positions that one assumes in the areas of christology and ecclesiology have serious implications for sacramental theology. Likewise, positions that one maintains in sacramental theology condition, either consciously or unconsciously, the pastoral stance one takes. All these factors influence, or should influence, the directives issued to promote and regulate sacramental ministry and practice.

It should also be noted that liturgical documents are often the result of compromise. They sometimes stress issues that have only passing significance; they rarely carry the same weight in all sections of the universal Church because of variations in cultural conditions and pastoral needs. It is not really possible to understand the liturgical legislation adequately without having some understanding of the Roman offices and personnel responsible for the texts. This is surely the case with the texts that have emanated from the Holy See since the Council of Trent.

When Pope Sixtus V established the Congregation for Sacred Rites and Ceremonies in 1588, he charged it with the protection of the legitimate rites of the Church and the prohibition of any spurious innovations. In his encyclical *Mediator Dei*, Pope Pius XII noted that that dicastery fulfilled the official function of supervising and formulating legislation with regard to all matters relating to the liturgy.[1] In general, the Congregation produced documents that regulated every detail of the liturgy and rarely allowed the minister or the community to change the rites in any way. The primary concern was with the external aspects of the rites; liturgy and rubrics were generally thought to be synonymous terms. The mentality of the Congregation is reflected in the 4,051 decisions concerning minute rubrical details that were collected in five volumes and issued by Pope Leo XIII between 1898 and 1901 under the title *Decreta authentica Congregationis Sacrorum Rituum*. Supplements were issued in 1912, 1927, and 1947.

As already noted, the narrow juridical mentality generally characteristic of the four centuries following Trent gradually changed, especially during the pontificate of Pius XII. Certainly the work of the commission for the general reform of the liturgy, which he inaugurated in 1946, did much to stimulate critical reflection not only on what was being celebrated in the Church's liturgy but also on the way the celebrations were executed. By the time the Second Vatican Council was convened, considerable work had already been done on projects requisite for a critical reform of the liturgical books. Certainly most of the experts involved in the modern liturgical movement had an appreciation of the history and theology of the liturgy vastly different from that presented in the traditional rubrical manuals.

[1] *AAS* 39 (1947) 544.

Although Cardinal Gaetano Cicognani, the president of the preparatory liturgical commission for the Second Vatican Council and prefect of the Sacred Congregation of Rites from December 7, 1953, until his death on February 5, 1962, was not what we would call an expert in liturgical matters, he did give basic support to the reform of the liturgy and was generally not an obstacle to others involved in the reform projects. His place in the Congregation was taken on February 22, 1962, by Cardinal A. M. Larraona, a Spanish Claretian who had long been associated with the Congregation for Religious. Cardinal Larraona was almost completely innocent of any comprehension of the true nature of liturgical reform. In fact, in the beginning he was strongly opposed to the reform and consequently often proved to be an annoying obstacle in the work of the conciliar liturgical commission.

On September 21, 1963, Pope Paul VI gave an allocution to the Roman curia in which he announced an eventual reform of that body.[2] The Pope praised the heritage of Pope John XXIII and called for full support of his ideals on the part of the curia. He stressed the close adherence and absolute obedience of the curia to the Roman pontiff and maintained that the curia itself should be an example to the Church and the world in the matter of renewal and reform. In closing, he said:

> The Roman Curia is not an anonymous body, insensitive to the great spiritual problems, dictating laws automatically; it is a living organ faithful and docile to the Head of the Church, aware of the grave responsibility of its functions and full of reverence and solicitude toward the prelates whom "the Holy Spirit has placed as Bishops to rule the Church of God." Let it not, therefore, be a bureaucracy, as some wrongly judge it to be, pretentious and apathetic, exclusively legalistic and ritualistic, a palestra of hidden ambitions and unreasoning antagonisms, as others accuse it of being; but let it be a true community of faith and charity; of prayer and action, a community of brothers and sons of the Pope, who, with due regard for the competency of others and with a sense of collaboration, do everything to help the Pope in the service which he gives to the brethren and sons of the universal Church and of the entire world.

Following the promulgation of the Constitution on the Sacred

[2] *AAS* 55 (1963) 793–800.

Liturgy and just before the end of the *vacatio legis*, the Holy Father, on January 25, 1964, issued the apostolic letter *Sacram liturgiam*, on the implementation of the constitution. The introduction to the document stated that a special commission was to be established to revise the liturgical rites and prepare new liturgical books. This was the origin of the Consilium. The Consilium was made up of bishops from various parts of the world together with a few cardinals from the curia; its consultors were drawn largely from European countries. However, continuity in members and consultors was preserved with both the preparatory and conciliar commissions on the liturgy. Pope Paul named Cardinal Giacomo Lercaro, archbishop of Bologna, the first president. The first and only secretary was Annibale Bugnini, who had served as secretary of the preparatory commission that had drawn up the schema of the liturgical constitution.

The Consilium's relationship to the Congregation of Rites was somewhat ambiguous and was defined as a compromise. Although the Consilium had some direct authority, such as the confirmation of decisions of the conferences of bishops concerning the vernacular, it was primarily a research and study body, with a group of experts assigned by subject matter to subcommittees. Its texts were submitted to the Congregation of Rites and were issued by that body over the signatures of both the prefect of the Congregation and the president of the Consilium. The principal work of the Consilium was the reform of the Roman liturgical books, as required by the Constitution on the Sacred Liturgy.[3] The reform of those books was thought to be the primary means of achieving the goals of the constitution in the area of actual ritual reform as distinguished from doctrinal and educational renewal. The Consilium ceased to be an autonomous body within the Roman curia with the creation of the Congregation for Divine Worship on May 8, 1969.

During the four years in which Cardinal Lercaro presided over the work of the Consilium, he moderated the work of the group with a keen pastoral sense. As noted in a tribute published in *Notitiae* on the occasion of his retirement, his leadership was distinguished, suave, dynamic, and courageous.[4] He submitted his resignation to

---

[3] *Sacrosanctum Concilium*, no. 25: *AAS* 56 (1964) 107.
[4] Vol. 4 (1968) 3.

the Holy Father on the occasion of his seventy-fifth birthday. It was accepted on January 9, 1968.

Another body that has had considerable influence on liturgical reform in English-speaking countries and whose origins go back to the days of the Council is the International Committee on English in the Liturgy. It seems the beginnings of ICEL, as it is now generally known, go back to Rome and an informal meeting that Archbishop Paul Hallinan of Atlanta held in October 1962 with bishops and others from various English-speaking countries. Hallinan had been nominated by the U.S. conference of bishops for election to the conciliar commission on the liturgy. The initial concern was not so much with the use of English in the liturgy as with contacts for cooperation among English-speaking bishops in liturgical matters in general.

Shortly after that meeting, Archbishop Hallinan and Archbishop Francis Grimshaw of Birmingham, England, were both elected to the conciliar liturgical commission, and Father Frederick McManus was named a *peritus*. That same year, in a general congregation of the Council, the first chapter of the Constitution on the Sacred Liturgy was approved by almost unanimous vote. The general principles of reform were agreed upon, and the introduction of the vernacular was left to the discretion of the conferences of bishops.[5] The Apostolic See was to confirm the decisions of the conferences concerning the extent of the use of the vernacular but not to confirm or ratify the actual versions. However, the Constitution on the Sacred Liturgy suggested that the conferences should take counsel with bishops of neighboring regions using the same language.[6]

Toward the end of the first period of the Council, it became evident to Archbishop Hallinan and others that formal collaboration among English-speaking peoples was desirable. At a dinner meeting in December 1962, common liturgical texts were discussed enthusiastically by English-speaking bishops, including Archbishops Grimshaw and Hallinan, Archbishop (later Cardinal) Lawrence J. Shehan, Bishops Michael Hyle and Christopher Weldon, and the English bishops George Beck and Edward Ellis. In the spring of 1963, Archbishop Denis E. Hurley of Durban, South Africa, sug-

---

[5] *Sacrosanctum Concilium*, no. 36: AAS 56 (1964) 109–10.

[6] *Sacrosanctum Concilium*, no. 36: AAS 56 (1964) 110.

gested a structure for an English-language liturgical committee and proposed that Archbishops Hallinan and Grimshaw convoke the body when the Fathers of the Council reassembled later in the year.

The interested conferences of bishops designated official representatives, and the initial meeting of the episcopal committee was held on October 17, 1963, at the Venerable English College in Rome. Ten countries were represented: United States, South Africa, Australia, Ireland, Canada, Scotland, India, New Zealand, England and Wales, and Pakistan. Archbishop Grimshaw was elected chairman; Archbishops Hallinan and Clyde Guilford Young of Hobart, Australia, were elected first and second vice-chairmen. During the initial stages of ICEL's development, two English-speaking *periti* took part in the meetings of the episcopal committee. They were Father McManus and Father Godfrey Diekmann, O.S.B., who had joined the conciliar liturgical commission as its second English-speaking *peritus*.

Since the work of the international committee had not proceeded as quickly as expected, the episcopal committee agreed in 1963 that there would necessarily be a period during which provisional texts would have to be used. With the promulgation of the Constitution on the Sacred Liturgy on December 4, 1963, and its *vacatio legis* set for February 16, 1964, each episcopal conference was obliged to approve vernacular texts if it decided to allow the introduction of the vernacular.

The meetings of the episcopal committee were resumed on October 10, 1964. A constitution was adopted for the body, and an advisory committee on English in the liturgy was established. This latter group, made up of priests and lay people, was entrusted with the actual work of planning and coordinating the project of liturgical translation into English. The actual mandate given to the advisory committee by the hierarchies of the member countries was "to work out a plan for the translation of liturgical texts and the provision of original texts where required."[7]

The membership of the advisory committee was conceived to represent the diversity of specializations requisite for planning and executing a program of translating liturgical texts into English. The committee met for the first time in London in January 1965. A deci-

[7] *Notitiae* 1 (1965) 341; 11 (1975) 245.

sion had already been made by the episcopal committee to establish a permanent secretariat in Washington. That office was opened in September 1965.

Although the episcopal committee met occasionally during the fourth period of the Second Vatican Council, the advisory committee, together with the newly appointed executive secretary, set about developing plans for the prosecution of the ICEL program. The first annual report of ICEL was issued to the participating episcopal conferences in November 1966. The work of the body from that time to the present may be traced in the successive reports that have regularly been submitted to the participating conferences of bishops.[8]

When Cardinal Lercaro's resignation was accepted on January 9, 1968, the Holy Father also accepted the resignation of Cardinal Larraona as prefect of the Congregation of Rites. The guidance of both departments was given over to Cardinal Benno Gut. He was a Swiss Benedictine from the Abbey of Einsiedeln and had served as abbot primate of the Benedictine Confederation from September 24, 1959, until he was made an archbishop and a cardinal by Pope Paul VI in June 1967. A trained biblical scholar, Cardinal Gut loved the liturgy and understood it rather well. He was a pleasant but reserved man who rarely interfered in the work of others. His monastic background helped him understand the doctrinal aspects of the liturgy, but it did not develop in him a keen pastoral sense or a deep appreciation of the need to take into account the diverse cultural backgrounds in the Church.

When Pope Paul VI mandated a general structural reform of the Roman curia in 1967, the Congregation of Rites was relatively unaffected. It retained its competence in the matter of ordering divine worship, in its pastoral and ritual aspects, for the Roman and other Latin rites. As a temporary arrangement, the revision of liturgical books and the implementation of liturgical renewal, along with relations with episcopal conferences, were still handled by the Consilium.

By an apostolic constitution, *Sacra Rituum Congregatio*, issued

---

[8] A more detailed history of the first years of ICEL has been prepared by Father Frederick McManus and has been issued by ICEL. It is available from the Secretariat in Washington, D.C.

on May 8, 1969,[9] Pope Paul VI divided the original Congregation of Rites into two Congregations: the Congregation for Divine Worship, corresponding generally to the existing section of the Congregation pertaining to worship, and the Congregation for the Causes of Saints, which took over the Congregation of Rites' competence in beatification and canonization processes.

The new Congregation for Divine Worship succeeded to the liturgical competence of the Congregation of Rites, but in effect it succeeded the Consilium, whose work was much more extensive than that done within the section for worship in the Congregation of Rites. The membership of the Congregation for Divine Worship and in large part its personnel were derived from the Consilium: the cardinal members of the Consilium became members of the Congregation; the bishop members of the Consilium elected from their number the seven bishops who became members of the new Congregation. The president of the Consilium, Cardinal Gut, was named first prefect of the Congregation for Divine Worship, and Father (later Archbishop) Annibale Bugnini, the secretary of the Consilium, became secretary of the new Congregation.

The competence of the Congregation was defined as "everything which directly and proximately pertains to divine worship in the Roman and other Latin rites," while the authority of the other dicasteries of the Roman curia remained intact "in matters which touch upon the doctrine of faith or which require the juridical order."[10] This competence was specified in a threefold enumeration of matters handled, entrusted to three different offices. The first category included liturgical worship, in both its ritual and pastoral aspects; the creation and correction of liturgical texts; the review and approval of special calendars of dioceses and religious institutes, together with their proper Mass and office texts; the concession of dispensations in such matters; the correct and lawful interpretation of the norms and rubrics contained in the liturgical books; the cult of relics; the confirmation of patron saints; and the concession of the title of minor basilica.

The second category included relations with the episcopal conferences in regard to their liturgical decisions that required the con-

[9] *AAS* 61 (1969) 297–305.
[10] *AAS* 61 (1969) 296.

firmation of the Apostolic See, as well as the liturgical adaptations mentioned in number 40 of the Constitution on the Sacred Liturgy, adaptations that the episcopal conferences might propose in the light of cultural and other needs. This category also included the extra-liturgical forms of worship, i.e., popular or devotional exercises of piety, but doctrinal questions concerning such practices were reserved to the competence of the Congregation for the Doctrine of the Faith.

The third category concerned the Congregation's relations with liturgical commissions, international commissions for the preparation of vernacular liturgical translations, and institutes that promote the liturgical apostolate, music, and sacred art. Those responsible for this third category were to gather written material and information on the Church's liturgical life, to study the use of communications media in relation to worship, and to encourage associations and congresses on liturgical matters.

The work that was set out for the new Congregation in the apostolic constitution certainly had a positive thrust. Its responsibility was to promote growth in the Church's liturgical life, not simply to supervise its celebrations. In accord with the directive of the Constitution on the Sacred Liturgy,[11] it was to share responsibility for the moderation of the liturgy of the Latin Church with the local bishops and the episcopal conferences. It is indeed unfortunate that the three offices described in the apostolic constitution of May 8, 1969, were in fact never actually developed.

Cardinal Benno Gut died on December 8, 1970. On February 20, 1971, Pope Paul VI named Cardinal Arturo Tabera Aroaz to head the Congregation for Divine Worship. A member of the Claretian Fathers and a trained canon lawyer, he had taught canon law in Spain and worked on the editorial staff of *Commentarium pro Religiosis.* He was general prefect of studies for the Claretians when he was named a bishop on February 16, 1946. In 1968 he was made archbishop of Pamplona and was created a cardinal by Pope Paul VI on April 28, 1969. He was involved in the preparation of the Oriental Code of Canon Law. He took over as prefect of the Congregation for Divine Worship on March 9, 1971. As prefect he tried above all to promote good relations with the various episcopal conferences

---

[11] *Sacrosanctum Concilium*, no. 22: AAS 56 (1964) 106.

and liturgical commissions throughout the world; he personally visited Central and South America, Poland, England, Spain, and Germany. He was made prefect of the Sacred Congregation for Religious and Secular Institutes in September 1973, a post for which he was well suited both by training and experience. He died on June 13, 1975.

When Cardinal Tabera was transferred to the Congregation for Religious and Secular Institutes, Pope Paul VI appointed Cardinal James Knox prefect of the Congregation for Divine Worship and also head of the Congregation for the Discipline of the Sacraments, replacing Cardinal Antonio Samoré. Cardinal Knox was born in Australia; he served in the Vatican secretariat of state and then in the apostolic delegation in Japan. He was made a bishop on December 8, 1953, and was appointed apostolic delegate in East Africa, then internuncio in India, Burma, and Ceylon. He was made archbishop of Melbourne on April 13, 1967. It was while he was ordinary there that the Eucharistic Congress was held in Australia. Since he had not been deeply involved in liturgical renewal, his appointment to the two Roman Congregations was met by a less than enthusiastic response on the part of most liturgists. Unfortunately, it seems that liturgical expertise has never been a primary qualification of any of the cardinals who have headed the dicastery responsible for the Church's worship.

On July 17, 1975, Pope Paul VI issued an apostolic constitution, *Constans Nobis*, suppressing the Sacred Congregations for the Discipline of the Sacraments and for Divine Worship and establishing a new Sacred Congregation for the Sacraments and Divine Worship.[12] The document noted that the new dicastery would be divided into two sections: one for the discipline of the sacraments and one for divine worship. The Congregation would have a prefect and a secretary and a subsecretary for each section.

To the section for the discipline of the sacraments were entrusted all the matters previously handled by the Sacred Congregation for the Discipline of the Sacraments, as determined by the apostolic constitution *Regimini Ecclesiae universae*, nos. 54–57, which Pope Paul VI had issued in 1967.[13] The Congregation was established by

[12] *AAS* 67 (1975) 417–20.
[13] *AAS* 59 (1967) 903–4.

Pius X, and its competency was determined by his constitution *Sapienti consilio*, issued on June 29, 1908.[14] The scope of its work remained much the same from that time to the reorganization of the curia by Pope Paul VI.

What is customarily decreed and granted in the discipline of the sacraments and in the celebration of the Eucharistic sacrifice pertained to that Congregation. It also had the power to grant dispensations that went beyond the competence of the local bishops, even from the Eucharistic fast either of the faithful, or, after consultation, if necessary, with the Congregation for the Doctrine of the Faith, of priests celebrating Mass. It also passed judgment on the fact of non-consummation of marriage, oversaw the obligations attached to major orders, and examined questions on the validity of sacred ordination.

To the second section of the Congregation for Sacraments and Divine Worship belong all those matters previously handled by the Sacred Congregation for Divine Worship, which was established by the apostolic constitution *Sacra rituum*, nos. 1–4.[15]

Archbishop Antonio Innocenti, secretary of the former Congregation for the Discipline of the Sacraments, was named secretary of the new Congregation; Monsignor Virgilio Noe was named subsecretary of the section for divine worship, and Monsignor Antonius Magnoni was named subsecretary for the discipline of the sacraments.

As Pope Paul VI noted in the apostolic constitution *Constans Nobis*, the two former Congregations were concerned with what is actually one single theological reality in which the juridical, pastoral, and disciplinary aspects are inseparably linked. The name given to the new Congregation is unfortunate, however, for the sacraments are in fact divine worship.

In order to bring the work of the section for divine worship into greater prominence within the Congregation, Pope Paul VI, on October 21, 1977, appointed Monsignor Noe associate secretary of the Congregation for the Sacraments and Divine Worship, in the section for divine worship. At the same time, Father Luis Alessio, rector of the major seminary of Cordoba, Argentina, was named

---

[14] *AAS* 1 (1908) 7–15.
[15] *AAS* 61 (1969) 299–301.

undersecretary of the Congregation for Sacraments and Divine Worship, in the section for divine worship.

Of special significance is the fact that with the establishment of the new Congregation, Archbishop Annibale Bugnini, secretary of the former Congregation for Divine Worship, was retired from his central role in the implementation of liturgical reform. He had been deeply involved in liturgical renewal for years and was especially active from 1952, when Pope Pius XII initiated the reform of the Holy Week liturgy. As secretary of the preparatory liturgical commission, he was one of the principal architects of the Constitution on the Sacred Liturgy. In the years after the Council, he served as secretary of the Consilium. His frequent role as mediator between those in the Church who wanted more reform and those who wanted less was a delicate and difficult one. Although he was often criticized by both sides, he manifested a growing sensitivity to the pastoral perspective of liturgical celebration and an openness to the need for liturgical adaptation and indigenization.

Chapter 13

CANONICAL SIGNIFICANCE OF CONCILIAR, PAPAL, AND CURIAL PRONOUNCEMENTS

A survey of the documents that have been issued to initiate and implement liturgical renewal will show that the texts fit in various categories whose legal import is not readily grasped by those who are not specialists in canon law. Moreover, a number of the documents have not been widely publicized; hence, often through ignorance, they have not been effectively implemented. It should be helpful, then, to clarify the significance of the various categories and the legal importance that should be attached to a particular document.

Canon 9 of the Code of Canon Law requires that the laws enacted by the Apostolic See shall be promulgated by the publication of them in the official journal of the Holy See, *Acta Apostolicae Sedis*, except when under special circumstances a different mode of promulgation is prescribed. The canon is not, of course, applicable to the conciliar documents, which were all promulgated in public sessions of the Second Vatican Council. Canon 9 says that laws published in the *Acta* become effective three months after the date affixed to the number of that journal in which publication occurred, unless the nature of the law requires that it become effective at once, or unless the text of the law itself expressly specifies a shorter or longer period of suspension or "vacation," a technical expression designating the time that is permitted to elapse between the date of publication and the date on which the law takes effect. This has been the general practice since 1870 and was confirmed by Pope Pius X in an apostolic constitution, *Promulgandi*, issued on September 29, 1908.

This arrangement seemed both wise and convenient, and avoided much confusion and doubt in matters of ecclesiastical law. In the years since the Second Vatican Council, however, the ordinary method of promulgating laws has often not been followed. Most of the documents issued since that time have determined the day on which they take effect. The majority of them have been printed in the *Acta Apostolicae Sedis*, but a number of significant documents have not appeared there. Perhaps it should be noted that the liturgical books as such are not published in the *Acta*, as this would be impractical.

To facilitate familiarity with documents emanating from the Holy See, various editors have collected and translated legal texts, but they have often neglected to distinguish texts according to their proper categories, so that documents that are relatively unimportant are given the same weight as those that are in fact weighty. In an effort to clear up misunderstanding, a brief comment will be made on the various sources of ecclesiastical legislation and the categories of documents issued by each source.

Documents of the Second Vatican Council

Since an ecumenical council represents the whole Church and has full power over it, documents originating in that context are of supreme importance in the Church. Four types of documents were issued by the Second Vatican Council: constitutions, decrees, declarations, and messages. Messages, however, are not included in the official compilation of documents by the secretary general of the Council. Distinctions among the various categories are not always easily and clearly drawn, but in general, *constitutions* are addressed to the universal Church and are concerned with doctrinal, disciplinary, or pastoral topics of the greatest importance. Four constitutions were issued by the Second Vatican Council: on the liturgy, the Church, divine revelation, and the Church in the modern world.

Decrees are concerned with a specific aspect of the Church's life and mission. They are characterized primarily as disciplinary, although they contain much doctrine and policy. The Second Vatican Council issued nine decrees: on communication, ecumenism, Eastern Catholic Churches, the bishops' pastoral office in the Church, priestly formation, religious life, the apostolate of the laity, the ministry and life of priests, and the Church's missionary activity.

Declarations are generally policy statements that reflect the Church's stand on particular issues at a particular time. The Second Vatican Council issued three declarations: on Christian education, the relationship of the Church to non-Christian religions, and religious freedom.

Messages are exhortations addressed to various groups of people during solemn ceremonies marking the beginning and end of the ecumenical council. They are characterized as acts agreed to in principle by the Council Fathers but not enacted like constitutions, decrees, and declarations. At the Second Vatican Council such messages were addressed to the Council Fathers, rulers, priests, intellectuals and scientists, artists, women, the poor, the sick and the suffering, workers, and youth.

Obviously, constitutions are much more important than decrees, and decrees are more important than declarations. Messages are relatively unimportant, since they are ephemeral exhortations. Of all the documents that have been issued concerning liturgical renewal, the Constitution on the Sacred Liturgy is by far, then, the most important. As a constitution, the Council document on the sacred liturgy is not only doctrinal but also disciplinary in content. This is clear from the fact that the motu proprio *Sacram liturgiam*, of January 25, 1964, as well as the three instructions of September 26, 1964; May 4, 1967; and September 5, 1970, provided for the implementation of that document. Pope Paul VI affirmed the legislative import of this and other conciliar texts in an address given during a general audience on August 17, 1966:

> The Council laid down laws, and they must be respected. But on other occasions it formulated principles, criteria, and desires which must be given concrete expression in new laws and instructions, in new structures and offices, in spiritual, cultural and moral developments and in organizations. This will require much work for many people for quite a number of years.[1]

[1] *AAS* 58 (1966) 800.

PAPAL PRONOUNCEMENTS

The scope of papal pronouncements is very broad, ranging from bulls to messages of greeting and condolence sent to various people throughout the world. For example, during the ceremonies marking the end of the Year of Faith (1967–68), Pope Paul VI issued a new statement of Catholic faith.[2] The text is a solemn proclamation reaffirming basic dogmas of the Church, and so is purely doctrinal. It is not legislative, since no prescriptions were laid down concerning the liturgical or extra-liturgical use of the formula.

A very solemn form of papal proclamation is a *decretal letter*, used, for example, to reaffirm the beatification of servants of God and the canonization of the blessed. The issuance of such letters is a very special act of the papal magisterium, but is not considered to be legislative in nature.

Encyclicals are divided into two categories: encyclical epistles and encyclical letters. Those of the first category are more solemn in form, although the content may not always be more important than that of other papal letters. Encyclicals are generally pastoral letters written by the pope for the universal Church. Rather than affirming dogmatic definitions, they usually attempt to clarify doctrinal issues. They express the pope's ordinary teaching authority; their content, then, is capable of development and change. Encyclicals are not legislative in the sense that they modify existing laws of the Church. An example of an encyclical epistle issued in recent years would be *Mense maio*, the letter addressed by Pope Paul VI on April 29, 1965, to all the ordinaries of the world on the subject of prayers to be offered in honor of the Virgin Mary during the month of May. The most important encyclical letter concerning the liturgy that has been issued since the opening of the Second Vatican Council is *Mysterium fidei*, addressed on September 3, 1965, to all the ordinaries of the world, and through them to all the clergy and faithful, on the doctrine and worship of the Holy Eucharist.

An *apostolic epistle* is a less solemn papal letter, sometimes addressed to one person or a group in the Church but usually not to the universal Church. Its subject matter is regularly not of great importance. An example is *Investigabiles divitias Christi*, the apostolic

[2] *AAS* 60 (1968) 436–45.

epistle that Pope Paul VI sent on February 6, 1965, to the bishops of the Catholic world on the anniversary of the institution of the liturgical feast in honor of the Sacred Heart of Jesus.

Like apostolic epistles, *apostolic exhortations* are usually addressed to a limited group in the Church, such as clergy, religious, or the bishops of the world. They are mainly exhortative in nature and are not legislative. An example is *Marialis cultus*, the document issued on February 2, 1974, by Pope Paul VI on the right ordering and development of devotion to the Blessed Virgin Mary. It is somewhat curious that this document was issued in the form of a simple apostolic exhortation, since it is an excellent doctrinal statement clearly elaborating on the eighth chapter of the Constitution on the Church and explaining the implications of liturgical reform affecting the cult of the Virgin Mary.

Apostolic constitutions are generally considered to be the most solemn form of document issued by the pope in his own name. They may deal with both doctrinal and disciplinary matters, and are generally reserved for papal acts related to very important matters regarding either the universal or a particular Church. Much of the recent liturgical reform was promulgated in the form of apostolic constitutions, although details were often worked out in complementary documents. Examples include *Indulgentiarum doctrina*, the apostolic constitution of January 1, 1969, on the revision of indulgences; *Pontificalis Romani*, the apostolic constitution of June 8, 1969, revising the rites for confirmation; *Missale Romanum*, the apostolic constitution of April 3, 1969, on the new Roman Missal; and *Sacram Unctionem infirmorum*, the apostolic constitution of November 11, 1972, on the revision of the matter and form of the sacrament of anointing of the sick. The recently issued apostolic constitutions on liturgical matters have regularly been both doctrinal and disciplinary. In other words, the disciplinary norms have been put in a doctrinal context, so that the revised laws are shown to be based on and derived from theological principles. There is no doubt that apostolic constitutions are legislative texts. It might well be noted here that the major liturgical books, such as the Roman Missal and the Liturgy of the Hours, were issued with accompanying constitutions as well as decrees, but the individual sections or titles of the Roman Ritual and Roman Pontifical were accompanied by apostolic constitutions only if a change in the form of a sacrament was at issue.

When a papal document is issued motu proprio, it means that it comes from the pope on his own initiative. These documents are called *apostolic letters motu proprio*. Such documents are concerned with serious matters, are generally legislative in nature, and are addressed to the universal Church. Since the Second Vatican Council, the popes have issued about fifty documents motu proprio. In one way or another they have modified existing legislation; hence, they have been a source of new laws. Examples of documents issued motu proprio that have been concerned with the liturgy are *Sacram liturgiam* (January 25, 1964), on the implementation of the Constitution on the Sacred Liturgy; *Ministeria quaedam* (August 15, 1972), establishing certain norms regarding the order of the diaconate; and *Ad pascendum* (also August 15, 1972), reforming the discipline of first tonsure, minor orders, and subdiaconate in the Latin Church. It should be noted that the relative importance of the content of a document is not always the key to the form chosen for its promulgation. For example, the restoration of the diaconate was done in an apostolic letter motu proprio, but the doctrine of indulgences was revised in an apostolic constitution.

There are other types of papal pronouncements, such as declarations, allocutions, homilies, and radio and television messages, but it is correct to say that the legislative acts of the pope are found primarily in apostolic constitutions and in apostolic letters issued motu proprio. The Constitution on the Church issued by the Second Vatican Council acknowledged that the pope may use a wide variety of documents to communicate his teachings; it states, however, that "his mind and will . . . may be known chiefly either from the character of the documents, from his frequent repetition of the same doctrine, or from his manner of speaking."[3]

Documents Issued by the Roman Curia

Among the most important documents issued by the Roman Congregations, Secretariats, and Offices are decrees, instructions, declarations, circular letters, directories, official responses, and

---

[3] *Lumen gentium*, no. 25: AAS 57 (1965) 30.

norms. *Decrees* are new laws promulgated by the Roman Congregations with the special approval of the Holy Father; they carry the same weight as general laws of the Code of Canon Law. Many of the documents relating to liturgical renewal belong to this category. Examples include *Ecclesiae semper* (March 7, 1965), the decree on concelebration and communion under both kinds; and *Dum canonicarum* (December 8, 1970), the decree on the use and celebration of the sacrament of penance by religious. The various sections of the reformed liturgical books were generally promulgated by decrees.

An *instruction* is a doctrinal explanation or a set of directives, recommendations, or admonitions issued by the Roman curia. It usually elaborates on prescriptions so that they may be more effectively implemented. Strictly speaking, an instruction does not have the force of universal law or definition. If by chance an instruction cannot be reconciled with a given law, the law itself is to be preferred over the instruction.

Numerous instructions have been issued since the Second Vatican Council. Of special significance in the area of liturgy have been the three instructions implementing the Constitution on the Sacred Liturgy: *Eucharisticum mysterium* (May 25, 1967), the instruction on Eucharistic worship; the instruction sent on January 25, 1969, to the presidents of the episcopal conferences on the translation of liturgical texts; *Actio pastoralis Ecclesiae* (May 15, 1969), the instruction on group Masses; and *Memoriale Domini* (May 29, 1969), the instruction on the manner of administering holy communion.

Because of the rather ambiguous character of instructions, their interpretation has caused considerable difficulty since the Second Vatican Council. Of their nature they are not strictly legislative; their application therefore allows for more flexibility than decrees. They certainly do not carry the same weight as conciliar documents or decrees issued by the Roman curia.

There have been several instructions issued since the Council, however, that have authorized changes in the existing legislation. The instruction of September 26, 1964, and that of May 4, 1967, both of which were meant to implement the Constitution on the Sacred Liturgy, did in fact alter existing liturgical discipline. Likewise, changes in existing law were made by *Renovationis causam* (January 6, 1969), the instruction on the renewal of religious life, and *Venite seorsum* (August 15, 1969), the instruction on the contemplative life and on the enclosure of nuns.

These latter documents both have two principal parts. The first section is primarily doctrinal, providing guidelines and principles; the second section is devoted to special norms. It would seem that the term "instruction" is not used in its accepted sense in these cases. Because of the prescriptions found in these documents, the content would have been better placed in a decree. In terms of their structure, these two documents are similar to the "directives" jointly issued by the Sacred Congregation for Religious and Secular Institutes and the Sacred Congregation for Bishops concerning the mutual relations between bishops and religious in the Church (May 14, 1978). In some cases it is only by a careful study of both text and context that one can determine whether an instruction contains material that according to strict definition should have been issued in the form of a decree or apostolic constitution.

Declarations are pronouncements that give an interpretation to existing laws or facts, or provide a reply to a contested power of law. There are four types of declarations: a simple declaration, an authentic interpretation, a non-authentic interpretation, and an extensive declaration. A *simple declaration* is not a new law; it is to be interpreted in the light of existing legislation. One such declaration that caused great confusion was the declaration on first confession and first communion issued jointly by the Congregation for the Clergy and the Congregation for the Discipline of the Sacraments on May 24, 1972. The text is a simple declaration, not a new law; it should be understood as such. If another intention existed in the minds of those who issued the document, a different form of pronouncement should have been used.

An *authentic declaration* or *interpretation* refers to interpretations given with official authority as opposed to doctrinal interpretations given privately by anyone who knows the law. Authentic interpretation of laws is the subject of canon 17 of the Code of Canon Law. Laws are authentically interpreted by the legislator or his successor and by those to whom the legislator or his successor has committed the power of interpretation. A superior may authentically interpret the laws of a subordinate legislator. Thus the pope and an ecumenical council have authority to issue an authentic interpretation of any ecclesiastical law. Moreover, the Sacred Congregations, within the limits of their competency, may issue, in the form of law or of general rescript, authentic interpretations of even universal laws. The Pontifical Commission for the Authentic Interpretation of the Canons of the Code established by Benedict XV on September 15, 1917, may give authentic interpretations of particular canons, and the Pontifical Commission for the Interpretation of the Decrees of the Second Vatican Council established by Paul VI on January 3, 1966, may give authentic interpretations of the various decrees of the Second Vatican Council and postconciliar legislation as well. These commissions are not bound to give reasons for their interpretations. An example of an authentic interpretation given by the Commission for the Interpretation of the Decrees of the Second Vatican Council would be the responses given on March 26, 1968, and on April 4, 1969, to the effect that deacons who will not remain in that order but wish to advance to priesthood have the functions listed under number 29 of the Constitution on the Church and under number 22 of the apostolic letter *Sacrum diaconatus ordinem*, of June 18, 1967. The tribunals of the Roman curia may also give authentic interpretations of universal laws in the form of judicial sentences, but in such cases reasons for the interpretation must be given.

Authentic interpretation, given in the form of a law, has the force of law. An interpretation is so given when it is expressed as a general norm, inclusive of all cases and persons involved in the subject matter of the law. When the interpretation appears in the *Acta Apostolicae Sedis* in the form of a general rescript showing no indication that the rescript was addressed to a particular place or person, the interpretation should be regarded as directed to the entire Church and binding on all who have a concern in the issue.

A *non-authentic interpretation*, sometimes called a simple doctrinal interpretation, is that which is given by a theologian or canonist acting as a private person. Certainly every theologian and canonist may interpret the law privately, with the authority warranted by their own learning. Their interpretations, however, bear only that weight that attaches to the reasons on which they base their positions. The various liturgical studies that appear in periodicals such as *Notitiae, The Jurist, Worship, Ephemerides Liturgicae,*

La Maison-Dieu, and *Rivista Liturgica* would fall under the category of non-authentic interpretations.

The final type of declaration, not regularly issued in recent years, is the *extensive declaration*. Like a restrictive interpretation or one that is explanatory of a doubtful law, it must be promulgated according to the norms of law and is not retroactive. It becomes effective only at the expiration of a period of "vacation," unless otherwise indicated.

The use of *circular letters* as forms to communicate information from the Roman curia is of relatively recent origin. They have never been specified as an authoritative source of ecclesiastical law, and frequently are not published in the *Acta Apostolicae Sedis*. Hence it seems correct to say that they are not legislative documents but simply expressions of the views of the bodies that have issued them. They should be interpreted as exhortative in scope. Frequently circular letters are used to communicate information from one Roman Congregation to the personnel of another Congregation or from a Roman Congregation to national hierarchies or conferences of religious superiors.

Circular letters have often been used to promote liturgical renewal since the promulgation of the Constitution on the Sacred Liturgy. For example, on June 30, 1965, Cardinal Lercaro, as president of the Consilium, sent a letter to the presidents of episcopal conferences concerning the promotion of liturgical renewal. He sent similar letters on January 25, 1966, and June 21, 1967. The Sacred Congregation of the Clergy sent a circular letter on March 19, 1966, to local ordinaries on the celebration of liturgy for tourists. On June 2, 1968, Cardinal Gut, as president of the Consilium, sent a circular letter to the presidents of episcopal conferences outlining ways to provide catechesis concerning the new Eucharistic anaphoras that had just been published. Another letter on Eucharistic prayers was sent on April 27, 1973, by the Congregation for Divine Worship; it was also addressed to the presidents of episcopal conferences.

Another relatively new form for circulating information and policies by the Roman dicasteries is the *directory*, which provides guidelines for the application of generally accepted principles. In that sense directories are quite similar to instructions. Directories issued since the Second Vatican Council include the one on tourism issued on April 30, 1969, by the Congregation for the Clergy; the general catechetical directory issued by the same Congregation on April 11, 1971; the directory on Masses with children issued by the Congregation for Divine Worship on November 1, 1973; and the directory for ecumenical affairs issued by the Secretariat for Christian Unity on May 14, 1967 (Part I) and April 16, 1970 (Part II). It should be noted here that the directory on Masses with children is in effect a supplement to the General Instruction of the Roman Missal; it was approved by the Holy Father, who ordered it to become a matter of public law. The ecumenical directory is really an instruction that has the force of law. Its status was clarified in a declaration issued by the Secretariat for Christian Unity on January 7, 1970.[4]

The intent of a directory is to provide norms for pastoral practice. The text usually combines theory and disciplinary norms; the theological foundations of the norms are quite clearly elaborated. Directories usually provide broad guidelines for various kinds of ministry in the Church. It is difficult to specify the weight that should be attached to them. Some are clearly legislative documents and contain statements to that effect; others are not legislative in character. The advantage of issuing statements in the form of directories is that the legislation can be adequately situated in its proper theological context.

Somewhat similar to a directory is the *ratio fundamentalis* or basic program on priestly formation published on January 6, 1970, by the Congregation for Catholic Education. It was addressed to national conferences of bishops and specifically referred to the obligatory character of its prescriptions. The document mentioned three types of norms: those obligatory throughout the whole Latin Church, those whose application will vary from place to place, and those which are given simply as examples. There is no doubt that this *ratio fundamentalis* is legislative.

The Roman dicasteries also issue *notifications* and *norms*. Usually a notification is used to clarify existing law; it is closely related to a declaration. A notification was issued on June 14, 1971, by the Congregation for Divine Worship concerning the use of the Roman Missal, the liturgy of the hours, and the calendar. On August 6,

---

[4] *AAS* 62 (1970) 184–88.

1972, the same Congregation issued a notification concerning the use of the liturgy of the hours by certain religious communities. The Secretariat of State issued a notification on November 29, 1971, on the subject of Mass stipends. Norms are regulations that are to be applied in specific instances. For example, the pastoral norms for general absolution were issued on June 16, 1972, by the Congregation for the Doctrine of the Faith. On March 25, 1973, the Congregation for Divine Worship issued norms concerning the crowning of images of the Blessed Virgin Mary. Such norms are clearly legislative in intent. Sometimes a set of norms is accompanied by a circular letter that is used to clarify or explain the norms.

In addition to the various kinds of documents that have been discussed, the Roman curia also issues official *responses* to questions, such as the responses issued by the Pontifical Commission for the Interpretation of the Decrees of the Second Vatican Council. If a response is given in the form of a rescript in a particular matter, it does not have the force of public law, but binds only the person or persons to whom it is given and in the specific matters affected by it. Responses to various liturgical questions have regularly been printed in *Notitiae*. Since the Consilium was not established as a legislative body, its responses to liturgical questions did not constitute part of the liturgical law of the Church. In fact, the Consilium went out of its way to say that its responses in *Notitiae* were not official. They were classified as *officiosa*, i.e., unofficial. Responses given by the Pontifical Commission for the Interpretation of the Decrees of the Second Vatican Council include the three responses concerning the capacity of deacons to solemnize marriages (March 26, 1968; April 4, 1969; and July 19, 1970) and the one concerning homilies given by lay persons at Mass (January 11, 1971). Some canonical commentators maintain that these responses are legislative in scope, but others do not agree.

Reference should also be made to *indults*, which are special favors granted to some physical or moral person by the Holy See or by the local ordinary, conferring faculties contrary to or beyond the prescriptions of the law. These concessions are given in particular instances; they do not change the common law or modify its substance. They simply authorize a person or a body to act contrary to the law or beyond its prescriptions in view of special circumstances.

Such an indult would be the faculty given to alcoholic priests to use grape juice rather than wine in the celebration of the Eucharist.

A number of general conclusions emerge from this brief survey of the types of legislative documents emanating from the Roman curia. First of all, there is a great need for the legislator to clarify the legal import of his documents. Because of the current ambiguity, some documents that are relatively unimportant in content are given as much weight as those that are in fact very important. It often takes a skilled canonist to determine the legal import of texts, but at times not even the canonist can be sure of their weight. Since the documents are frequently intended for those who are not in fact skilled canonists, their legal import should be quite evident.

Another conclusion is that documents should be carefully promulgated, and there should be consistency in the mode of promulgation. Finally, a clear distinction should be made between authentic ecclesiastical legislation and private opinion. Particular rescripts limited to particular cases or persons do not constitute ecclesiastical law.

Chapter 14

LITURGICAL ADAPTATION, INDIGENIZATION, AND PARTICULAR LAW

In many parts of the world, liturgical reform and renewal must be viewed in the context of popular efforts to regain a cultural identity. There are at the present time strong movements to rediscover and foster traditional values and customs that have shaped the life of various peoples for many generations. Furthermore, in those parts of the world where Western theology and the Roman liturgy have been imposed on people whose thought patterns and symbol systems are more Eastern than Western, the Church and her rituals have regularly maintained an immigrant status. "Folk" liturgies rather than "official" liturgies often provide the focus for religious and ecclesial identity, because they enable people to synthesize their own cultural elements with the heritage of Western theology and Roman liturgical patterns. The question that confronts the Roman Catholic Church throughout the world, then, is how to bring the Roman liturgy closer to the hearts of people coming from such diverse cultural backgrounds. This is of course a challenge that has faced the Church from its inception.

LITURGICAL ADAPTATION

The liturgical renewal envisaged by the Second Vatican Council may be described as a process whereby the liturgy is made pastorally meaningful for modern people in a way that is congruent with the

Church's liturgical tradition. If encumbrances and intrusions that the liturgy has suffered in the past have confused or obstructed its meaning and if a sound tradition is now to be maintained, it is imperative that we both know the historical facts and be in possession of a sound theology with which we can critique the facts.

Essential aspects of that tradition are the phenomena of liturgical adaptation and the reinterpretation of historical data.[1] For example, Jesus himself gave a new orientation to the Jewish rites to which he and his disciples were heirs; he situated them in the context of his own life and mission. A fresh interpretation was given to the paschal meal whereby it was no longer looked upon simply as a memorial of the Exodus but of Christ's own passing over to the Father for the salvation of his people. Likewise, the baptism preached and practiced by John was adapted by Christ as a symbol of participation in the life of the Trinity. While Christ's own disciples continued to frequent the temple and to pray in the Jewish tradition, they also infused new meanings into Jewish worship and read the scriptures in the light of Christ's life, death and resurrection.

But Christianity not only adapted Jewish religious practices to its own purposes; it also adapted itself to the culture of prospective converts beyond Judaism. This was certainly not an easy process. In fact, it took a special council of the apostles and elders to establish the legitimacy of such a procedure against strong protests of the early Christians, who had a marked disdain for pagan religions. Until the peace of Constantine, efforts at liturgical adaptation met not only with success but also with failure. As the Church moved into the age of persecutions, there was a conscious effort to remain within the Jewish liturgical tradition and to weave both Old and New Testament themes through the liturgical prayers. During this period, adaptation meant instilling Christian liturgy with a sense of salvation history. Efforts to retain Jewish practices and to imbue them with a new spirit, however, existed alongside vehement denunciations of both Jews and their customs.

[1] See Josef Jungmann, *The Early Liturgy to the Time of Gregory the Great* (Notre Dame, Ind.: University of Notre Dame Press, 1959); Bernard Botte, "Le problème de l'adaptation en liturgie," *Revue du Clergé Africain* 18 (July 1963) 308–19; Joachim Jeremias, *The Eucharistic Words of Jesus* (New York: Scribner, 1966) 41–88, 218–37; Cyril Pocknee, *Water and the Spirit* (London: Darton, Longman and Todd, 1967) 17–29.

Improvisation and spontaneity were also features of the Church's liturgy during these early centuries. Since there were no sacramentaries or missals as we know them today, prayers for the liturgical celebrations had to be improvised. Although the actual formulation and length of the prayers were left to the discretion of the leader, he was expected to follow approved models and to conform to the rule of faith. While praying extemporaneously, the leader was obliged to be faithful to orthodox doctrine.

Creativity and adaptation likewise characterized the Church's liturgy from the Edict of Milan to the eighth century. The Bible was the principal source of inspiration for new prayer forms, but contact with Greek and Roman culture had lasting influence on the liturgy.[2] For example, precision, sobriety, and brevity, marks of secular language during this period, came to characterize the language of the liturgy also. Kissing the altar was derived from pagan rituals of reverence; processions, prostrations, and the use of candles and incense were adapted from usages in effect in the imperial court. Liturgical vestments, which have undergone considerable modification throughout the centuries, were originally the clothes worn by the Romans in their secular life: the *tunica*, *toga* and *mappula*.

The Church's general attitude during this period was one of respect for all that was good and noble in life. In contrast to its earlier reluctance to assimilate any elements of pagan culture, the Church during this period engaged in compromise. In some instances it replaced pagan cultic elements with Christian observances, being careful not to abolish something without putting something else in its place. An example would be the suppression of the feast of the birth of the sun-god in Mithraic religion and the institution of the feast of Christmas in its place. In other instances the Church assimilated pagan rituals and infused into them a specifically Christian meaning. For example, the Church readily accepted the custom inspired by solar cults of facing the east during prayer but looked on the east as the direction from which Christ, the Sun of Justice, would come at the end of time.

Since paganism was gradually declining and was no longer a major threat, the Church felt free to assimilate select cultic elements

[2] Jungmann, *op. cit.*, 122–63; Hugo Rahner, *Greek Myths and Christian Mystery* (London: Burns and Oates Ltd., 1963); Botte, *art. cit.*, 311–16.

from paganism. One would have expected that the result of such assimilation would have been an extension in liturgical diversity, but that does not seem to have been the case. In fact, one of the basic characteristics of liturgical history is the trend from diversity to uniformity. Improvisation and spontaneity have regularly been abandoned in favor of fixed formulas. Communication among the various local churches resulted not only in closer doctrinal bonds but also in more uniform liturgical practices. It is interesting to note, however, the open-minded attitude of Gregory the Great toward liturgical pluriformity and his reluctance to impose the Roman forms on people from other parts of the world. Writing to Augustine of Canterbury, who resented the lack of uniformity among churches in celebrating the Eucharist, Gregory encouraged the adoption of practices from any church if they proved useful.[3] He was implicitly asserting that fidelity to the Church's tradition did not necessarily mean a slavish copying of the Roman rite.

Of special interest in the history of liturgical adaptation are the changes that took place in the Roman rite when it was transplanted to the land of the Franco-Germanic peoples in the eighth century.[4] Coming into contact with markedly different cultural forms, austere Roman rituals were embellished with drama and florid ceremonials. With the decline in active participation in the liturgy, lay people more and more found their religious sustenance not so much in the liturgy as in extra-liturgical devotions.

Although the period from the tenth to the thirteenth century is recognized as one of the more significant epochs in Church history, it was not significant from the standpoint of liturgical enrichment and adaptation, apart from practices surrounding devotion to the Eucharist.[5] Throughout the fourteenth, fifteenth, and the first half of the sixteenth centuries, liturgical life declined, although dramas inspired by the texts of the liturgy played an important role in the religious life of many people. These performances functioned as

[3] Epist. 64, lib. XI: *PL* 77, col. 1187.

[4] See Theodor Klauser, "Die liturgischen Austauschbeziehungen zwischen der römischen und der fränkisch-deutschen Kirche vom 8. bis zum 11. Jahrhundert," *Historisches Jahrbuch* 53 (1933) 169–89.

[5] See Anton Mayer, *Die Liturgie in der europäischen Geistesgeschichte* (Darmstadt: Wissenschaftliche Buchgesellschaft, 1971) 68–97.

vehicles for Christian catechesis, but they did not deepen the community's understanding of the liturgy or involvement in its celebration.[6]

The Council of Trent (1545–63) sought to correct various liturgical abuses, but rather than foster adaptation as a means of reform and renewal, it legislated rigid uniformity. With the establishment of the Sacred Congregation of Rites and Ceremonies in 1588 by Sixtus V, liturgical spontaneity was terminated and adaptation of the liturgy to local conditions was forbidden. Since the Church was in many ways divorced from popular experience, the religious life of the people was generally sustained by exercises of piety, a situation that gave rise to the religious culture of the baroque.

In a sense, the liturgy during the baroque manifested the triumphal attitude of the Church, which had survived the crisis of the Reformation. Although the liturgy was uniformly celebrated, its essential symbols and rituals were submerged in grand art forms. "The external elements were excessively magnified and the essential dwarfed and relegated to the periphery of the celebration."[7] Such festive occasions have been described as "church concerts with liturgical accompaniments."[8]

Of special significance in the history of liturgical adaptation is the unfortunate Chinese rites controversy, which began after the death of Matteo Ricci in 1610 and continued until the publication of the papal bull of 1742, which forbade the participation of Chinese Catholics in their traditional ancestral rites.[9] With acute cultural sensitivity and an amazing ability to distinguish between the essentials and the accidentals of Christian faith and worship, the Jesuit missionaries had selected Chinese terms that approximated Christian concepts and infused them with Christian meaning. They also

[6] Jungmann, "The State of Liturgical Life on the Eve of the Reformation," *Pastoral Liturgy* (New York: Herder and Herder, 1962) 64–80.

[7] Anscar J. Chupungco, *Towards a Filipino Liturgy* (Manila: Benedictine Abbey, 1976) 43. The author wishes to acknowledge his special dependence on this work in various sections of this chapter.

[8] Jungmann, *The Mass of the Roman Rite* (New York: Benziger Brothers, 1961) 112.

[9] See George Dunne, *Generation of Giants* (Notre Dame, Ind.: University of Notre Dame Press, 1962); Arnold H. Rowbotham, *Missionary and Mandarin: The Jesuits at the Court of China* (New York: Russell & Russell, 1966).

had permitted newly initiated Church members to perform, under specific restrictions, various rites in honor of Confucius and their own ancestors. Their efforts, however, were denounced as a continuation of pagan idolatry. This unhappy event indicates that a basic hostility to other world religions has not been confined to Christians of the primitive Church. In fact, the relationship between the Catholic Church and other world religions continues to be an issue in need of much sympathetic study.

Firsthand experience by Christians of worship patterns among other world religions and also serious dialogue between Roman Catholics and representatives from other Christian Churches as well as non-Christian religions continue to surface the question of liturgical adaptation and the more complicated question of liturgical indigenization. The Constitution on the Sacred Liturgy has lifted many of the restrictions imposed by the Council of Trent and has once again authorized liturgical adaptation. The conciliar Decree on the Church's Missionary Activity has specifically addressed the question of indigenization.

LITURGICAL INDIGENIZATION

Anscar Chupungco opens a discussion of liturgical indigenization with the following remarks:

> When the signs of the times indicate that a country wishes to preserve its family and national traditions or return to them, the Church will do well to follow in the same train or else face the embarrassment of an overstaying alien. In matters which are not essential to the gospel the Church can learn from the wisdom of a Chinese aphorism: "The stiffest tree is readiest for the axe; the strong and mighty topple from their place; the soft and yielding rise above them."[10]

But Chupungco goes on to affirm that expedience is not the primary reason for indigenization. The principal reason is to be found in the nature of the Church as the symbolization of the incarnate Word of God in all times and places.[11] The mystery of the incarnation provides the theological foundation for indigenization.

[10] *Op. cit.*, 47.

[11] Cyprian Vagaggini, *Theological Dimensions of the Liturgy* (Collegeville, Minn.: The Liturgical Press, 1976) 300–307; Yves Raguin, "Indigenization of the Church," *Teaching All Nations, International Study Week on Missionary Catechetics* 6 (1969) 151–68.

In becoming man, the Word of God bound himself to human nature, and in so doing he committed himself to be bound up inextricably with the history, culture, and traditions of human beings. But he did not become a man in general; he became a Jew, a member of God's chosen people. He inherited the traits and endowments of the Jewish people. This lineage, however, did not limit the sphere of the incarnation. The fact that Jesus was born a Jew, a member of the chosen people to whom God entrusted the promise of universal salvation, gives us assurance that in his resurrection he pours out his Spirit on all different races and cultures called to share in the fulfillment of the saving promise made to Abraham. If the Church is called to be the body of Christ and to incarnate his Spirit in all times and places, it will be faithful to that mission to the extent that it incarnates itself in the various races and cultures of the world. "Indigenization is thus not an option, but a theological imperative arising from incarnational exigency."[12]

The Church must become incarnate in every race, just as the mystery of the incarnation necessitated that Christ become incarnate in the Jewish people. As the Decree on the Church's Missionary Activity states: "The Church must become part of all these groups for the same motive which led Christ to bind Himself, in virtue of His Incarnation, to the definite social and cultural conditions of those human beings among whom He dwelt."[13] This pluralistic view of the Church will not destroy the universality of the Church; rather it will promote it, since there can be no universal Church unless there are in fact local churches. But these local churches will be truly local only if they have their own distinctive culture and traditions. In the words of the conciliar decree, "particular traditions, together with the individual patrimony of each family of nations, can be illumined by the light of the gospel, and then be taken up into Catholic unity."[14]

When the incarnational principle is truly applied to the Church, the life of the Church is actually enriched by cultural pluriformity. By being faithful to its mission, the Church plays its role in the establishment of the Kingdom when God will be all in all. Likewise,

---

[12] Chupungco, op. cit., 49.

[13] Ad gentes, no. 10: AAS 58 (1966) 959.

[14] Ad gentes, no. 22: AAS 58 (1966) 974.

the various cultures of the world are illumined by the light of Christ. In this wonderful exchange, world cultures and traditions are themselves enriched.

The exchange between the Church and various world cultures will necessarily involve adjustments on both sides. Traditions and cultural traits will have to undergo critical evaluation; they will have to abandon any claim to ultimacy or finality in human life and be subsumed as symbols of divine revelation, just as Jewish rituals were subsumed by Christ and primitive Christians, and regarded as types and shadows of Christian realities. In practice this procedure may be very simple, as when kneeling as a symbol of reverence is replaced by standing or bowing; at other times the procedure may be very complex, as when the Church is confronted with the possibility of introducing the scriptures of other world religions into the Christian liturgy of the Word. The appropriation of such readings must certainly be supported by sound theological reasons consonant with the requirements of Christian faith. A failure to discuss the possibility, however, may well result in broadening the distance between the Catholic Church and other world religions. Relationships between the Church and indigenous cultures, then, may also involve accommodations on the part of the Church and its liturgy. Since cultures are always dynamic, the Church and its liturgy will always be asked to make certain modifications.

Liturgical pluralism, then, is not simply a concession made by the Second Vatican Council; it is rather a theological imperative resulting from the incarnational principle that is basic in Christian christology, ecclesiology, and sacramental theology and practice. The Church must prolong the incarnation of Christ in time and space through the proclamation and celebration of its faith. Liturgical pluralism, then, is a necessary corollary to the Church's nature to be local. If the Church is an indigenous Church, its liturgy must also be indigenous.

Adaptation and indigenization, then, are not simply concerns of missionaries in areas where the gospel of Christ has not yet been proclaimed. They are cultural exigencies. Just as grape vines that are transplanted from one country to another do not simply adjust externally to a new environment but are rather transformed from within by assimilating different minerals and moisture from new soil and hence produce a new variety of grapes, so also the Church is called upon not only to adjust to new environments externally but also to be transformed from within. Indigenization must not be restricted to Third World countries; all countries must respond to the challenge of indigenization. In our own country, this means a response to the great variety of cultures prevalent in the United States, ranging from black and Chicano cultures to Indian and Eskimo cultures. It means that the Church must attend seriously to the great cultural differences that extend from urban centers in the East to rural communities in the South and Midwest. It implies an awareness of cultural differences that distinguish mobile or migrant peoples from stable people who live in our small towns and villages.

Culture itself is a complex term. Although it expresses itself in monuments, rituals, and language, it is above all the sum total of human meanings and values; it includes social and religious traditions and the various forms in which people express their identity. It is above all rooted in the native genius of people. Each culture is in a constant state of evolution; it moves both forward and backward. An analysis of culture is especially difficult in areas of rapid transition from a rural agricultural condition to an industrialized or urbanized environment. Such mutations provoke profound changes in world views, basic philosophies of life, and attitudes toward social institutions, especially religious and ecclesial institutions. It should be noted, however, that both cultural anthropologists and psychologists are in agreement that no traditional culture disappears completely from the consciousness or subconsciousness of the people who have nurtured it for generations.

The question that is then posed for the Church is what level or stage of cultural development should be selected as the one best suited for indigenization. Should older cultural forms be discarded in favor of newer ones, or should the newer ones be discarded in favor of those that are older? Indigenization does not imply a return to a fossilized culture, nor does it mean that one should reject everything that is old in favor of what is modern. Above all, the Church's task is to discover what values have been deeply rooted in the life of people and how they have shaped the religious, family, social, and national life of various generations. If the goal of indigenization is to work toward the integration of liturgy and culture, the Church must ascertain which cultural elements have been stable and have been truly expressive of a people's identity. Ultimately, a people's approval is the best proof that the process of indigenization has been authentic.

Although religion regularly plays a significant role in the development of culture, it is important to remember that the religious aspects can be so thoroughly secularized that they are no longer religious. For example, in certain areas of the world that have traditionally been called Catholic, the baptism of infants has sometimes degenerated into a mere social celebration with scarcely any deeply religious connotations. But the opposite may also be true. Religion can be the means whereby certain secular aspects of culture can be retained for generations. For example, various secular rituals and customs associated with Christmas, such as the Christmas tree and the hanging of mistletoe, have been preserved because Christians have continued to celebrate the feast of Christ's birth. It is to be expected that the indigenization of the liturgy in predominantly Christian cultures will introduce cultural forms that already have Christian connotations or readily admit of Christian interpretations. In non-Christian cultures the process is bound to be more complex.

THE CONSTITUTION ON THE SACRED LITURGY, NOS. 37–40

The Constitution on the Sacred Liturgy addresses the general educative and pastoral nature of the liturgy in articles 33–36; specific norms for adapting the liturgy to the genius and traditions of various people are set out in articles 37–40.[15] Although so-called mission territories were uppermost in the minds of the Council Fathers when the subject of adaptation was discussed, the concern broadened so as to include the diverse cultures in areas where the Church has long been established.

[15] For background material and commentary on these articles, see Josef Jungmann, "Constitution on the Sacred Liturgy," *Commentary on the Documents of Vatican II*, ed. H. Vorgrimler, vol. 1 (New York: Herder and Herder, 1967) 1–8; Boniface Luykx, "Norms for Adapting the Liturgy to the Genius and Traditions of Various Peoples," *The Commentary on the Constitution and on the Instruction on the Sacred Liturgy*, ed. A. Bugnini-C. Braga (New York: Benziger Brothers, 1965) 100–107; Godfrey Diekmann, "The Constitution on the Sacred Liturgy in Retrospect," *Worship* 40 (August–September 1966) 408–423; Frederick McManus, "Commentary on the Constitution on the Liturgy," *Worship* 38 (May 1964) 350–67.

Liturgical adaptation is but one species of cultural adaptation that the Church must make if it is to be faithful to its mission to bring the gospel to all people. In its first article the Constitution on the Sacred Liturgy recognized such accommodation as one of the general goals of the Second Vatican Council: "to make more responsive to the requirements of our times those Church observances which are open to adaptation."[16]

Certainly the theory and techniques of liturgical adaptation are closely related to the theory and techniques of missionary adaptation. For that reason the Constitution on the Sacred Liturgy speaks of adaptation "especially in missionary lands."[17] That concern, however, does not in any way rule out the possibility or the propriety of liturgical adaptation in other regions as well.

Liturgical adaptation refers to any kind of accommodation, adjustment, or modification whereby a liturgical symbol or rite is changed from one form to another while preserving something of the original. Hence it is different from the creation of wholly original symbols and rites. When addressing itself to the question of liturgical adaptation, the constitution does not speak of indigenization; it refers rather to what might be called minor and major adaptations.

Article 37 of the Constitution on the Sacred Liturgy provides the theoretical basis for adaptation. It calls to mind the fundamental principle set down in article 21, which underlies this later section of the document:

> In order that the Christian people may more securely derive an abundance of graces from the sacred liturgy, holy Mother Church desires to undertake with great care a general restoration of the liturgy itself. For the liturgy is made up of unchangeable elements divinely instituted, and elements subject to change. The latter not only may but ought to be changed with the passing of time if features have by chance crept in which are less harmonious with the intimate nature of the liturgy, or if existing elements have grown less functional.[18]

Article 21 seems to presuppose that there is universal agreement concerning the parts of the liturgy that have been established by

---

[16] *Sacrosanctum Concilium*, no. 1: *AAS* 56 (1964) 97.

[17] *Sacrosanctum Concilium*, no. 38: *AAS* 56 (1964) 110.

[18] *AAS* 56 (1964) 105–106.

Christ, but recent scholarship has raised unresolved questions about which parts have in fact been so established and hence which parts are in fact unchangeable.[19] While leaving the question unresolved, and in fact presuming an answer to the question, article 37 does reject the efforts of earlier epochs to "Europeanize" the liturgy and affirms the value of other cultures and the contributions they may make in the reformed Roman liturgy. Recognition of cultural pluriformity and the need to adapt Christian worship to the genius of people go hand in hand with a clearer understanding of the accessory, accidental nature of ecclesiastical customs, including liturgical customs. When the Church ceases to urge complete uniformity, it does not mean that she has become permissive; rather it shows that she has genuine respect for the divine gifts that God has given to his people, gifts that are to be used and fostered even in a liturgical context.

Manifesting, then, a clear intention to abandon the principle supporting the strict uniformity of the Roman liturgy, carefully maintained since the Council of Trent, article 37 quotes in part the encyclical letter *Summi pontificatus* of Pius XII, which declared that the Church should struggle for unity rather than mere external uniformity, and that the Church has approved of and fostered the diverse gifts that have sprung from the deep resources of every race.[20] Although the assertion that the Church studies world cultures "with sympathy" may seem somewhat patronizing, the text does go on to open the door to liturgical pluralism within the Roman rite by acknowledging that sometimes the Church admits the gifts of various cultures into the liturgy, provided they harmonize with its true and authentic spirit.

The long-term consequences of such a provision are hard to predict, but whatever developments do occur, the new forms that are adopted should in some way grow organically from forms already existing.[21] The process whereby a single Roman rite develops into different rites to form a single Roman liturgical family of rites may be described as branches growing out of one trunk.[22] It

[19] See Chupungco, *op. cit.*, 70–73.
[20] *AAS* 31 (1939) 429.
[21] See *Sacrosanctum Concilium*, no. 23: *AAS* 56 (1964) 106.
[22] Chupungco, *op. cit.*, 7.

is possible that in the future the distinctly "Roman" rite will be confined more and more to Rome and other Italian dioceses as the responsibility for cultural adaptation is taken seriously by the local and regional churches throughout the world.[23]

The liturgical pluralism envisioned by article 37 is based on certain liturgical and ecclesial principles. First of all, the Church does not wish to impose liturgical uniformity in matters that do not touch on the basic faith and well-being of the Catholic community. Although we are all called to unity in faith, this can be achieved while allowing for diversity of forms in matters that do not directly affect the faith. The liturgy pertains to the genus of symbol; its Christian meaning is communicated by means of symbols that of necessity must be interpreted. It is Christian faith that enables those who celebrate the Christian liturgy to find Christian meaning there. Although it is this Christian meaning that is of primary importance, a certain uniformity of liturgical symbols and rites may well be expedient in order to foster the essential unity of faith. The degree of liturgical uniformity should be determined by cultural uniformity in each region. In this regard, the Constitution on the Sacred Liturgy notes that "as far as possible, notable differences between the rites used in adjacent regions are to be carefully avoided."[24] Marked cultural variants, then, determine the scope to which uniformity is abandoned in favor of pluriformity.

Article 37 establishes both negative and positive conditions for admitting cultural variants into the liturgy. On the one hand, anything that is not indissolubly bound up with superstition and error may be admitted; on the other hand, elements that are admitted must harmonize with the liturgy's true and authentic spirit. Experience has already shown that we must not be too quick to label practices as superstitious and bound up with error; they may in fact be simple and unsophisticated expressions of genuine faith.[25]

---

[23] This was a fear expressed during the Council. It was linked with the fear that the Latin rite itself would sink into oblivion. See *Schema Constitutionis de Sacra Liturgia, Modi I, Prooemium — Caput I* (Typis Polyglottis Vaticanis, 1962) 25: "Periculosum videtur permittere mutationes in ipsa liturgia derivatas ex moribus populorum, nam ansa dabitur destructionis ritus latini."

[24] *Sacrosanctum Concilium*, no. 23: *AAS* 56 (1964) 106.

[25] See Chupungco, *op. cit.,* 9.

Greater authority in this matter of adaptation, then, is given to the national body of bishops, since they are more directly in contact with the life of the people and are therefore apt to be better judges in such matters. For a people to have their own rite is no longer to be considered as a derogation from the law but rather as a normal situation, thoroughly in accord with both the spirit and the letter of the law.

Article 38 maintains that liturgical adaptation may certainly be made, "provided that the substantial unity of the Roman rite is maintained."[26] However, the constitution does not explain what is meant by the substantial unity of the Roman rite. Furthermore, it is unlikely that a comparative analysis of the structures of Eastern and Western rites will yield a clear understanding of what is distinctively Roman. Hence, for some degree of understanding we must refer to the common canonical norms for the interpretation of laws, namely, the context in which the statement is found and the sources from which it is derived.

The context of article 38 does not suggest preserving uniformity but rather providing for the needs of adaptation that enjoys the favor of the law, at least as much as uniformity does. Such adaptation, however, is to be done within the limits of faith and with the common good in mind. Furthermore, the basic sources of the Roman rite are the primitive nucleus of worship patterns common to all Catholic liturgies and of those symbols and rituals proper to the Western culture that have given the Roman rite its own special form and expression. Fidelity to the first source implies that all Catholic liturgy should spring from the tradition of the universal Church, which in matters of both faith and worship provides norms for Christian life. Although a comparative study of Eastern and Western Catholic liturgies indicates a common structure composed of introductory rite, liturgy of the Word, ritual action such as the Eucharist or baptism, and a concluding rite, history clearly shows that there have been significant modifications in the symbols and rituals that surround these basic elements. In some instances these ancillary symbols and rites have been distinctively Western and have distinguished the Roman rite from various Eastern rites. They are also the symbols and rites that have been modified in the course

[26] *Sacrosanctum Concilium,* no. 38: *AAS* 56 (1964) 110.

of history. These are the aspects of the liturgy that are subject to various degrees of adaptation when the substance of the Roman rite is to be accommodated to the needs of various peoples.

It should be clear that adaptation does not apply simply to relatively unimportant aspects of the celebration, such as liturgical colors or specific gestures such as kneeling, but it may extend to the structures and texts of the rites themselves. To facilitate the work of adaptation, the liturgical books revised since the Council have indicated what parts of celebrations must be altogether preserved and what place is to be left to legitimate accommodation.

Article 39 indicates the broad areas where minor adaptations may be made. They include the relatively simple changes that can be readily noted in the rubrical directions given in the liturgical books. The areas include "the administration of the sacraments, the sacramentals, processions, liturgical language, sacred music, and the arts,"[27] according to the fundamental norms laid down in the Constitution on the Sacred Liturgy. It should be noted that article 39 does not present a taxative list. Other articles of the constitution note specific areas for adaptation, for example, the degrees and rites of the catechumenate (art. 65), rites of matrimony (art. 77), funeral rites (art. 81), sacred music (art. 119), liturgical arts (art. 123, 128), the sacramentals (art. 79), and the liturgical year (art. 111).

The provision for minor adaptations made by the Constitution on the Sacred Liturgy has been implemented in the revised liturgical books of the Roman rite; the introductions and the descriptive rubrics frequently refer to adaptations within the competence of the episcopal conferences. In some instances the books also indicate adaptations within the competence of the local ordinary or even the individual celebrant. Examples of minor adaptations listed in the revised books include the use or omission of baptismal anointings, the form of baptismal promises, congregational postures at the celebration of the Eucharist, choice of biblical readings at Mass, the mode of exchanging the sign of peace, and the place appropriate for the celebration of the sacrament of penance.

It should be noted here that the Constitution on the Sacred Liturgy expressly states that the Church holds all lawfully acknowledged rites to be of equal authority and dignity and that it wishes to

---

[27] *Sacrosanctum Concilium*, no. 39: *AAS* 56 (1964) 110.

preserve them in the future and to foster them in every way (art. 4).[28] This would include the liturgical traditions and distinctive rituals of religious orders. Unless they have been expressly forbidden, they enjoy the express favor of the law and so stand alongside more recent adaptations as examples of liturgical accommodations made within the context of the Roman rite.

Article 40 deals with the subject of major adaptations of the liturgy. In its original version, the article focused on the liturgy in mission areas, but in the text finally approved by the Council Fathers the missionary thrust was softened at the request of several bishops who maintained that conditions in mission areas are not different from those in other parts of the world.[29] The detail is significant, for it implies that major adaptation or indigenization is not necessarily restricted to mission countries. Whenever and wherever translations of the typical books containing the substance of the Roman rite together with provision for minor adaptations are inadequate to respond to pastoral needs, more profound adaptations must be undertaken. In the case of minor adaptations, it is a question of merely inserting secondary symbols or rites into the substantial unity of the Roman rite or of eliminating such symbols and rites, but in the case of major adaptations it is a question of adapting the basic structure of the liturgy to a religious sensitivity that is different from the mentality manifested in the Roman rite.

Article 40 outlines the procedures for major adaptation in three paragraphs. The first asserts that it belongs to the national body of bishops to decide whether it is appropriate to make such adaptations and "which elements from the traditions and genius of individual peoples might appropriately be admitted into divine worship."[30] Such deliberations must be submitted to the Holy See for approval.

The second paragraph concerns experimentation. So that the territorial bodies of bishops may make their deliberations after mature consideration and sufficient experience, the Holy See will empower them to select for a determined period of time special groups among whom they can carry out preliminary experiments involving liturgical changes to be proposed to the Holy See for approval.

[28] *Sacrosanctum Concilium*, no. 4: AAS 56 (1964) 98.
[29] *Schema Constitutionis de Sacra Liturgia*, Emend. IV, Appendix, 27.
[30] *Sacrosanctum Concilium*, no. 40: AAS 56 (1964) 111.

The final paragraph addresses the special difficulty that arises when liturgical changes are to be expressed in new liturgical laws. Experts are to be employed in writing these laws, so that a spirit favorable to adaptation will be preserved in the laws themselves.

The distinction between minor and major adaptations is not always clear. For example, the Constitution on the Sacred Liturgy considers as minor such matters as the form and material of liturgical vessels and furnishings,[31] whereas the General Instruction of the Roman Missal maintains that proposed changes in the form and even the color of liturgical vesture are major issues that must be approved by the Apostolic See.[32] Certainly the creation of new Eucharistic prayers, a radical restructuring of rites in the liturgical books, the omission of substantial elements in celebrations, or the development of a distinctly new rite would all be major adaptations.

Minor adaptations may be made by episcopal conferences without the consent of the Holy See, although the Holy See may require confirmation of the episcopal decisions. Major adaptations must be preceded by a period of study and experimentation. The Holy See must authorize such experimentation and must ultimately approve the implementation of major adaptations. In 1972 the episcopal conference in the United States decided that individual bishops may petition, through the Bishops' Committee on the Liturgy, the requisite permission to undertake experimentation with a view to future major adaptation.[33]

Experimentation refers to a process of trial and error in order to test a hypothesis. It is used in article 40 of the Constitution on the Sacred Liturgy to refer to limited efforts in controlled groups to test the effectiveness of a proposed change before it is approved for more general use. The Constitution on the Sacred Liturgy certainly presumes that such experimentation will take place, since what seems to be ideal in theory is often not at all ideal in practice.

The third instruction on the proper implementation of the Constitution on the Sacred Liturgy, issued on September 5, 1970, directed

[31] *Sacrosanctum Concilium*, no. 128: *AAS* 56 (1964) 132–33.

[32] *Institutio generalis Missalis Romani*, nos. 304, 308: *Missale Romanum* (Rome: Typis Polyglottis Vaticanis, 1971) 82–84.

[33] Frederick McManus, "Liturgical Experimentation," *New Catholic Encyclopedia* 16 (Washington, D.C.: McGraw-Hill Book Company, 1974) 257.

that experiments must be conducted by prudent persons who have been given a special mandate for the purpose; they may not take place during large liturgical celebrations, and they may not be publicized; and they are to be limited in number and not extended beyond one year.[34] The same instruction specified the major adaptations for which prior experimentation is expected as those that involve "the structure of rites or order of parts, any matter foreign to the traditional usage, or the introduction of new texts."[35]

Where options are specifically allowed within the liturgical rites approved by the Holy See, experimentation may take place without any special permission. Experimentation within the limits of the authority of the episcopal conferences or the diocesan bishops may take place under the direction of the respective episcopal conference or bishops.

The careful wording of the procedures regulating experimentation indicates a grave concern lest illegitimate innovations be introduced into the liturgy. Since thirst for novelty and impatience at the slowness of the episcopal conferences to initiate experimentation are often responsible for haphazard experiments, the Constitution on the Sacred Liturgy places a heavy burden on the episcopal conferences both to support liturgical indigenization and to set out the plans for requisite experimentation. For legitimate experiments and their evaluation to take place, the bishops will need the services not only of liturgists but also of experts in other areas such as theology, anthropology, psychology, linguistics, sociology, and the arts. Adaptation, especially major adaptation, is a complex operation.

PARTICULAR LAW AND THE JURIDICAL POWER OF THE BISHOP

From what has already been said, it should be clear that liturgical laws emanate not only from the Holy See but also from episcopal conferences and local bishops. The Constitution on the Sacred Liturgy affirms that "regulation of the sacred liturgy depends solely on the authority of the Church, that is, on the Apostolic See and, as laws may determine, on the bishop."[36] Article 22 also acknowledges that the right to regulate the liturgy "within certain defined limits

---

[34] *Liturgicae instaurationes*, no. 12: AAS 62 (1970) 703.
[35] *Ibid.*
[36] *Sacrosanctum Concilium*, no. 22, §1: AAS 56 (1964) 102.

belongs also to various kinds of competent territorial bodies of bishops legitimately established."[37] That article is significant in that it acknowledges that each bishop has genuine authority and regulatory power over the liturgy. Since the Council of Trent, the regulation of the liturgy has generally been reserved to the Apostolic See. For example, in *Mediator Dei* Pius XII taught that "the supreme pontiff alone has the right to permit or establish any liturgical practice, to introduce or approve new rites, or to make any changes in them he considers necessary." The responsibility of the bishop was "to enforce vigilantly the observance of the canonical rules on divine worship."[38] Above all he was to correct abuses.

In contrast to this stance, the Constitution on the Sacred Liturgy firmly establishes the regulatory power of the bishop affecting the liturgy. Since the bishop "is to be considered the high priest of his flock," from whom "the faithful under his care derive and maintain their life in Christ,"[39] he needs the proper authority to fulfill his mission. The presumption is no longer that the bishop lacks authority until it is specifically given to him, but rather that he has authority unless it is reserved to the pope or the Apostolic See.

Article 22 also speaks of the exercise of juridical power over the liturgy by competent territorial bodies of bishops legitimately established. The regional exercise of juridical power by bodies of bishops, whether in provincial and plenary councils or in episcopal conferences, is certainly a manifestation of episcopal collegiality and of the corporate responsibility of all bishops for all the churches. If each individual bishop has responsibility for churches other than his own, this concern is surely stronger in relation to the dioceses of the province, region, or nation to which he belongs. In most parts of the world, this authority noted in article 22.2 is exercised by national bodies of bishops; in some parts of the world, the bishops of several nations have united to form an association. In exercising their lawmaking authority, a two-thirds majority by secret ballot is required.[40] In a number of instances, the decrees of territorial bodies of bishops must be confirmed by the Apostolic See.

---

[37] *Sacrosanctum Concilium*, no. 22, §2: AAS 56 (1964) 102.

[38] AAS 39 (1947) 544.

[39] *Sacrosanctum Concilium*, no. 41: AAS 56 (1964) 111.

[40] *Sacram liturgiam*, no. 10: AAS 56 (1964) 143.

It is clear that liturgical laws on a great variety of topics may be enacted by and truly proceed from the legislative authority of territorial bodies of bishops. Although such laws receive an additional juridical and moral force because they are subsequently confirmed by the Apostolic See, their nature as truly episcopal law is not changed.

Certainly the preparation and promulgation of the Constitution on the Sacred Liturgy set a plateau in the reform of the liturgy in that it established a broad doctrinal statement and a specific project for liturgical reform. The preparation and promulgation of the revised liturgical books in Latin and their official translations into vernacular languages was another plateau; it represented a further stage of development called for by the Council. In a sense these books have established the substantial unity of the Roman rite. It is imperative, however, that we always keep in mind the further stage of development involving the adaptation to local and regional conditions and the more radical accommodations of the liturgy to the diverse cultures of the world. The initiative and responsibility for this final stage rests above all with the episcopal conferences and the local bishops.

It is quite easy to document liturgical reform that is preoccupied with changes in liturgical structures but quite difficult to document liturgical renewal that is preoccupied with vital participation in the liturgical celebrations. Liturgical reform calls for and necessitates liturgical renewal. If the latter does not happen, we end up simply with a new kind of empty formalism. Neither liturgical reform nor renewal, however, is at its final stage, since both reform and renewal are to be constantly promoted by the principles of liturgical adaptation sanctioned by the Constitution on the Sacred Liturgy. Without liturgical adaptation and cultural indigenization, it is unlikely that the majority of people in the Church will achieve that kind of ecclesial renewal that has been called for by the Second Vatican Council.[41]

[41] Achille Triacca, "Adattamento liturgico: Utopia, velleità o strumento della pastorale liturgica?" *Notitiae* 15 (1979) 26–45.

Chapter 15

FIDELITY TO LAW AND
FIDELITY TO PASTORAL NEEDS

From what has already been said, it should be clear that the Constitution on the Sacred Liturgy is a document that is evangelical, theological, juridical, and pastoral. It is evangelical in that it has been framed in the spirit of the New Testament — the words of the constitution are often the very words of the gospel. It is theological in that it elaborates at great length the theological foundations for the way in which the Church is sanctified and worships — in Christ and through his Holy Spirit. It is juridical in the sense that it proposes definite practical lines of action in matters of the liturgy. Finally, it is pastoral in that its object is "to intensify the daily growth of Catholics in Christian living; to make more responsive to the requirements of our times those Church observances which are open to adaptation; to nurture whatever can contribute to the unity of all who believe in Christ; and to strengthen those aspects of the Church which can help summon all of mankind into her embrace."[1]

Most liturgical documents that have been issued since the Second Vatican Council also have evangelical, theological, juridical, and pastoral characteristics. One of the greatest challenges confronting ministers in the Church has been that of keeping these characteristics in a poised tension with one another. Because of training and background, some people respond only to commands and ignore

---

[1] *Sacrosanctum Concilium* no. 1: *AAS* 56 (1964) 97.

counsels. Such persons tend to give little response to the theological values set forth in liturgical documents and often feel free to ignore liturgical renewal unless they are subject to sanctions and commands. Other people, steeped in a legalistic mentality, give a strict juridical interpretation where it least of all belongs. Failing to understand the positive nature of Church law, still others manifest only contempt for practical norms in an exaggerated effort to counteract legalism.

If Christian theology is the science that is built on the Word that God speaks to his people, canon law as a science is concerned with the practical life of the Church founded on God's Word. Although it has its source in God's Word, its formulation is the work of those human agents who are responsible for ordering the life of the Church. It is by reflecting on the Word of God that the Church concludes how people should act. As the history of the liturgy shows, in the early centuries of the Church the practical expression of the Church's worship was not separated from its inner spirit. The patristic writers, who were steeped in a theology of the Church and her worship, were also responsible for the concrete expression of the liturgy in the life of the Christian people. The same may be said of certain medieval authors.

When the Sacred Congregation of Rites and Ceremonies was created in 1588, Pope Sixtus V manifested a special concern for the interior transformation of the faithful through the Church's liturgy. As he noted in the decree establishing the Congregation, "sacred rites and ceremonies contain valuable instruction for the Christian people and for the profession of the true faith; they recommend the majesty of the sacred mysteries, lift up the mind of the faithful to the contemplation of the highest things, and inflame them with the fire of devotion. Since this is so, we desire to increase the piety of the Church's sons and daughters and of divine worship by the maintenance and restoration of sacred rites and ceremonies."[2] In other words, the Congregation was established to put into effect and promote the theological and liturgical reforms that were an outgrowth of the Council of Trent.

But under the strong influence of nominalism, which prevailed

[2] *Bullarum diplomatum et privilegiorum Romanorum pontificum Taurinensis Editio*, VIII, 989–90.

even among the Tridentine Fathers, the intelligent, meaningful celebration of the liturgy gave way to a concern mainly for the validity of the sacraments. Consequently, the rubrics came to be interpreted simply as rigid norms for mere ceremonial, often devoid of theological significance. The centuries following the Council of Trent saw a widening rift between the Church's worship and the norms that regulate the external organization and manifestation of that worship.

Contemporary liturgical studies, however, have rediscovered the fundamental theological nature of the Church's worship; hence the emphasis is not so much on validity as on meaningful celebrations of the paschal mystery of Christ. The sacraments are no longer viewed as magical founts where people are automatically made holy, but rather as rich symbols through which men and women as total persons are sanctified by Christ and in union with him worship the Father.

If people understand the true nature of liturgical law as the complexus of practical norms ordering the rituals in and through which people are sanctified and in turn worship God, surely they will admit that a canonical study of the liturgy is important; but ministers who blindly follow the ritual directives in the reformed liturgical books will run the risk of producing a new form of liturgical pageantry that might be externally correct but interiorly dead.

To a great extent, canonists must depend on the insights of the theologians. Actions should proceed from sound ideas. The Church is the living Christ, and its worship is the worship of Christ, who sanctifies the members of his body and leads them back to the Father, all through the outpouring of the Holy Spirit. But in order that the new inspirations of the Spirit may be put into practice, the legal regulations must be formulated in such a way that there is still room for constant growth and development. If the practical life of the Church is to reflect her ever-deepening understanding of the faith, it is imperative that the body of the Church's law should have an elastic quality so that new insights may be assimilated to what is already good in the Church's life.

The Constitution on the Sacred Liturgy certainly established the principle of historical relevance. As we have already indicated, the document conceives of the people of God in a historical context; that

history is constantly changing, revealing God to his people in varying ways. The document does not visualize a fully developed form of
worship that the Church wants to impose on all people for all time.
Instead, the constitution insists on respect for the whole tradition of
the Church's worship, but it leaves open the possibility that new
forms of worship may always be accepted if they are recommended
as being the fruit of serious scholarship and experimentation and are
felt to be beneficial to the Church as it exists in concrete situations.

Furthermore, the constitution is based on the principle of personal consciousness and responsibility. Worship cannot be legislated, for it is the free and loving response of the whole person to a
loving God. It is not magic nor is it mere ceremony, but it is the conscious acknowledgment of the sanctifying power of God that finds
expression through the ritual celebrations of the Church. Worship is
based on the fundamental principle of our total dependence on God.
When law is internalized in human consciences, when people have
an awareness of God's power to save them and of his desire to save
them through the liturgy of the Church, the written law of the
Church does not have to address minute details. When consciences
have been developed and sound theological awareness has been
deepened, it is best that Church law emphasize only the basic norms
and principles. In this way there is room for the free development
and assimilation of wholesome customs and usages. This is the best
way of promoting that unity in diversity that should be characteristic of the Church of Christ.

Certainly the Constitution on the Sacred Liturgy and most of the
liturgical documents that have been issued to implement it have
been formulated in this spirit. Usually the norms that have been set
down have been general and have been concerned with major issues,
not with picayune details. Provision has been made for experimentation before final texts have been promulgated. In many instances options have been given in the celebration of the liturgy. Extensive
power has been transferred from the Holy See and placed in the
hands of national episcopates, thus providing for more diversifica-
tion in the Church's rites as determined by culture and need.

In matters of liturgical music and liturgical art, only directives of
a very general nature have been issued, and rightly so, for the creation of art, like morality, is something that cannot be legislated.

Artists, architects, and musicians who agree to work for the Church should have a clear understanding of the theology of the liturgy and the role of their proper arts in the liturgy, but talent and genius should not be stifled by legislators who are not themselves conversant with the arts. It is above all in these areas that the law should say little, once the role of the arts in the liturgy has been established. This seems to have been the attitude behind the formulation of chapters 6 and 7 of the Constitution on the Sacred Liturgy.

It is indeed fortunate that the Constitution on the Sacred Liturgy and most of the subsequent liturgical documents have taken theology as a starting point in the formulation of practical norms. Surely such laws as reflect a deep understanding of the faith should be a great asset in the sanctification of God's people and in their worship of the Father. Unfortunately, the spirit that has been reflected in the Church's universal legislation has not always been manifested in the directives emanating from authorities on the diocesan and parochial levels. If legislation on all levels is grounded in theology, the law of the Church will be a sturdy framework in which the Spirit of God can freely operate and recreate the face of the earth.

The primary liturgical questions that continue to challenge Christian communities are how to implement to best advantage the reform embodied in the revised service books; how to foster the growth of faith-communities that can genuinely express their life and deepen that life in the liturgical forms approved by the Church; how to carry out the liturgical catechesis that is always essential to liturgical renewal; and how to be liturgically creative and responsive to pastoral needs without being antinomian and frivolously iconoclastic.[3] These questions, however, must be confronted along with the complicated question of how one should maintain fidelity to clearly established norms while being pastorally responsible. The challenge is underlined in article 11 of the Constitution on the Sacred Liturgy: "Pastors of souls must therefore realize that, when the liturgy is celebrated, more is required than the mere observance of laws governing valid and lawful celebration. It is their duty also

---

[3] Frederick McManus, "Liturgical Law and Difficult Cases," *Worship* 48 (1974) 347.

to ensure that the faithful take part knowingly, actively, and fruit-fully."[4]

The text is clear that the responsibility of ministers is not only to the faithful observance of norms but also to the enrichment of the Christian lives of all those who take part in the celebrations. No longer may ministers feel that they have done their duty if they have carried out the norms in the liturgical books; they must go beyond the norms, in the sense that they must bring the liturgy to life for people. Consequently, they must develop a sensitive ministerial style that enables them to be aware of the pastoral needs of the people and to structure and execute celebrations in such a way that they truly respond to people's needs. This presupposes an understanding of both the theological and aesthetic dimensions of the liturgy. Without undermining liturgical discipline, ministers may and should explore opportunities for creativity within the liturgy.

There are various areas where creativity is explicitly authorized and encouraged. For example, according to article 11 of the General Instruction of the Roman Missal, the president of the assembly may exercise creativity in introducing the liturgy of the day, the liturgy of the Word, the Eucharistic prayer, and in concluding the liturgy. The homily and general intercessions also provide opportunities for spontaneity.[5] Furthermore, the texts provided in the Roman Missal for introducing the penitential rite, the Lord's Prayer, the kiss of peace, and the communion rite are not unchangeable texts; they are models or examples to be adapted to the needs of diverse assemblies.[6] Many times the new rites explicitly sanction verbal creativity by the phrase *his vel similibus verbis*, "in these or similar words."

It is also important that ministers be aware of the canonical axiom derived from Roman law: *De minimis non curat praetor*. This means that sometimes matters are of such minimal significance that it is not appropriate to make them the object of a canonical norm. For example, the rubrics of the post-Tridentine missal did not specify that the collection may be taken up after the creed on Sundays, yet no reasonable pastor hesitated to authorize the Sunday col-

---

[4] *Sacrosanctum Concilium* no. 11: AAS 56 (1964) 103.

[5] *Institutio generalis Missalis Romani, Missale Romanum* (Rome: Typis Polyglottis Vaticanis, 1971) 30.

[6] G. Fontaine, "Créativité dans la liturgie d'aujourd'hui," *Notitiae* 8 (1972) 151–56.

lection at that time, even without explicit authorization in the rubrics. Likewise, symbols and rituals not explicitly authorized are sometimes introduced into celebrations, but they are of such minor significance that they do not call for authorization. Examples would be the introduction of additional popular acclamations into the structure of the Eucharistic prayer so as to provide more active participation on the part of the community, or the introduction of liturgical dance at various appropriate times during the liturgy.[7] The former practice would find precedent in the liturgies of the Eastern Churches and in the canons authorized for use at Masses with children; the latter practice would find precedent in the disciplined choreography that has often been part of the liturgy of religious institutes. Monastic communities and enclosed communities of women religious have regularly had traditions involving ritual bows, prostrations, processions, and arm gestures that have something in common with modern liturgical dance. Unless such creative elements have been explicitly forbidden, ministers should feel free to respond to pastoral needs by introducing them into the liturgy, provided they are based on sound theological, liturgical, and aesthetic principles.

It is also important that ministers be aware of the difficulties that are sometimes unwittingly created by the vernacular translation of liturgical norms. When a subjunctive verb is used in Latin, the precise sense is often unclear. Sometimes it means "may"; at other times it means "should." In one case an option is being given; in another, a directive is being set forth. The translator should not needlessly restrict the freedom of the minister, but should give as much latitude as possible. In liturgical matters as well as in other ecclesial areas, the translation of a text is something one can understand and critique adequately only with the help of the original text.

It is important for the minister to scrutinize the language and the content of the liturgical books in order to see whether the rubrics are clearly intended as binding precepts or simply as useful and helpful guidelines. In this regard, one must remember that the supplementary and interpretative instructions and commentaries that have been issued by various liturgical committees are usually only inform-

[7] Lucien Deiss, *Spirit and Song in the New Liturgy*, rev. ed. (Cincinnati: World Library Publications, Inc., 1976) 91–99.

ative. They do not have the weight or favor of law that the norms of the official liturgical books carry. This applies also to the various replies and explanations contained in *Notitiae*.[8]

It should also be remembered that liturgical laws can become obsolete and that even without a formal act of abrogation, they can cease to have the force of law for the Christian community. This may happen over a long period of time or it may happen quickly. The Eastern Churches have long been comfortable with the assertion that acceptance by the community is a requisite for the reasonableness and hence the authority of a Church law; this doctrine needs to be more widely asserted and accepted in the West. A law may be so far removed from the goal it intends to achieve and so foreign to the experiences and cultural situations of a community that it can in no way function as an effective law for such a community.[9]

Canonists are in general agreement that when a law has become counterproductive, when it is no longer suitable for its purpose, it no longer has the force of law. It is of course difficult to decide when the literal observance of a norm becomes harmful or impossible for a particular community. The ability to make such an accurate decision surely depends on a well-formed and adequately informed conscience. The minister must have not only an accurate understanding of the norm and what it requires but also a proper assessment of the pastoral situation.

If observance of a law occasions the rejection of the liturgy or the Church by a large segment of the community, surely the traditional teaching on *epikia* justifies the non-observance of the law. This affirmation is in keeping with the medieval axiom that sacraments are for people; people do not exist for the sacraments. The Church is likewise for people; people do not exist for the Church. For example, in communities that are aware of and committed to efforts to assure justice for women and minorities in the Church, the use of sexist

---

[8] McManus, *art. cit.*, 354. For further treatment of the binding force of liturgical law, see Walter J. Kelly, "The Authority of Liturgical Law," *The Jurist* 28 (1968) 397–424; A. Turck, "Le Problème de la loi: Réflexions pastorales," *Paroisse et Liturgie* 47 (1965) 3–13; Thomas Vismans, "Liturgy or Rubrics?" *The Church Worships*, Concilium 12 (1966) 83–91.

[9] McManus, *art. cit.*, 358.

language in the liturgy is often both irritating and alienating; in some instances it arouses deep hostility. Sometimes the bias against women is built into the vernacular translation but not into the original Latin text. There is no reason why the words *pro multis* in the text of institution within the anaphora need to be translated "for all men." To avoid harm and insult to the community, ministers have rightly changed the text and avoided sexist language.

Similarly, the refusal to offer the cup to all of the faithful has at times resulted in the widespread feeling within certain communities that the Church is elitist and that clergy and religious are more privileged than lay people. There is the feeling that the practice is not in accord with the basic teaching on Christian equality and the universal call to holiness as set out in the Constitution on the Church. Surely the conciliar constitution carries more weight than later instructions and decrees. Such hostility has at times been lessened or alleviated by offering the cup to all at each celebration of the Eucharist.

In the recent past, the refusal to give communion in the hand often resulted in distressing confrontations between communicants and ministers of the Eucharist. In such instances it probably would have been more prudent for the minister to give communion in the hand rather than observe the liturgical norm. Avoidance of hostility and division would have been more in keeping with the symbolism of the Eucharist as the expression and cause of Christian unity than strict adherence to liturgical discipline was.

In each of these examples it is a case of discerning the greater good to be achieved. It is a case of weighing the observance of the law and response to pastoral need in the balance. And as the Constitution on the Sacred Liturgy clearly affirmed, ministers must not only be concerned with the laws governing valid and lawful celebrations; they must see that the faithful are actively engaged in the rites and are truly enriched by the celebrations.

Since the promulgation of the Constitution on the Sacred Liturgy, scholars have continued to study the liturgy in the light of developments in theology. Those responsible for the pastoral life of the Church have made serious efforts to implement the reform set in motion by the Second Vatican Council. The result has been a genuine renewal of the Church's life of prayer. This has been made possible above all by a rediscovery of the fuller ecclesial dimensions of the Eucharist, by a richer celebration of the liturgy of the Word, especially through the revised lectionary, and by other revised sacramental rites.

Although the progress has been striking, the years following the Council have not always been peaceful. The majority of people in the Church, both clergy and laity, have accepted the reform of the liturgy, but some have been confused and even hurt by the changes. The latter include both those who were not adequately prepared or were psychologically unable to change, as well as those who sought to implement the changes but were rebuffed and even ridiculed. Efforts to heal divisions and wounds must continue if the liturgy is to be the symbol of unity and charity it is meant to be.

Adequate formation must be given to leaders of prayer and other ministers so they may serve the community of faith well. Efforts to initiate the faithful into the meaning of the Church's liturgy must be given priority so that their participation will be enlightened and the mystery of Christ interiorized in the lives of his people.[10] The most profound change has to be that of the heart which takes in the Spirit offered by the Church in the celebration of the liturgy.[11] In other words, the new liturgy and its new laws must always be related to the pastoral situation in the Church. In that way both liturgy and law promote fullness of life in preparation for the day when all things will be new.

[10] U.S. Bishops' Committee on the Liturgy, "Fifteenth Anniversary of the Constitution on the Liturgy: A Commemorative Statement," *Bishops' Committee on the Liturgy Newsletter* 14 (December 1978) 141–44.

[11] Max Thurian, "Créativité et spontanéité dans la liturgie," *Notitiae* 14 (1978) 169–75.

OFFICIAL DOCUMENTS PERTAINING TO LITURGICAL RENEWAL

I. Documents of the Second Vatican Council

1. Constitution on the Sacred Liturgy (*Sacrosanctum Concilium*), December 4, 1963: *AAS* 56 (1964) 97–134; W. Abbot (ed.), *Documents of Vatican II* (New York 1966) 137–178.
2. Decree on the Instruments of Social Communication (*Inter mirifica*), December 21, 1964: *AAS* 56 (1964) 145–153; *Documents of Vatican II* 319–331.
3. Dogmatic Constitution on the Church (*Lumen gentium*), November 21, 1964: *AAS* 57 (1965) 5–67; *Documents of Vatican II* 14–96.
4. Decree on the Eastern Catholic Churches (*Orientalium Ecclesiarum*), November 21, 1964: *AAS* 57 (1965) 76–85; *Documents of Vatican II* 373–386.
5. Decree on Ecumenism (*Unitatis redintegratio*), November 21, 1964: *AAS* 57 (1965) 90–107; *Documents of Vatican II* 341–366.
6. Decree on the Pastoral Office of Bishops in the Church (*Christus Dominus*), October 28, 1965: *AAS* 58 (1966) 673–696; *Documents of Vatican II* 396–429.
7. Decree on the Adaptation and Renewal of the Religious Life (*Perfectae caritatis*), October 28, 1965: *AAS* 58 (1966) 702–712; *Documents of Vatican II* 466–482.
8. Decree on Priestly Formation (*Optatam totius*), October 28, 1965: *AAS* 58 (1966) 713–727; *Documents of Vatican II* 437–457.
9. Declaration on Christian Education (*Gravissimum educationis*), October 28, 1965: *AAS* 58 (1966) 728–739; *Documents of Vatican II* 637–651.

II. Organization of the Liturgical Reform by the Apostolic See

of Saints (*Sacra Rituum Congregatio*), May 8, 1969: *AAS* 61 (1969) 297–305; *The Pope Speaks* 14 (1969) 174–180.

13. Address of Pope Paul VI to the Consilium at the Completion of Its Work, April 10, 1970: *AAS* 62 (1970) 272–274; *L'Osservatore Romano* (English edition), April 23, 1970; 2, 5.

14. Apostolic Constitution on the Congregation for the Sacraments and Divine Worship (*Constans Nobis studium*), July 11, 1975: *AAS* 67 (1975) 417–420; *Canon Law Digest* 8:224–227.

III. General Documents for the Liturgical Renewal

1. Pontifical Biblical Commission, Instruction on the Historical Truth of the Gospels, April 21, 1964: *AAS* 56 (1964) 712–718; *Canon Law Digest* 6:789–797.

2. Congregation of Rites, First Instruction on the Constitution on the Liturgy (*Inter Oecumenici*), September 26, 1964: *AAS* 56 (1964) 877–900; *The Pope Speaks* 10 (1965) 186–200.

3. Consilium, Statement on Unauthorized Experiments, June 15, 1965: *Notitiae* 1 (1965) 145.

4. Consilium, First Letter to Presidents of Conferences of Bishops, June 30, 1965: *Notitiae* 1 (1965) 257–264.

5. Encyclical Letter on the Doctrine and Cult of the Eucharist (*Mysterium fidei*), September 3, 1965: *AAS* 57 (1965) 753–774; *The Pope Speaks* 10 (1965) 309–328.

6. Congregation of Seminaries and Universities, Instruction on Liturgical Training of Seminarians, December 25, 1965, and January 14, 1966.

7. Consilium, Letter on Guidelines for Liturgical Reform, January 25, 1966: *Notitiae* 2 (1966) 157–161.

8. Congregation of Rites, Clarification on Liturgical Renewal, December 29, 1966: *Notitiae* 3 (1967) 37–38; *The Pope Speaks* 12 (1967) 30–33.

9. Congregation of Rites, Second Instruction on the Constitution on the Liturgy (*Tres abhinc annos*), May 4, 1967: *AAS* 59 (1967) 442–448; *The Pope Speaks* 12 (1967) 244–249.

10. Congregation of Rites, Instruction on the Eucharistic Mystery (*Eucharisticum mysterium*), May 25, 1967: *AAS* 59 (1967) 539–573; *The Pope Speaks* 12 (1967) 211–236.

11. Consilium, Letter on Questions about Liturgical Renewal, June 21, 1967: *Notitiae* 3 (1967) 289–296.

12. Apostolic Letter on the Revision of Beatification and Canonization Processes (*Processus de causis*), March 19, 1969: *AAS* 61 (1969) 149–153.

13. Congregation of Rites, Third Instruction on the Constitution on the Liturgy (*Liturgicae instaurationes*), September 5, 1970: *AAS* 62 (1970) 692–704; A Flannery (ed.), *Vatican Council II: The Conciliar and Post Conciliar Documents* 209–221.

14. Congregation for the Discipline of the Sacraments, Instruction on Sacramental Communion (*Immensae caritatis*), January 29, 1973: *AAS* 65 (1973) 264–271; Bishops' Committee on the Liturgy, *Study Text I* (1973) 3–10.

15. Congregation for the Doctrine of the Faith, Statement Defending the Church Doctrine Against Some Present-day Errors (*Mysterium Ecclesiae*), June 24, 1973: *AAS* 65 (1973) 396–408; *Catholic Mind* 71 (October 1973) 54–64.

16. Congregation for the Doctrine of the Faith, Clarification on Sacramental Forms and Their Approbation, January 25, 1974: *AAS* 66 (1974) 661; *Canon Law Digest* 8:72–73.

17. Letter of Pope Paul VI, Written to the Benedictine Congregation of Solesmes on the Centenary of the Death of Dom Guéranger, January 20, 1975: *Notitiae* 11 (1975) 170–172.

18. Address of Pope Paul VI to the Consistory, on Fidelity to the Council, May 24, 1976: *AAS* 68 (1976) 369–378; *The Pope Speaks* 21 (1976) 204–212.

19. Letter of Pope Paul VI to Archbishop Lefebvre, October 11, 1976: *Origins* 6 (1976/1977) 416–420.

20. Encyclical Letter of Pope John Paul II on the Redeemer of Man (*Redemptor hominis*), March 4, 1979: *Origins* 8 (1979) 625–644.

21. Apostolic Constitution of Pope John Paul II promulgating the New Typical Vulgate Edition of the Bible (*Scripturarum thesaurus*), April 25, 1979: *Notitiae* 15 (1979) 233–235.

22. Congregation for the Doctrine of the Faith, Letter on Certain Questions Concerning Eschatology, May 17, 1979: *Origins* 9 (1979) 131–133.

23. Congregation for Catholic Education, Instruction on Liturgical Education and Formation of Seminarians, June 3, 1979: *Notitiae* 15 (1979) 526–565.

IV. Norms for Translations and Publication
    of Liturgical Texts and Books

1. Consilium, Letter on Using Only One Vernacular Version, October 16, 1964: *Notitiae* 1 (1965) 195–196.

2. Congregation of Rites, Instruction on Proper Masses and Offices, June 1, 1965; June 2, 1965: *Notitiae* 1 (1965) 197–198.

3. Consilium, Instruction on Translations for Celebrations with the People, January 25, 1969: *Notitiae* 5 (1969) 3–12.

4. Congregation of Rites, Decree on the Publication of Liturgical Books, January 27, 1969.

5. Consilium, Statement on Provisional Texts, January 1969.

6. Congregation for Divine Worship, Statement on the Integrity of Vernacular Texts, September 15, 1969: *Notitiae* 5 (1969) 333–334.

7. Congregation for Divine Worship, Clarification on Using Only One Vernacular Version, February 6, 1970: *Notitiae* 6 (1970) 84–85.

8. Congregation for Divine Worship, Letter on Liturgical Book Royalties, February 25, 1970.

9. Congregation for Divine Worship, Statement on Authorship and Copyright, May 15, 1970: *Notitiae* 6 (1970) 153.

10. Congregation for Divine Worship, Statement on *ad interim* Texts, November 11, 1971: *Notitiae* 7 (1971) 379–383.

11. Congregation for Divine Worship, Letter on Norms for Translating Liturgical Books, October 25, 1973: *AAS* 66 (1974) 98–99; *Canon Law Digest* 8:67–69.

12. Congregation for the Doctrine of the Faith, Decree on New Norms for Publication of Liturgical Books, March 19, 1975: *AAS* 67 (1975) 281–284; *Canon Law Digest* 8:991–996.

13. Congregation for Divine Worship, Letter on the Use of Dialects in the Liturgy, June 5, 1976: *Notitiae* 12 (1976) 300–302; *Newsletter of the Bishops' Committee on the Liturgy* 13 (1977) 49–50.

V. Reform of the Roman Calendar

1. Congregation of Rites, Change in the Date for the Feast of St. Joseph, May 13, 1966: *AAS* 58 (1966) 529.

2. Apostolic Letter on Norms for the Liturgical Year and the New General Roman Calendar, February 14, 1969: *AAS* 61 (1969) 222–226; *The Pope Speaks* 14 (1969) 181–184.

3. Congregation of Rites, Decree on the Revision of the Roman Calendar, March 21, 1969: *Notitiae* 5 (1969) 163–164.

4. Congregation for Divine Worship, Instruction on *ad interim* Local Calendars, June 29, 1969: *Notitiae* 5 (1969) 283.

5. Congregation for Divine Worship, Instruction on Local Calendars and Mass Propers, June 24, 1970: *AAS* 62 (1970) 651–663; *L'Osservatore Romano* (English edition), September 3, 1970, 3–4, 6.

6. Congregation for Divine Worship, Feast of the Immaculate Conception and the Second Sunday of Advent, 1974, January 20, 1973: *Notitiae* 9 (1973) 71.

7. Congregation for Divine Worship, Letter on Local Calendars and Mass Propers, February 1974: *Notitiae* 10 (1974) 87–88.

8. Secretariat for Christian Unity, Letter on a Possible Common Date for Easter, May 18, 1975: *Canon Law Digest* 8:86–88.

9. Congregation for Sacraments and Divine Worship on Concurrence of All Saints and All Souls Days in 1975, October 29, 1975: *Notitiae* 11 (1975) 349; *Canon Law Digest* 8:868.

10. Secretariat for Christian Unity, Letter on the Progress Toward a Common Date for Easter, March 15, 1977: *Notitiae* 13 (1977) 201–202; *Canon Law Digest* 8:91–93.

11. Congregation for Sacraments and Divine Worship, Transfer of the Feast of the Baptism of the Lord, October 7, 1977: *Notitiae* 13 (1977) 477–479; *Canon Law Digest* 8:93–94.
12. Congregation for Sacraments and Divine Worship, Norms for Revised Local Calendars, December 1977: *Notitiae* 13 (1977) 557–558.
13. Apostolic Letter of Pope John Paul II, Optional Memorial of St. Stanislaus Changed to Obligatory Memorial, May 8, 1979.
14. Congregation for the Sacraments and Divine Worship, Memorial of St. Stanislaus, May 29, 1979.

VI. THE ROMAN MISSAL (1963–1968)

1. Congregation of Rites, Decree on Prayer to the Holy Spirit, September 24, 1963: AAS 55 (1963) 838.
2. Congregation of the Holy Office, Decree on the Eucharistic Fast, January 10, 1964: AAS 56 (1964) 212.
3. Congregation of Rites, Decree on New Formula at Communion, April 25, 1964: AAS 56 (1964) 337–338.
4. Congregation of Rites, Decree on the Commemoration of Pope Paul VI's Anniversary at Mass, May 9, 1964: *L'Osservatore Romano*, May 10, 1964, 2; *Canon Law Digest* 6:73.
5. Congregation of the Council, Fulfillment of Sunday Mass Obligation on Saturday, June 12, 1964; June 16, 1964: Vatican Radio; *Canon Law Digest* 6:670–672.
6. Sacred Apostolic Penitentiary, Papal Blessing at First Mass by Newly Ordained Priest, November 5, 1964: AAS 56 (1964) 953; *Canon Law Digest* 6:569.
7. Concession by Pope Paul VI Concerning Eucharistic Fast, November 21, 1964: AAS 56 (1964) 953.
8. Congregation of Rites, Decree Promulgating a Simple Kyriale, December 14, 1964: AAS 57 (1965) 407; *Canon Law Digest* 6:102.
9. Congregation of Rites, Decree Concerning Chants for the Roman Missal and for Concelebration, December 14, 1964: AAS (1965) 408; *Canon Law Digest* 57 (1965) 408.
10. Consilium, on the Prayer of the Faithful or Common Prayer, January 13, 1965.
11. Congregation of Rites, on Revisions for the Order of Mass, January 27, 1965: AAS 57 (1965) 408–409.
12. Congregation of Rites, on Concelebration and Communion under Both Kinds, March 7, 1965: AAS 57 (1965) 410–412.
13. Congregation of Rites, on Changes in the Order of Holy Week, March 7, 1965: AAS 57 (1965) 412–413.
14. Congregation of Rites, on Reading the Passion by Non-deacons, March 25, 1965: AAS 57 (1965) 413–414.
15. Congregation for Extraordinary Ecclesiastical Affairs, on Lay Reli-

gious Distributing Communion, April 24, 1965: *Canon Law Digest* 6:560–561.

16. Secretariat of State, on Prefaces in the Vernacular, April 27, 1965: *Notitiae* 1 (1965) 149.

17. Congregation of Rites, on Proper Mass for the Feast of St. Benedict, May 26, 1965: *Notitiae* 1 (1965) 157.

18. Congregation of the Council, on the Eucharistic Fast and the Catechism of St. Pius X, June 18, 1965: *AAS* 57 (1965) 666.

19. Letter of Pope Paul VI, on the Blessed Sacrament, July 19, 1965: *AAS* 57 (1965) 719–721.

20. Congregation of Rites, on Texts of Anticipated Sunday or Holy Day Mass, September 25, 1965: *Notitiae* 2 (1966) 14.

21. Congregation of the Council, on Anticipated Sunday or Holy Day, October 19, 1965: *Canon Law Digest* 6:674.

22. Consilium, on the Use of Sign Language at Mass, December 10, 1965: *Canon Law Digest* 6:552–553.

23. Consilium, on Supplementary Weekday Biblical Readings, January 1966: *Notitiae* 2 (1966) 6–7.

24. Congregation of Rites, on Vestments for Reading the Gospel, January 12, 1966: *Notitiae* 2 (1966) 265–266.

25. Congregation of the Council, on Masses for Tourists, March 19, 1966: *Notitiae* 2 (1966) 185–189.

26. Consilium, Fascicle on the Prayer of the Faithful, April 17, 1966.

27. Congregation of Rites, on Changes in the Order of Mass, May 18, 1967: *Notitiae* 3 (1967) 195–211.

28. Consilium, on Translations of the Roman Canon, August 10, 1967: *Notitiae* 3 (1967) 326–327.

29. Congregation of Rites, on the Simple Gradual for Small Churches, September 3, 1967: *Notitiae* 3 (1967) 311.

30. Consilium, on Translations of the Simple Gradual, January 23, 1968: *Notitiae* 4 (1968) 10.

31. Congregation of Rites, on New Eucharistic Prayers and Prefaces, May 23, 1968: *Notitiae* 4 (1968) 156.

32. Consilium, on the Catechesis of the New Eucharistic Prayers, June 2, 1968: *Notitiae* 4 (1968) 148–155.

33. Consilium, Letter Concerning New Eucharistic Prayers, June 2, 1968: *Notitiae* 4 (1968) 146–148.

34. Consilium, on Translations of the New Eucharistic Prayers, November 6, 1968: *Notitiae* 4 (1968) 356.

VII. THE NEW ROMAN MISSAL (1969–1979)

1. Congregation of Rites, General Instruction of the Roman Missal, April 3, 1969.

2. Apostolic Constitution on the New Roman Missal (*Missale Romanum*),

April 3, 1969: *AAS* 61 (1969) 217–222; *The Pope Speaks* 14 (1969) 165–169.

3. Congregation of Rites, on the Promulgation of the New Roman Missal, April 6, 1969: *Notitiae* 5 (1969) 147.

4. Consilium, on the Adaptation of the Liturgy to India, April 25, 1969: *Notitiae* 5 (1969) 365–366.

5. Congregation for Divine Worship, on Masses for Special Groups, May 15, 1969: *AAS* 61 (1969) 806–811; *The Furrow* 21 (1970) 327–331.

6. Congregation for Divine Worship, Promulgation of the New Mass Lectionary, May 25, 1969: *AAS* 61 (1969) 548–549.

7. Congregation for Divine Worship, General Introduction to the New Mass Lectionary, May 25, 1969: *Notitiae* 5 (1969) 240–255.

8. Congregation for Divine Worship, Instruction on the Manner of Distributing Holy Communion, May 29, 1969: *AAS* 61 (1969) 541–545.

9. Congregation for Divine Worship, Letter on Distributing Holy Communion in the Hand, May 29, 1969: *AAS* 61 (1969) 546–547.

10. Congregation for Divine Worship, on Lay Persons Distributing Holy Communion, June 25, 1969: *Canon Law Digest* 7:650–651.

11. Congregation for Catholic Education, on Weekday Bination, July 24, 1969: *Canon Law Digest* 7:616.

12. Congregation for Divine Worship, Instruction on the New Mass Lectionary, July 25, 1969: *Notitiae* 5 (1969) 238–239.

13. Congregation for Divine Worship, Letter on New Norms for the Roman Missal, November 10, 1969: *Notitiae* 5 (1969) 442–443.

14. Congregation for Divine Worship, Declaration on the General Instruction, November 18, 1969: *Notitiae* 5 (1969) 417–418.

15. Address of Pope Paul VI on the New Order of Mass, November 19, 1969: *AAS* 61 (1969) 777–780; *The Pope Speaks* 14 (1969) 326–332.

16. Congregation for Divine Worship, on Renewal of Priestly Promises at the Chrism Masses, March 6, 1970: *Notitiae* 6 (1970) 87–89.

17. Congregation for Divine Worship, on the New Edition of the Roman Missal, March 26, 1970: *AAS* 62 (1970) 554; *Canon Law Digest* 7:632.

18. Congregation for Divine Worship, Instruction on Communion under Both Kinds, June 29, 1970: *AAS* 62 (1970) 664–666; *The Pope Speaks* 15 (1970) 245–248.

19. Congregation for the Clergy, on Mass for the People, July 25, 1970: *AAS* 63 (1971) 943–944.

20. Congregation for Divine Worship, on the New Latin Lectionary, September 30, 1970: *AAS* 63 (1971) 710.

21. Congregation for Divine Worship, on the Small Missal, October 18, 1970.

22. Congregation for Divine Worship, Notification about the Roman Missal, Liturgy of the Hours, and Calendar, June 14, 1971: *AAS* 63 (1971) 712–715; *Canon Law Digest* 7:54–57.

23. Secretariat of State, on the Application of Masses for the Donor's Intention, November 29, 1971: *AAS* 63 (1971) 841.

24. Congregation for the Doctrine of the Faith, on Fragments of the Host, May 2, 1972: *Notitiae* 8 (1972) 227; *Canon Law Digest* 7:635.

25. Secretariat for Christian Unity, on Other Christians and the Eucharist, June 1, 1972: *AAS* 64 (1972) 518–525; *The Furrow* 23 (1972) 501–505.

26. Congregation for Divine Worship, Letter and Instruction on the Order of Chant at Mass, June 24, 1972: *AAS* 65 (1973) 274.

27. Congregation for Divine Worship, on Concelebration, August 7, 1972: *AAS* 64 (1972) 561–563; *Canon Law Digest* 7:612–614.

28. Congregation for Divine Worship, on Naming the Bishop in the Eucharistic Prayer, October 9, 1972: *AAS* 64 (1972) 692–694; *Canon Law Digest* 7:59–60.

29. Congregation for Divine Worship, on Changes in the General Instruction for the Roman Missal, December 23, 1972: *Notitiae* 9 (1973) 34–38.

30. Congregation for the Discipline of the Sacraments, Instruction on Greater Access to Sacramental Communion, January 29, 1973: *AAS* 65 (1973) 264 – 271; Bishops' Committee on the Liturgy, *Study Texts I* (1973) 3–10.

31. Congregation for Divine Worship, on New Vestment for Mass, March 15, 1973: *Notitiae* 8 (1973) 96–98.

32. Congregation for Divine Worship, Letter on the Eucharistic Prayers, April 27, 1973: *AAS* 65 (1973) 340–347.

33. Congregation for Divine Worship, Directory for Masses with Children, November 1, 1973: *AAS* 66 (1974) 30–46.

34. Congregation for the Clergy, Letter on Preaching by Lay Persons, November 20, 1973: *Canon Law Digest* 8:941–944.

35. Apostolic Letter of Pope Paul VI, on Mass Stipends, June 13, 1974: *AAS* 66 (1974) 308–311; *Canon Law Digest* 8:530–533.

36. Congregation for Divine Worship, on the Use of the Roman Missal, October 28, 1974: *Notitiae* 10 (1974) 353.

37. Congregation for Divine Worship, on Eucharistic Prayers for Masses with Children and for Masses of Reconciliation, November 1, 1974: *Notitiae* 11 (1975) 4–6.

38. Congregation for Divine Worship, Letter on Vernacular in the Liturgy, June 5, 1976: *Notitiae* 12 (1976) 300–302.

39. Congregation for the Doctrine of the Faith, on Celebration of Public Masses for Deceased Non-Catholics, June 11, 1976: *AAS* 68 (1976) 621–622.

40. Congregation for Divine Worship, on Mass for Peace, November 24, 1977: *Notitiae* 13 (1977) 609; *Canon Law Digest* 8:94–95.

41. Congregation for Sacraments and Divine Worship, Letter Concerning

Eucharistic Prayers in Masses for Children and Masses of Reconciliation: *Notitiae* 13 (1977) 555–556; *Canon Law Digest* 8:95–97.

VIII. THE LITURGY OF THE HOURS

1. Congregation of Rites, on the Vernacular in the Divine Office, January 9, 1965: *Commentarium pro Religiosis* 44 (1965) 206–207; *Canon Law Digest* 6:501.

2. Consilium, on a Dispensation from the Hour of Prime, August 22, 1965: *Commentarium pro Religiosis* 44 (1965) 297; *Canon Law Digest* 6:114.

3. Congregation of Rites, Instruction on the Language to be Used in the Divine Office and Mass for Religious, November 23, 1965: *AAS* 57 (1965) 1010–1013; *Canon Law Digest* 6:117–120.

4. Apostolic Penitentiary, on Indulgence for Prayer before Office, January 31, 1966: *AAS* 58 (1966) 332.

5. Apostolic Letter of Pope Paul VI to Clerical Institutes Bound by Choir (*Sacrificium laudis*), August 15, 1966: *Notitiae* 2 (1966) 252–255.

6. Congregation for Religious, on the Divine Office in the Vernacular, September 20, 1967: *Commentarium pro Religiosis* 49 (1968) 64; *Canon Law Digest* 7:101–102.

7. Congregation for Religious, on the Divine Office in the Vernacular, March 21, 1969: *Commentarium pro Religiosis* 51 (1970) 182–183; *Canon Law Digest* 7:546–547.

8. Congregation for Religious and Secular Institutes, on Reciting the Divine Office in Common, May 31, 1969: *Commentarium pro Religiosis* 51 (1970) 183–184; *Canon Law Digest* 7:547–548.

9. Apostolic Constitution of Pope Paul VI, on the Restored Divine Office (*Laudis canticum*), November 1, 1970: *AAS* 63 (1971) 527–535; *The Pope Speaks* 16 (1971) 129–135.

10. Congregation for Divine Worship, Announcement of the General Instruction on the Liturgy of the Hours, February 2, 1971.

11. Congregation for Divine Worship, General Instruction on the Liturgy of the Hours, February 2, 1971.

12. Congregation for Divine Worship, on the Publication of the Liturgy of the Hours, April 11, 1971: *AAS* 63 (1971) 712.

13. Congregation for the Clergy, Letter on the Historico-Artistic Patrimony of the Church, April 11, 1971: *AAS* 63 (1971) 315–317.

14. Congregation for Divine Worship, Norms for Thursday, Friday, and Saturday of Holy Week and Easter Octave, March 3, 1972: *Notitiae* 8 (1972) 96–99.

15. Congregation for the Doctrine of the Faith, on an Optional Patristic Lectionary, July 9, 1972: *Canon Law Digest* 7:108–109.

16. Congregation for Divine Worship, on an Optional Patristic Lectionary, October 1972: *Notitiae* 8 (1972) 249–250.

17.   Congregation for the Sacraments and Divine Worship, Approval of the Treasury of the Monastic Office for the Confederation of Benedictines, February 10, 1977: *Notitiae* 13 (1977) 157–191.

IX. THE ROMAN PONTIFICAL

1.   Congregation of Rites, on the Use of the Vernacular in the Ordination Rite, July 17, 1965: *Ephemerides Liturgicae* 79 (1965) 417–419; *Canon Law Digest* 6:587–588.

2.   Congregation of Rites, on Concelebration of an Ordination Mass, November 26, 1965: *Notitiae* 2 (1966) 184; *Canon Law Digest* 6:589.

3.   Apostolic Letter of Pope Paul VI, on the Restoration of a Permanent Diaconate (*Sacrum diaconatus ordinem*), June 18, 1967: *AAS* 59 (1967) 697–704; *The Pope Speaks* 12 (1967) 237–243.

4.   Apostolic Constitution of Pope Paul VI, on a New Rite of Ordination for Deacons, Priests, and Bishops: June 18, 1968: *AAS* 60 (1968) 369–373; *L'Osservatore Romano* (English edition), June 27, 1968, 2, 5.

5.   Congregation of Rites, on the New Ordination Rite, August 15, 1968: *Ephemerides Liturgicae* 83 (1969) 4; *Canon Law Digest* 7:704–705.

6.   Congregation of Sacraments, on a Temporary Deacon Assisting at Marriage, August 30, 1968: *Canon Law Digest* 7:689.

7.   Congregation for the Evangelization of Peoples, on Blessing of Holy Oils on Wednesday of Holy Week, January 14, 1969: *Canon Law Digest* 7:35–36.

8.   Congregation for Divine Worship, on the New Rite of Consecration of Virgins, May 31, 1970: *AAS* 62 (1970) 650.

9.   Pontifical Commission for Interpreting Decrees of the Council, on General Delegation for Parochial Deacon, July 19, 1970: *AAS* (1970) 571; *Canon Law Digest* 7:752.

10.   Congregation for Divine Worship, on the Order of Blessing an Abbot and Abbess, November 9, 1970: *AAS* 63 (1971) 710–711.

11.   Congregation for Divine Worship, on Blessing of Oils and Consecration of Chrism, December 3, 1970: *AAS* 63 (1971) 711.

12.   Congregation for the Doctrine of the Faith, on Procedures for the Return to the Lay State, January 13, 1971: *AAS* 63 (1971) 303–308; *Canon Law Digest* 7:110–121.

13.   Apostolic Constitution of Pope Paul VI, on Confirmation (*Divinae consortium naturae*), August 15, 1971: *AAS* 63 (1971) 657–664; *The Pope Speaks* 16 (1971) 223–228.

14.   Congregation for Divine Worship, on the New Order for Confirmation, August 22, 1971: *AAS* 64 (1972) 77.

15.   Pontifical Commission for Interpreting Decrees of the Council, on the Imposition of Hands in Confirmation, June 9, 1972: *AAS* 64 (1972) 526; *Canon Law Digest* 7:611.

16. Apostolic Letter of Pope Paul VI, on Tonsure, Minor Orders, and Subdiaconate (*Ministeria quaedam*), August 15, 1972: *AAS* 64 (1972) 529–534; *The Furrow* 23 (1972) 751–755.

17. Apostolic Letter of Pope Paul VI, on Norms for the Diaconate (*Ad pascendum*), August 15, 1972: *AAS* 64 (1972) 534–540; *The Furrow* 23 (1972) 747–751.

18. Congregation for Divine Worship, on Rites for Lector and Acolyte, and Admission to Diaconate and Priesthood, December 3, 1972: *AAS* 65 (1973) 274–275.

19. Pontifical Commission for Interpretation of Decrees of the Council, on the Office of Auxiliary Bishop, April 25, 1975: *AAS* 67 (1975) 348.

20. Pontifical Commission for Interpretation of Decrees of the Council, on the Minister of Confirmation, April 25, 1975: *AAS* 67 (1975) 348.

21. Congregation for Divine Worship, on English Formula for Confirmation, May 5, 1975: *Notitiae* 11 (1975) 172; *Canon Law Digest* 8:474–475.

22. Congregation for the Doctrine of the Faith, on Unlawful Ordinations, September 17, 1976: *AAS* 68 (1976) 623; *Canon Law Digest* 8:1216–1217.

23. Congregation for the Doctrine of the Faith, on the Admission of Women to the Priesthood, October 15, 1976: *AAS* 69 (1977) 98–116.

24. Apostolic Letter of Pope Paul VI, on the Status of Abbeys "Nullius Dioeceseos" (*Catholica Ecclesia*), October 23, 1976: *Notitiae* 13 (1977) 3–5.

25. Congregation of Sacraments and Divine Worship, on New Order of Dedication of a Church and Altar, May 29, 1977: *Notitiae* 13 (1977) 364–390.

X. THE ROMAN RITUAL

Christian Initiation

1. Congregation for Divine Worship, on the Order of Baptism of Infants, May 15, 1969: *AAS* 61 (1969) 548.

2. Congregation for Divine Worship, on the Revised Order of Baptism of Infants, July 10, 1969: *AAS* 61 (1969) 549–550.

3. Congregation for the Doctrine of the Faith, on the Baptism of Infants of Non-Catholics, July 13, 1970: *Notitiae* 7 (1971) 64–69; *Canon Law Digest* 7:592–594.

4. Congregation for Divine Worship, on Baptizing the Aged and Infants, August 19, 1970: *Notitiae* 7 (1971) 59–63; *Canon Law Digest* 7:599–603.

5. Congregation for Religious and Secular Institutes, on Lay Religious Administering Baptism, October 12, 1970: *Commentarium pro Religiosis* 52 (1971) 188–189; *Canon Law Digest* 7:591–592.

6. Secretariat for Christian Unity, on Non-Catholic Christian Sponsors,

December 3, 1970: *Notitiae* 7 (1971) 92–93; *Canon Law Digest* 7:597–599.

7. Congregation for Divine Worship, on the Order for Christian Initiation of Adults, January 6, 1972: *AAS* 64 (1972) 252.

8. Congregation for Divine Worship, on a New Edition of the Order for the Baptism of Infants, August 29, 1973: *Notitiae* 9 (1973) 268–272.

9. Congregation for the Sacraments, on the Delegation of the Minister of Confirmation, May 9, 1975: *Canon Law Digest* 8:475–476.

Sacraments of the Sick and Dying

1. Congregation of Rites, on Priests Carrying Oil for the Sick, March 4, 1965: *Commentarium pro Religiosis* 44 (1965) 202–204; *Canon Law Digest* 6:576–577.

2. Congregation of Rites, on Giving Communion in Hospitals, February 14, 1966: *Notitiae* 2 (1966) 328.

3. Congregation of Divine Worship, on the Revised Order of Blessing Holy Oils, December 3, 1970: *AAS* 63 (1971) 711; *Canon Law Digest* 7:590–591.

4. Apostolic Constitution of Pope Paul VI, on the Anointing of the Sick (*Sacram Unctionem infirmorum*), November 30, 1972: *AAS* 65 (1973) 5–9; *Canon Law Digest* 7:682–686.

5. Congregation for Divine Worship, on Anointing and Pastoral Care of the Sick, December 7, 1972: *AAS* 65 (1973) 275; *Canon Law Digest* 7:686–687.

6. Congregation for Divine Worship, on Sacramental Formulas for Confirmation and Anointing of the Sick, n.d.: *Notitiae* 10 (1974) 89–91.

7. Congregation for Divine Worship, on the Extension of the Suspension of Law Relative to the Order of Anointing of the Sick, January 10, 1974: *AAS* 66 (1974) 100; *Canon Law Digest* 8:618–619.

Holy Communion

1. Congregation for Extraordinary Affairs, on Lay Religious as Distributors of Holy Communion, April 24, 1965: *Commentarium pro Religiosis* 45 (1966) 337; *Canon Law Digest* 6:560.

2. Congregation for the Propagation of the Faith, on Lay Religious as Distributors of Holy Communion, May 31, 1966: *Canon Law Digest* 6:560–561.

3. Congregation for Divine Worship, on Holy Communion and Worship of the Eucharist outside of Mass, June 21, 1973: *AAS* 65 (1973) 610; *Canon Law Digest* 8:485–497.

Penance

1. Congregation for the Doctrine of the Faith, on Absolution from Grave

Sin before Communion, July 11, 1968: *Vida Religiosa* 26 (1969) 389; *Canon Law Digest* 7:664.

2. Congregation for Religious and Secular Institutes, on Confession and Religious, December 8, 1970: *AAS* 63 (1971) 318–319; *Canon Law Digest* 7:531–533.

3. Congregation for the Doctrine of the Faith, Pastoral Norms for General Absolution, June 16, 1972: *AAS* 64 (1972) 510–514; *Canon Law Digest* 7:667–672.

4. Congregation for the Doctrine of the Faith, on the Sacrament of Penance, March 23, 1973: *AAS* 65 (1973) 678; *Canon Law Digest* 8:1214.

5. Congregation for the Discipline of the Sacraments, on the Sacrament of Penance before First Communion, May 24, 1973: *AAS* 65 (1973) 410; *Canon Law Digest* 8:563–564.

6. Congregation for the Clergy, on Ending the Experimentation Concerning First Communion and First Confession, June 20, 1973: *Canon Law Digest* 8:565–570.

7. Congregation for Divine Worship, on the Rite of Penance, December 2, 1973: *AAS* 66 (1974) 42–43; *Canon Law Digest* 8:550–552.

8. Address of Pope Paul VI, on the New Order of Penance, April 3, 1974: *Notitiae* 10 (1974) 225–227.

9. Congregation for the Doctrine of the Faith, on General Absolution, January 20, 1978: *Notitiae* 14 (1978) 6–7.

Marriage

1. Congregation for the Doctrine of the Faith, Instruction on Mixed Marriages, March 18, 1966: *AAS* 58 (1966) 235–239; *The Pope Speaks* 11 (1966) 114–118.

2. Congregation for the Oriental Churches, on Marriages between Catholics and Baptized Oriental Non-Catholics, February 22, 1967: *AAS* 59 (1967) 165–166; *The Pope Speaks* 12 (1967) 122–124.

3. Congregation for the Doctrine of the Faith, on Mixed Marriage in a Catholic Church before a Minister, September 3, 1968: *Canon Law Digest* 7:764–765.

4. Congregation of Rites, on New Order of Marriage, March 19, 1969: *Notitiae* 5 (1969) 203; *Canon Law Digest* 7:763.

5. Apostolic Letter of Pope Paul VI, on Norms for Mixed Marriages, March 31, 1970: *AAS* 62 (1970) 257–263; *The Furrow* 21 (1970) 388–394.

6. Congregation for Divine Worship, on Appropriate Music for Weddings, January 1972: *Notitiae* 8 (1972) 25–29.

Christian Burial

1. Congregation of Rites, on Funeral Mass the Evening before Certain

Liturgical Days, October 15, 1965: *Notitiae* 2 (1966) 181; *Canon Law Digest* 6:114.

2. Congregation for the Doctrine of the Faith, on Funeral Services at a Crematory Chapel, July 9, 1966: *Canon Law Digest* 8:851.

3. Congregation for Divine Worship, on the Revised Order for Funerals, August 15, 1969: *Notitiae* 5 (1969) 423–424; *Canon Law Digest* 7:777–778.

4. Congregation for the Doctrine of the Faith, on Ecclesiastical Burial of Manifest Sinners: *AAS* 65 (1973) 500; *Canon Law Digest* 8:864.

5. Congregation for the Doctrine of the Faith, on Public Mass for Deceased Non-Catholic Christians, June 11, 1976: *AAS* 68 (1976) 621–622; *Canon Law Digest* 8:864–866.

Religious Profession

1. Congregation for Divine Worship, on a New Order for Religious Profession, February 2, 1970: *AAS* 62 (1970) 553; *Canon Law Digest* 7:515–516.

2. Congregation for Divine Worship, Norms for Religious Profession, July 15, 1970: *Notitiae* 6 (1970) 114–117; *Canon Law Digest* 7:516–520.

3. Congregation for Divine Worship, on Vernacular Translation of the New Order for Religious Profession, July 15, 1970: *Notitiae* 6 (1970) 317–318; *Canon Law Digest* 7:521–522.

4. Congregation for Divine Worship, on Adaptations of the New Order for Religious Profession, July 15, 1970: *Notitiae* 6 (1970) 318–322; *Canon Law Digest* 7:522–526.

5. Congregation for Religious and Secular Institutes, on Formula of Religious Profession, February 14, 1973: *Notitiae* 11 (1973) 283; *Canon Law Digest* 8:365–366.

XI. RELIGIOUS DEVOTIONS

1. Apostolic Exhortation of Pope Paul VI, on Prayer and Penance for Christian Renewal, January 15, 1964: *AAS* 56 (1964) 183–188; *The Pope Speaks* 9 (1964) 288–291.

2. Congregation of Rites, on the Invocation of the Holy Spirit, April 25, 1964: *AAS* 56 (1964) 338; *American Ecclesiastical Review* 151 (1964) 55.

3. Apostolic Letter of Pope Paul VI, on Veneration of the Sacred Heart, February 6, 1965: *AAS* 57 (1965) 298–301.

4. Sacred Penitentiary, on Indulgences Attached to Objects with Blessing, March 6, 1965: *AAS* 57 (1965) 547; *Canon Law Digest* 6:568–569.

5. Announcement by Pope Paul VI, on Jubilee Year, December 7, 1965: *AAS* 57 (1965) 945–951; *Canon Law Digest* 6:243–249.

6. Sacred Penitentiary, on Indulgences on the Occasion of the Jubilee

Year, December 20, 1965: *AAS* 57 (1965) 1018; *Canon Law Digest* 6:251-252.

7. Sacred Penitentiary, on Indulgences on the Occasion of the Jubilee Year, January 6, 1966: *AAS* 58 (1966) 105; *Canon Law Digest* 6:255-256.

8. Apostolic Constitution of Pope Paul VI, on Penitential Discipline (*Paenitemini*), February 17, 1966: *AAS* 58 (1966) 177-198; *The Pope Speaks* 11 (1966) 362-371.

9. Apostolic Constitution of Pope Paul VI, on the Jubilee Year, May 3, 1966: *AAS* 58 (1966) 337-341.

10. Encyclical Letter of Pope Paul VI, on the Rosary, September 15, 1966: *AAS* 58 (1966) 745-749.

11. Apostolic Constitution of Pope Paul VI, on Indulgences, January 1, 1967: *AAS* 59 (1967) 9-24; *The Pope Speaks* 12 (1967) 124-135.

12. Congregation of the Council, on Days of Penance, February 24, 1967: *AAS* 59 (1967) 229.

13. Apostolic Address of Pope Paul VI, on Our Lady, May 13, 1967: *AAS* 59 (1967) 465-475.

14. Sacred Penitentiary, on Papal Blessing with Indulgences for Jubilee Year, June 28, 1967: *AAS* 59 (1967) 764.

15. Congregation of Rites, on Formulas for General Absolution for Religious Orders, April 9, 1968: *Commentarium pro Religiosis* 51 (1970) 82-83; *Canon Law Digest* 7:26-27.

16. Sacred Penitentiary, on New Edition of Treasury of Indulgences, June 29, 1968: *AAS* 60 (1968) 413-414.

17. Sacred Penitentiary, on Norms for Granting Indulgences, n.d.: *AAS* 60 (1968) 414-419.

18. Congregation of Rites, on Celebrations for the Recently Canonized or Beatified, September 12, 1968: *AAS* 60 (1968) 602; *Canon Law Digest* 7:32-33.

19. Apostolic Address of Pope Paul VI, on the Rosary, October 7, 1969: *AAS* 61 (1969) 137-149; *The Pope Speaks* 14 (1969/1970) 247-251.

20. Vicariate of Rome, Instruction on Forty Hours, May 28, 1970: *Notitiae* 6 (1970) 257-262.

21. Congregation for Divine Worship, on the Litany of the Saints, n.d.: *Notitiae* 6 (1970) 375.

22. Congregation for Divine Worship, on Norms for Patron Saints and Images of Mary, March 19, 1973: *AAS* 65 (1973) 276-279; *Canon Law Digest* 8:912-916.

23. Congregation for Divine Worship, on Coronation of an Image of Mary, March 25, 1973: *AAS* 65 (1973) 280-281; *Canon Law Digest* 8:908-909.

24. Apostolic Exhortation of Pope Paul VI, on Devotion to Mary, February 11, 1974: *Notitiae* 10 (1974) 153-157.

25. Commission for the Interpretation of the Decrees of the Second Vatican

Council, on Faculties of Deacons Relative to Sacramentals and Blessings, November 13, 1974: *AAS* 66 (1974) 667; *Canon Law Digest* 8:849.

26. Allocution of Pope Paul VI, on the Feast of the Presentation of the Lord and Dedication to Christ, February 2, 1977: *Notitiae* 13 (1977) 49–50.

XII. OTHER DOCUMENTS OF LITURGICAL IMPLEMENTATION

Music and Dance in the Liturgy

1. Letter of Pope Paul VI to the International Association for Sacred Music, November 22, 1963: *AAS* 56 (1964) 231–234.
2. Congregation of Rites, on Music in the Liturgy, March 5, 1967: *AAS* 59 (1967) 300–320; *The Pope Speaks* 12 (1967) 173–186.
3. Allocution of Pope Paul VI to the Saint Cecilia Society, September 18, 1968: *AAS* 60 (1968) 711–715; *The Pope Speaks* 13 (1968/1969) 347–351.
4. Allocution of Pope Paul VI to the International Association for Sacred Music, October 12, 1973: *Notitiae* 10 (1974) 3–4; *The Pope Speaks* 18 (1973) 262–264.
5. Congregation for Divine Worship, Letter accompanying *Jubilate Deo*, Easter 1974: *Notitiae* 10 (1974) 123–126.
6. Congregation for Divine Worship, on Melodic Musical Formulas in Missals, n.d.: *Notitiae* 11 (1975) 129–132.
7. Congregation for Divine Worship, on Dance in the Liturgy, n.d.: *Notitiae* 11 (1975) 202–205.

Church Building

1. Apostolic Letter of Pope Paul VI, on Pontifical Altars in Roman Patriarchal Basilicas, February 8, 1966: *AAS* 58 (1966) 119–122; *Canon Law Digest* 6:555–557.
2. Congregation of Rites, on Minor Basilicas, June 6, 1968: *AAS* 60 (1968) 536–539; *Canon Law Digest* 7:28–33.
3. Congregation of the Council, on Historical and Artistic Patrimony, April 11, 1971: *AAS* 63 (1971) 315–317.

Insignia

1. Apostolic Letter of Pope Paul VI, on the Papal Household, March 28, 1968: *AAS* 60 (1968) 305–315; *Canon Law Digest* 7:314–322.
2. Congregation of Rites, on Pontifical Insignia and Rites, June 21, 1968: *AAS* 60 (1968) 406–412; *Canon Law Digest* 7:376–382.
3. Apostolic Letter of Pope Paul VI, on Revision of Pontifical Insignia, June 21, 1968: *AAS* 60 (1968) 374–377; *Canon Law Digest* 7:373–376.

4. Secretariat of State, on Dress, Titles and Coats of Arms, March 31, 1969: *AAS* 61 (1969) 334–340; *Canon Law Digest* 7:137–143.
5. Congregation for the Clergy, on Reform of Choir Vesture, October 30, 1970: *Notitiae* 8 (1972) 36–37; *Canon Law Digest* 7:382–383.
6. Apostolic Letter of Pope Paul VI, on the Concession of the Pallium, May 11, 1978: *AAS* 70 (1978) 441–442.

XIII. IMPLEMENTATION OF RELATED CONCILIAR DOCUMENTS

Decree on Ecumenism

1. Statement by Pope Paul VI and Archbishop Michael Ramsey, March 24, 1966: *AAS* 58 (1966) 286–287; *The Pope Speaks* 11 (1966) 166.
2. Secretariat for Christian Unity, Ecumenical Directory I, May 14, 1967: *AAS* 59 (1967) 574–592; *The Pope Speaks* 12 (1967) 250–263.
3. Statement by Pope Paul VI and Patriarch Athenagoras I, October 28, 1967: *AAS* 59 (1967) 1054–1055.
4. Secretariat for Christian Unity, on Common Celebration of the Eucharist, January 7, 1970: *AAS* 62 (1970) 184–188; *Canon Law Digest* 7:796–801.
5. Secretariat for Christian Unity, Ecumenical Directory II, April 16, 1970: *AAS* 62 (1970) 705–724; *Canon Law Digest* 7:801–819.
6. Statement by Pope Paul VI and Patriarch Vaskin I, May 12, 1970: *AAS* 62 (1970) 416–417; *The Pope Speaks* 15 (1970) 155–156.
7. Statement by Pope Paul VI and Patriarch Mar Ignatius Jacobus III, October 27, 1971: *AAS* 63 (1971) 814–815.
8. Secretariat for Christian Unity, on Admitting Other Christians to the Eucharist, June 1, 1972: *AAS* 64 (1972) 518–525; *Canon Law Digest* 7:583–590.
9. Commission for Jewish-Catholic Dialogue, on Christian and Jewish Liturgies, December 1, 1974: *AAS* 67 (1975) 73–79; *The Pope Speaks* 19 (1974) 352–357.
10. Secretariat for Christian Unity, on Ecumenical Collaboration, February 22, 1975: *Canon Law Digest* 8:870–872.

Ministerial Formation and Religious Training and Life

1. Apostolic Letter of Pope Paul VI, on Fulfilling the Decrees of the Second Vatican Council, August 6, 1966: *AAS* 58 (1966) 757–758; *The Pope Speaks* 11 (1966) 376–400.
2. Congregation for Religious and Secular Institutes, on Contemplative Life, August 15, 1969: *AAS* 61 (1969) 674–690; *The Pope Speaks* 14 (1969) 268–282.
3. Congregation for the Clergy, on the Education and Formation of the Clergy, November 4, 1969: *AAS* 62 (1970) 123–134; *The Pope Speaks* 15 (1970) 75–83.

4. Apostolic Exhortation of Pope Paul VI, on the Renewal of Religious Life, June 29, 1971: *AAS* 63 (1971) 497–526.
5. Declaration of Pope Paul VI, on the Ministerial Priesthood, November 30, 1971: *AAS* 63 (1971) 898–992; *The Pope Speaks* 16 (1971) 359–376.
6. Congregation for Bishops, on the Pastoral Ministry of Bishops, February 22, 1973: Issued in Latin and various languages by the Vatican Press.

Catechetics

1. Congregation for the Clergy, General Catechetical Directory, April 11, 1971: *AAS* 64 (1972) 97–176.
2. Commission for Social Communication Media, on Fulfilling the Decrees of the Council, May 23, 1971: *AAS* 63 (1971) 593–656; *The Pope Speaks* 16 (1971) 245–283.
3. Pope John Paul II, Apostolic Exhortation on Catechetics (*Catechesi tradendae*), October 16, 1979: *Origins* 9 (1979) 329–348.

Pastoral Care of Migrants

1. Congregation for Bishops, General Directory for Ministry to Tourists, April 30, 1969: *AAS* 61 (1969) 360–384; *The Pope Speaks* 14 (1969) 380–397.
2. Congregation for Bishops, Pastoral Care of Migrants, August 22, 1969: *AAS* 61 (1969) 614–643.
3. Apostolic Letter of Pope Paul VI, on Pontifical Commission for Migrants and Travelers, March 19, 1970: *AAS* 62 (1970) 193–197.

Faculties and Privileges

1. Apostolic Letter of Pope Paul VI, on Faculties of Local Ordinaries, November 30, 1963: *AAS* 56 (1964) 5–12; *Canon Law Digest* 6:370–378.
2. Secretariat of State, on Faculties of Religious Superiors of Clerical Exempt Institutes, November 6, 1964: *AAS* 59 (1967) 374–378; *Canon Law Digest* 6:147–152.
3. Congregation for Religious and Secular Institutes, May 31, 1966: *AAS* 59 (1967) 362–364; *Canon Law Digest* 6:153–156.
4. Congregation for Bishops, on Quinquennial Faculties of Local Ordinaries, January 1, 1968: *Commentarium pro Religiosis* 51 (1970) 179–180; *Canon Law Digest* 7:74–75.
5. Congregation for the Eastern Churches, on Faculties of Oriental Religious, June 27, 1972: *AAS* 64 (1972) 738–743; *Canon Law Digest* 7:19–24.
6. Congregation for the Evangelization of Peoples, on the Role of Women in Evangelization, November 15, 1975: *Documentation Catholique* 73 (1976) 612–619.

Appendix 2

SUPPLEMENTAL BIBLIOGRAPHY

The Liturgical Movement from 1946 until the Second Vatican Council

L. Brinkhoff, "Chronicle of the Liturgical Movement," in *Liturgy in Development*, ed. Altong von Geausau (London 1965) 40–67.

A. Bugnini, *Documenta pontificia ad instaurationem liturgicam spectantia*, Vol. I: 1903–1953; Vol. II: 1953–1959 (Rome 1953, 1959).

––––––, "L'opera del Card. Gaetano Cicognani per il rinnovamento liturgico dell' ultimo decennio," *L'Osservatore Romano* (March 5–6, 1962) 2.

A. Frutaz, *La sezione storica della Sacra Congregazione dei Riti: Origini e metodo di lavoro* (Vatican City 1963).

P.-M. Gy, "Esquisse historique de la Constitution 'De Sacra Liturgia'," *La Maison-Dieu*, no. 76 (1963) 7–17.

R. Laurentin, *L'Enjeu du Concile* (Paris 1962).

T. Richstatter, *Liturgical Law: New Style, New Spirit* (Chicago 1977) 27–60.

R. K. Seasoltz, *The New Liturgy: A Documentation 1903–1965* (New York 1966) xv–xli.

The Second Vatican Council and Its General Implementation

W. Barauna (ed.), *Liturgy of Vatican II*, 2 vols. (Chicago 1965).

L. Bouyer, *Liturgy Revived* (Notre Dame, Indiana 1964).

A. Bugnini and C. Braga (eds.), *The Commentary on the Constitution and on the Instruction on the Sacred Liturgy*, trans. V. Mallon (New York 1965).

J. D. Crichton, "The Instruction of September 1964," *Liturgy* 34 (January 1965) 1–8.

––––––, "The Instruction on Church Music," *Liturgy* 36 (July 1967) 57–63.

F. Dell'Oro, "I documenti della riforma liturgica del Vaticano II (1963–1973)," *Rivista Liturgica* 61 (January–February 1974) 102–163.

Enchiridion documentorum instaurationis liturgicae, I (1963–1973), compiled, with an index, by R. Kaczynski (Turin 1976).

G. Fontaine, "Dix ans de réforme liturgique: Une réussite ou un échec?" *Liturgie et Vie Chrétienne* 86 (October–December 1973) 335–361.

J. Gelineau, "Quelques remarques en marge de l'Instruction sur la traduction des textes liturgiques," *La Maison-Dieu*, no. 98 (1969) 156–162.

A. Gignac, "Une réforme qui s'achève ou une réforme qui commence?" *Liturgie et Vie Chrétienne* 86 (October–December 1973) 331–334.

P.-M. Gy, "La troisième instruction pour une juste application de la Constitution conciliaire sur la liturgie," *La Maison-Dieu*, no. 104 (1970) 167–171.

"Instruction on Liturgy: Second Instruction on the Proper Implementation of the Constitution on the Sacred Liturgy (with explanatory notes by Annibale Bugnini)," *Doctrine and Life* 17 (June 1967) 328–340.

P. Jounel, "Implementing the Liturgy Constitution," *Doctrine and Life* 15 (February 1965) 88–103.

_____, "Principles of Liturgical Reform," *Doctrine and Life* 15 (March 1965) 138–155.

_____, "Les principes directeurs de la IIe Instruction sur la liturgie," *La Maison-Dieu*, no. 90 (1967) 17–43.

R. Laurentin, *L'Enjeu du Concile: Bilan de la premiere session* (Paris 1963).

_____, *Bilan de la deuxième session* (Paris 1964).

_____, *Bilan de la troisième session* (Paris 1965).

_____, *Bilan du Concile: Histoire, textes, commentaires avec une chronique de la quatrième session* (Paris 1966).

E. J. Lengeling, *Die Konstitution des Zweiten Vatikanischen Konzils über die heilige Liturgie* (Münster 1964).

P. Levillain, *La mécanique politique de Vatican II: La majorité et l'unanimité dans un Concile* (Paris 1975).

La Maison-Dieu, no. 77 (1964). Commentary on the Constitution on the Sacred Liturgy by J. Gelineau, P.-M. Gy, P. Jounel, A.-M. Roguet and X. Seumois.

La Maison-Dieu, no. 86 (1966): *Les traductions liturgiques: Congrès International.*

G. Martimort, "La réforme liturgique: Le bilan," *Liturgie et Vie Chrétienne* 86 (October–December 1973) 377–394.

J. Megivern (ed.), *Worship and Liturgy* (Wilmington, North Carolina 1978).

A. Milner, "The Instruction on Sacred Music," *Worship* 41 (June–July 1967) 322–333.

F. McManus, *Sacramental Liturgy* (New York 1967).

F. Morrisey, "Ten Years of Liturgical Legislation," *Studia Canonica* 7 (1973) 289–308.

H. Schmidt, *Die Konstitution über die heilige Liturgie: Text-Vorgeschichte-Kommentar* (Freiburg 1965).

C. Vagaggini, "Riflessioni in prospettiva teologica sui dieci anni di riforma liturgica e sulla aporia del problema liturgico in questo momento," *Rivista Liturgica* 61 (January–February 1974) 35–72.

H. Vorgrimler (ed.), *Commentary on the Documents of Vatican II*, Vol. I (New York 1967).

G. Wainwright, "The Risks and Possibilities of Liturgical Reform," *Studia Liturgica* 8 (1971/1972) 65–80.

THE SACRAMENTS

Christian Initiation

A. Aubry, "Le projet du rituel de l'initiation des adultes," *Ephemerides Liturgicae* 88 (1974) 174–191.

Baptism in the New Testament: A Symposium, trans. D. Askew (Baltimore 1964).

Becoming a Catholic Christian: A Symposium on Christian Initiation (New York 1978).

R. Béraudy, "Recherches théologiques autour du rituel baptismal des adultes," *La Maison-L u,* no. 110 (1972) 25–50.

C. Davis, *Sacraments of Initiation: Baptism and Confirmation* (New York 1964).

B. Fischer, "Baptismal Exorcism in the Catholic Baptismal Rites after Vatican II," *Studia Liturgica* 10 (1974) 48–55.

J. Crichton, *Christian Celebration: The Sacraments* (London 1973) 29–113.

J. Fisher, *Christian Initiation. Baptism in the Medieval West* (London 1965).

———, *Christian Initiation. The Reformation Period* (London 1970).

R. Guerrette, "Ecclesiology and Infant Baptism," *Worship* 44 (1970) 433–437.

P.-M. Gy, "Un document de la Congrégation pour la Doctrine de la Foi sur le baptême des petits enfants," *La Maison-Dieu,* no. 104 (1970) 41–45.

———, "The Idea of 'Christian Initiation,'" *Studia Liturgica* 12 (1977) 172–175.

J. Jeremias, *Infant Baptism in the First Four Centuries,* trans. D. Cairns (Philadelphia 1962).

A. Kavanagh, *The Shape of Baptism: The Rite of Christian Initiation.* Studies in the Reformed Rites of the Catholic Church, Vol. I (New York 1978).

B. Kleinheyer, "Le nouveau rituel de la confirmation," *La Maison-Dieu,* no. 110 (1972) 51–71.

G. Lampe, *The Seal of the Spirit: A Study in the Doctrine of Baptism and Confirmation in the New Testament and the Fathers* (London 1967).

P.-A. Liégé, "Le baptême des enfants dans le débat pastoral et theologique," *La Maison-Dieu*, no. 107 (1971) 7–28.

L. Ligier, "Le nouveau rituel du baptême des enfants," *La Maison-Dieu*, no. 98 (1969) 7–31.

―――, *La confirmation* (Paris 1973).

Made, Not Born. New Perspectives on Christian Initiation and the Catechumenate. Ed. Murphy Center for Liturgical Research (Notre Dame, Indiana 1976).

T. Maertens, *Histoire et pastorale du rituel du catéchuménat et du baptême* (Bruges 1962).

La Maison-Dieu, no. 89 (1967): *Le Baptême des petits enfants*. Articles by A.-M. Roguet, L. Lécuyer, L. Villette, J. Von Allmen, F. Favreau, and J. Molin.

La Maison-Dieu, no. 98 (1976): *Le nouveau rituel du baptême des enfants*. Articles by L. Ligier, J. Molin and G. Becquet, and P. Reinhard.

T. Marsh, "Infant Baptism: The Role of the Community," *The Furrow* 22 (January 1971) 4–12.

National Bulletin on Liturgy, 29: *Rite of Baptism for Children* (April 1970) 61–160.

National Bulletin on Liturgy, 64: *Christian Initiation: Into Full Communion* (May–June 1978) 129–192.

B. Neunheuser, *Baptism and Confirmation*, trans. J. Hughes (New York 1964).

R. Redmond, "Infant Baptism: History and Pastoral Problems," *Theological Studies* 30 (1969) 79–89.

A. Ryder, "Parents' Faith and Infant Baptism," *The Clergy Review* 58 (October 1973) 746–759.

R. Schnackenburg, *Baptism in the Thought of St. Paul*, trans. G. Beasley-Murray (Oxford 1964).

A. Stenzel, *Die Taufe: Eine genetische Erklärung der Taufliturgie* (Innsbruck 1958).

J. Wagner (ed.), *Adult Baptism and the Catechumenate*. Concilium 22 (New York 1967).

E. Whitaker (ed.), *Documents of the Baptismal Liturgy* (London 1960).

―――, *The Baptismal Liturgy: An Introduction to Baptism in the Western Church* (London 1965).

G. Winkler, *Das armenische Initiationsrituale. Entwicklungsgeschichtliche und liturgievergleichende Untersuchung der Quellen des 3. bis 10. Jahrhunderts* (Rome 1978).

Reconciliation

Z. Alszeghy and M. Flick, *Il sacramento della riconciliazione* (Turin 1976).

E. Bhaldraithe, "General Absolution in Switzerland," *Doctrine and Life* 27 (June 1977) 3–18.

Bishops' Committee on the Liturgy, *Study Text IV: Rite of Penance* (Washington 1975).

Bishops' Committee on Pastoral Research and Practice, *Guidelines for General Sacramental Absolution* (Washington n.d.).

F. Buckley, *Children and God: Communion, Confession and Confirmation* (Denville, New Jersey 1974).

J. Crichton, *The Ministry of Reconciliation* (London 1974).

J. Dallen, *A Decade of Discussion on the Reform of Penance: 1963-1973.* S.T.D thesis, The Catholic University of America (Washington 1973).

Federation of Diocesan Liturgical Commissions, *The New Rite of Penance: Background Catechesis* (St. Pius X Abbey 1975).

_____, *General Absolution: Toward a Deeper Understanding* (Chicago 1978).

J. Gonzalez del Valle, *El sacramento de la penitencia* (Pamplona 1972).

T. Guzie, *What a Modern Catholic Believes about Confession* (Chicago 1974).

B. Haggerty, *What Does 'Quam Singulare' Really Say? A Study Document on the Practice of First Communion and First Confession* (West Mystic, Connecticut 1973).

E. Jeep (ed.), *The Rite of Penance: Commentaries Implementing the Rite* (Washington 1976).

R. Keifer and F. McManus, *The Rite of Penance — Commentaries*, Vol. 1: *Understanding the Document* (Washington 1975).

Liturgie et rémission des péchés. Conférences Saint-Serge, XXe Semaine d'Études Liturgiques (Rome 1975).

B. Marthaler, *Catechetics in Context* (Huntington, Indiana 1974) 260-281.

N. Mitchell (ed.), *The Rite of Penance — Commentaries*, Vol. 3: *Background and Directions* (Washington 1978).

R. Novak, *A Selected Bibliography on Reconciliation.* Liturgy Training Program (Chicago 1975).

L. Orsy, "The Sins of Those Little Ones," *America* 129 (1973) 438-441.

_____, *The Evolving Church and the Sacrament of Penance* (Denville, New Jersey 1978).

K. Osborne and others, *Committee Report: The Renewal of the Sacrament of Penance.* The Catholic Theological Society of America 1975.

K. Rahner, *Allow Yourself to Be Forgiven: Penance Today* (Denville, New Jersey 1974).

E. Schillebeeckx (ed.), *Sacramental Reconciliation.* Concilium 61 (Paramus, New Jersey 1971).

F. Sottocornola, "Il nuovo 'Ordo Paenitentiae,'" *Notitiae* 10 (1974) 63-79.

_____, *A Look at the New Rite of Penance*, trans. T. Krosnicki (Washington 1975).

T. Sullivan, "The First Confession: Law and Catechesis," *America* 137 (1977) 128-131.

J. Tillard, "Pénitence et eucharistie," *La Maison-Dieu*, no. 90 (1967) 103–131.

U.S. Catholic Conference, *A Study Paper for First Confession* (Washington 1973).

C. Vogel, "Sin and Penance: A Survey of the Historical Evolution of the Penitential Discipline in the Latin Church," *Pastoral Treatment of Sin*, ed. P. Delhaye (New York 1968) 117–182.

J. Wright, "The New Catechetical Directory and Initiation to the Sacraments of Penance and Eucharist," *Homiletic and Pastoral Review* 72 (December 1971) 7–24.

Anointing of the Sick

Z. Alszeghy, "The Bodily Effects of Extreme Unction," *Theology Digest* 9 (1961) 105–110.

Bishops' Committee on the Liturgy, *Study Text II: Anointing and the Pastoral Care of the Sick* (Washington 1973).

B. Brown, *The Sacramental Ministry of the Sick* (New York 1968).

J. Crichton, *Christian Celebration: The Sacraments* (London 1973) 168–191.

C. Gusmer, "Liturgical Traditions of Christian Illness: Rites of the Sick," *Worship* 46 (1972) 528–543.

———, "I Was Sick and You Visited Me; The Revised Rites for the Sick," *Worship* 48 (1974) 516–525.

La Maison-Dieu, no. 113 (1973): *Le nouveau rituel des malades*. Articles by P. Jacob, P.-M. Gy, B. Reiche, J. Didier, D. Sicard, C. Ortemann, and F. Turquet.

National Bulletin on Liturgy, 57: *Rites for the Sick and the Dying* (January–February 1977) 1–64.

B. Newns, "Liturgical Bulletin: Reforming the Liturgy of the Sick," *The Clergy Review* 56 (1971) 279–286.

———, "Liturgical Bulletin: Anointing of Sick and Viaticum," *The Clergy Review* 56 (1971) 942–950.

C. Ortemann, *Le sacrement des malades: Histoire et signification* (Paris 1971).

B. Poschmann, *Penance and Anointing of the Sick*, trans. and rev. F. Courtney (New York 1964).

M. Slattery, "The New Rite for the Sacrament of the Sick," *The Furrow* 24 (1973) 131–137.

M. Taylor (ed.), *The Mystery of Suffering and Death* (New York 1973).

Marriage

P. Aries, "L'Amour dans le mariage et en dehors," *La Maison-Dieu*, no. 127 (1976) 139–145.

J.-P. Audet, *Structures of Christian Priesthood: A Study of Home, Marriage and Celibacy in the Pastoral Service of the Church* (New York 1968).

G. Baumann, "The Churches and Inter-Christian Marriages," *Worship* 42 (December 1968) 609–616.

L. Boff, "The Sacrament of Marriage," *The Future of Christian Worship*, Concilium 87 (New York 1973) 22–33.

A. Bugnini, "New Marriage Ritual," *Doctrine and Life* 19 (May 1969) 264–268.

J. Crichton, *Christian Celebration: The Sacraments* (London 1973) 114–136.

R. Didier, "Sacrement de mariage, baptême et foi," *La Maison-Dieu*, no. 127 (1976) 106–138.

R. Hovda, "Using the New Roman Rite," *Liturgy* 17 (May 1972) 16–19.

_____, "The Rite for Celebrating Marriage during Mass," *Manual for Celebration* (Washington 1972) 1–23.

International Theological Commission, "Propositions on the Doctrine of Christian Marriage," *Origins* 8 (September 28, 1978) 235–239.

D. Krouse, "Principles for Weddings from History," *Pastoral Music* 3 (October–November 1978) 13–17.

La Maison-Dieu, no. 99 (1969): *Le nouveau rituel du mariage.* Articles by P.-M. Gy, A. Duval, B. Fischer, N. Le Bousse, R. Mouret, M. Gaudillière.

National Bulletin on Liturgy, no. 59: *Celebrating Marriage* (May–June 1977) 129–181.

D. O'Callaghan, "Marriage as Sacrament," *The Future of Marriage as Institution.* Concilium 55 (New York 1970) 101–110.

P. Palmer, "Christian Marriage: Contract or Covenant," *Theological Studies* 33 (1972) 617–665.

K. Richter, *The Liturgical Celebration of Marriage. The Problems Raised by Changing Theological and Legal Views of Marriage.* Concilium 87 (New York 1973) 72–87.

E. Schillebeeckx, *Marriage: Human Reality and Saving Mystery*, 2 vols. (New York 1965).

G. Sloyan, "The New Rite for Celebrating Marriage," *Worship* 44 (May 1970) 258–267.

K. Smits, "The Wedding Ceremony: Unlimited Opportunities," *Pastoral Music* 3 (October–November 1978) 9–12.

G. Wilson, "Reflections on the Order of Marriage," *Worship* 42 (March 1968) 150–158.

Orders and Ministry

Bishops' Committee on the Liturgy, *Study Text III — Ministries in the Church: Commentary on the Apostolic Letters of Pope Paul VI, "Ministeria quaedam" and "Ad pascendum"* (Washington 1974).

Bishops' Committee on the Permanent Diaconate, *Permanent Deacons in the United States: Guidelines on Their Formation and Ministry* (Washington 1971).

C. Braga, *"Ministeria quaedam:* Commentarius," *Ephemerides Liturgicae* 87 (1973) 191–214.

N. Brockman, *Ordained to Service: A Theology of the Permanent Diaconate* (Hickville, New York 1976).

Y.-M. Congar, *Ministères et communion ecclésiale* (Paris 1971).

B. Cooke, *Ministry to Word and Sacraments: History and Theology* (Philadelphia 1976).

J. Crichton, *Christian Celebration: The Sacraments* (London 1973) 137–167.

J. Delorme (ed.), *Le ministère et les ministères selon le Nouveau Testament. Dossier exégétique et réflexion théologique* (Paris 1974).

A. Feuillet, *The Priesthood of Christ and His Ministers,* trans. M. O'Connell (New York 1975).

R. Gryson, *The Ministry of Women in the Early Church,* trans. J. Laporte and M. Hall (Collegeville, Minnesota 1976).

R. Hovda, *Strong, Loving and Wise: Presiding in Liturgy* (Washington 1976).

_____, *There Are Different Ministries* (Washington 1975).

P. Hunermann, "Conclusions Regarding the Female Diaconate," *Theological Studies* 36 (1975) 325–333.

International Theological Commission, *Report on the Priestly Ministry,* trans. J. Dupuis (Bangalore 1971).

F. Johannes (ed.), *Rethinking the Priesthood* (Dublin 1970).

J. Komanchak, "Theological Questions on the Ordination of Women," in *Women and Catholic Priesthood: An Expanded View,* ed. A. Gardiner (New York 1976) 241–257.

N. Lash and J. Rhymer (eds.), *The Christian Priesthood* (Denville, New Jersey 1970).

La Maison-Dieu, no. 102 (1970): *Ministères et ordinations dans l'Église aujourd'hui.* Articles by Y. Congar, J. Colson, K. Hruby, C. Vogel, I. Dalmais, J. Huard, J. Lécuyer, and J. de Benoist.

La Maison-Dieu, no. 115 (1973): *Les ministères dans l'assemblée chrétienne.* Articles by Y. Congar, A. Lemaire, A. de Vogüé, C. Vogel, R. Béraudy, J. de Baciocchi, F. Bussini, and H. Denis.

D. Power, *The Christian Priest: Elder and Prophet* (London 1973).

Eucharist (Celebration, Communion and Worship)

H. Ashworth, "The Prayer of the Faithful," *Liturgy* 37 (July 1968) 67–72.

_____, "The New Prefaces," *The Clergy Review* 58 (November 1968) 839–860.

R. Avery, "A Preview of the New Prefaces, I," *Worship* 42 (November 1968) 514–531; II: *Worship* 42 (December 1968) 587–608.

Bishops' Committee on the Liturgy, *The Body of Christ* (Washington 1977).

_____, *Study Text I: Holy Communion (Immensae caritatis)* (Washington 1973).

_____, *Study Text V: Eucharistic Concelebration* (Washington 1978).

R. Boeckler (ed.), *Interkommunion-Konziliarität* (Stuttgart 1974).

L. Bouyer, *Eucharist* (Notre Dame, Indiana 1968).

M. Collins, "Ritual Symbols: Something Human between Us and God: Reflections on the Directory for Masses with Children," *Living Light* 12 (1975) 438–448.

P. Coughlan, "The New Eucharistic Prayers," *The Furrow* 19 (July 1968) 381–389.

_____, "The New Order of the Mass," *The Furrow* 20 (June 1969) 294–301.

J. Crichton, *Christian Celebration: The Mass* (London 1971).

G. Danneels, "Communion under Both Kinds," *The Church and the Liturgy.* Concilium 2 (Glen Rock, New Jersey 1964) 153–160.

E. Dekkers, "Concelebration: Limitations of Current Practice," *Doctrine and Life* 22 (1972) 190–202.

J. Delorme and others, *The Eucharist in the New Testament* (Baltimore 1965).

A. Dulles, "Eucharistic Sharing as an Ecumenical Problem," *The Resilient Church* (New York 1977) 153–171.

Federation of Diocesan Liturgical Commissions, *Take and Eat* (Chicago 1977).

J. Fitzsimmons, "Learning to Live with the Lectionary," *The Clergy Review* 57 (June 1972) 419–431.

E. Flynn, "The Eucharist under Both Kinds," *Doctrine and Life* 19 (August 1969) 399–410.

T. Guzie, *Jesus and the Eucharist* (New York 1974).

P. Hocken, "On Eucharistic Devotions," *The Clergy Review* 53 (April 1968) 296–305.

R. Jasper and G. Cuming, *Prayers of the Eucharist: Early and Reformed* (London 1975).

P. Jounel, "The Mystery of the Eucharist," *Doctrine and Life* 15 (April 1965) 202–227.

A. Kavanagh, "Thoughts on the New Eucharistic Prayers," *Worship* 43 (January 1969) 2–12.

M. Kay (ed.), *It Is Your Own Mystery: A Guide to the Communion Rite* (Washington 1977).

A. King, *Eucharistic Reservation in the Western Church* (London 1965).

J. Kolesar, *Ministers of Life: The Role of Lay Ministers of the Eucharist* (Phoenix 1973).

La Maison-Dieu, no. 94 (1967): *Les nouvelles prières eucharistiques*. Articles by P. Jounel, M. Thurian, J. Orchampt, J. Gelineau, and G. Huyghe.

La Maison-Dieu, no. 100 (1969): *La nouvelle liturgie de la messe*. Articles by R. Cabié, C. Rozier, N. Rasmussen, R. Béraudy, A.-M. Roguet, P. Cneude, J. Gelineau, and B. Soudé.

La Maison-Dieu, no. 103 (1970): *Le nouveau missel*. Articles by P. Jounel and C. Duchesneau.

H. Manders, "Concelebration," *The Church and the Liturgy*. Concilium 2 (New York 1964) 135–152.

A. G. Martimort (ed.), *The Church at Prayer: The Eucharist* (New York 1973).

P. McGoldrick, "The Synod and the Mass," *The Furrow* 19 (March 1968) 123–130.

_____, "Aspects of the Order of Mass," *The Furrow* 20 (December 1969) 657–664.

J. McGowan, *Concelebration* (New York 1964).

J. Megivern, *Concomitance and Communion* (New York 1963).

R. Mumm and M. Lienhard (eds.), *Eucharistische Gastfreundschaft* (Kassel 1974).

J. Kent and R. Murray (eds.), *Church Membership and Intercommunion* (Denville, New Jersey 1973).

A. Nocent, "La Prière commune des fideles," *Nouvelle Revue Théologique* 86 (1964) 948–964.

J. O'Connell, "The Bidding Prayer," *The Clergy Review* 50 (September 1965) 685–691.

J. Powers, *Eucharistic Theology* (New York 1967).

J. Pruisken, *Interkommunion im Prozess* (Essen 1974).

P. Purdue, "The New Lectionary," *Doctrine and Life* 19 (December 1969) 666–674.

K. Rahner and A. Häussling, *The Celebration of the Eucharist* (New York 1968).

A.-M. Roguet, "Pour une théologie de la concélébration," *La Maison-Dieu*, no. 88 (1966) 116–126.

J. Ryan, *The Eucharistic Prayer* (New York 1974).

V. Ryan, "The New Mass Rite," *Doctrine and Life* 20. Part I (January 1970) 3–12; Part II (February 1970) 91–101.

A. Ryder, "The Theology of the New Order of the Mass," *The Clergy Review* 55 (February 1970) 101–111.

_____, "Adoration of the Eucharist," *The Clergy Review* 57 (June 1972) 439–451.

E. Schillebeeckx, *The Eucharist*, trans. N. Smith (New York 1968).

H. Skillin, *Concelebration: A Historical Synopsis and Canonical Commentary*. The Catholic University of America Canon Law Studies 450 (Washington 1968).

L. Soubigou, *A Commentary on the Prefaces and Eucharistic Prayers of the Roman Missal*, trans. J. Otto (Collegeville, Minnesota 1971).

L. Swidler (ed.), "The Eucharist in Ecumenical Dialogue," *Journal of Ecumenical Studies* 13 (1976) 191–344.

J. Tillard, "Commentaire de l'Instruction sur le culte eucharistique," *La Maison-Dieu*, no. 91 (1967) 45–63.

F. Van Beeck, "Intercommunion: A Note on Norms," *One in Christ* 12 (1976) 124–141.

Liturgy of the Hours

Bishops' Committee on the Liturgy, *A Call to Prayer* (Washington 1977).

P. Coughlan, "The Reform of the Breviary," *The Furrow* 21 (June 1970) 355–360.

J. Crichton, *Christian Celebration: The Prayer of the Church* (London 1976).

A. Flannery (ed.), *Making the Most of the Breviary* (Dublin n.d.).

J. Gallen (ed.), *Christians at Prayer* (Notre Dame, Indiana 1977).

P. Jounel, "The Divine Office," *Doctrine and Life* 15 (July 1965) 386–391.

E. J. Lengeling, "Liturgia Horarum: Zur Neuordnung des kirchlichen Stundengebets," *Liturgisches Jahrbuch* 20 (1970) 141–160.

———, "Liturgia Horarum: Die Lesungen und Responsorien im neuen Stundengebet," *Liturgisches Jahrbuch* 20 (1970) 231–249.

La Maison-Dieu, no. 95 (1968): *L'Office divin aujourd'hui*. Articles by Gantoy, Dupont, Besnard, Weakland, Geradon, Besret, Lheureux, Emery, and Leclercq.

La Maison-Dieu, no. 105 (1971): *La liturgie des heures*. Articles by Lengeling, Leclercq, David, Rose, Wiéner, Raciti, de Bourmont, Gelineau, Isabelle-Marie.

J. Mateos, "The Morning and Evening Office," *Worship* 42 (1968) 31–47.

———, "The Origins of the Divine Office," *Worship* 41 (1967) 477–485.

J. Pascher, "Die Psalmen als Grundlage des Stundengebets," *Ephemerides Liturgicae* 85 (1971) 260–280.

P. Purdue, "The New Breviary," *Doctrine and Life* 20 (June 1970) 336–340.

———, "The New Office: General Instruction," *Doctrine and Life* 21 (April 1971) 191–200.

A. Roguet, *The Liturgy of the Hours: The General Instruction with Commentary*, trans. P. Coughlan and P. Purdue (Collegeville, Minnesota 1974).

A. Rose, "La répartition des lectures bibliques dans le livre de la liturgie des heures," *Ephemerides Liturgicae* 85 (1971) 281–305.

W. Storey, "The Liturgy of the Hours: Principles and Practice," *Worship* 46 (1972) 194–203.

———, "Parish Worship: The Liturgy of the Hours," *Worship* 49 (1975) 2–12.

———, "The Liturgy of the Hours: Cathedral versus Monastery," *Worship* 50 (1976) 50–70.

G. Winkler, "Das Offizium am Ende des 4. Jahrhunderts und das heutige chaldäische Offizium, ihre strukturellen Zusammenhänge," *Ostkirchliche Studien* 19 (1970) 289–311.

———, "Über die Kathedralvesper in den verschiedenen Riten des Ostens und Westens," *Archiv für Liturgiewissenschaft* 16 (1974) 53–102.

OTHER LITURGICAL RITES

Blessing of an Abbot/Abbess and Use of Pontifical Insignia

A. Nocent, "L'Ordo benedictionis abbatis et abbatissae,'" *Rivista Liturgica* 60 (1973) 321–325.

Pontificalia insignia. Text with commentary. *Ephemerides Liturgicae* 82 (1968) 344–348; *Notitiae* 4 (1968) 224–226.

Instructio de ritibus et insignibus pontificalibus. Text with commentary. *Ephemerides Liturgicae* 82 (1968) 348–358; *Notitiae* 4 (1968) 246–252, 312–324.

Dedication of a Church and Altar

I. Calabuig, "L'Ordo dedicationis ecclesiae et altaris: Appunti di una lettura," *Notitiae* 13 (1977) 391–450.

Funeral Rite

J. Crichton, "The Rite of Funerals," *Christian Celebration: The Sacraments* (London 1973) 192–209.

K. Donovan, "The New Funeral Rite," *Life and Worship* 40 (April 1971) 19–24.

C. Howell, "The Revised Funeral Rite," *Life and Worship* 41 (July 1972) 12–19.

La Maison-Dieu, no. 101 (1970): *Les funérailles.* Articles by Gy, Sicard, Benoît, Puthanangady, Ariès, Hameline, Brisacier, Turck, and Tissier.

G. Rowell, *The Liturgy of Christian Burial: An Introductory Survey of the Historical Development of Christian Burial Rites* (London 1977).

Religious Profession and Consecration of Virgins

M. Auge, "I riti della professione religiosa e della consacrazione delle vergini," *Rivista Liturgica* 60 (1973) 326–340.

I. Calabuig, "La professione dei consigli evangelici," in *Nelle vostre assemblée,* ed. J. Gelineau (Brescia 1970) 689–714.

La Maison-Dieu, no. 110 (1972): *La consécration des vierges.* Articles by Metz and Croiset.

P. Raffin, "Liturgie de l'engagement religieux: Le nouveau rituel de la profession religieuse," *La Maison-Dieu,* no. 104 (1970) 151–166.

REFORM OF THE LITURGICAL CALENDAR

J. Crichton, "The Calendar," *Christian Celebration: The Mass* (London 1971) 107–114.

G. McGinty, "The Reform of the Church Calendar," *Doctrine and Life* 19 (November 1969) 594–601.

La Maison-Dieu, no. 100 (1969): *Le nouveau calendrier.* Articles by Jounel and Dubois.

R. Nardone, "The Roman Calendar in Ecumenical Perspective," *Worship* 50 (1976) 238–246.

SACRED ART AND ARCHITECTURE

Bishops' Committee on the Liturgy, *Environment and Art in Catholic Worship* (Washington 1978).

F. Debuyst, *Modern Architecture and Christian Celebration* (Richmond, Virginia 1968).

La Maison-Dieu, no. 136 (1978): *Des lieux pour célébrer.* Articles by Carrière, Jounel, Gy, Hameline, Boiret, Vallet and Violle.

LITURGICAL MUSIC

Bishops' Committee on the Liturgy, *Music in Catholic Worship* (Washington 1972).

L. Deiss, *Spirit and Song of the New Liturgy* (Cincinnati 1976).

R. Hayburn, *Papal Legislation on Sacred Music 95 A.D. to 1977 A.D.* (Collegeville, Minnesota 1979).

LITURGICAL ADAPTATION AND INDIGENIZATION

B. Botte, "Le problème de l'adaptation en liturgie," *Revue du Clergé Africain* 18 (July 1963) 308–319.

A. Chupungco, *Towards a Filipino Liturgy* (Manila 1976).

_____, "Greco-Roman Culture and Liturgical Adaptation," *Notitiae* 15 (1979) 202–218.

P. Gy, "La responsabilité des évêques par rapport au droit liturgique," *La Maison-Dieu*, no. 112 (1972) 9–24.

C. Hanson, "The Liberty of the Bishop to Improvise Prayer in the Eucharist," *Vigiliae Christianae* 15 (1961) 173–176.

F. McManus, "The Juridical Power of the Bishop in the Constitution on the Sacred Liturgy," *The Church and the Liturgy.* Concilium 2 (New York 1965) 33–49.

_____, "The Scope of Authority of the Episcopal Conference," in *The Once and Future Church*, ed. J. Coriden (New York 1971) 129–178.

B. Neunheuser, "Unità e molteplicità di forme liturgiche nella prospettiva postconciliare," in *La collegialità episcopale per il futuro della Chiesa. Dalla prima alla seconda assmblea del Sinodo dei vescovi*, ed. Fagiolo and Concetti (Florence 1969) 598–648.

_____, "Possibilities and Limits of Liturgical Spontaneity," *Monastic Studies* 8 (1972) 103–111.

_____, *Storia della liturgia attraverso le epoche culturali* (Rome 1977).

A. Nocent, "Souplesse et adaptation de la liturgie depuis Vatican II," *La Maison-Dieu*, no. 97 (1969) 76–94.

Y. Raguin, "Indigenization of the Church," *Teaching All Nations: International Study Week on Missionary Catechetics* 6 (1969) 151–168.

Notes de Pastorale Liturgique, no. 117 (1975): *Souplesse et adaptation.*

M. Thurian, "Créativité et spontanéité dans la liturgie," *Notitiae* 14 (1978) 169–175.

A. Triacca, "Improvvisazione o fissismo eucologico? Asterisco ad un periodica problema di pastorale liturgica," *Salesianum* 32 (1970) 149–164.

———, "Adattamento liturgico: Utopia, velleità o strumento della pastorale liturgica?" *Notitiae* 15 (1979) 26–45.

FIDELITY TO LITURGICAL LAWS AND TO PASTORAL RESPONSIBILITY

B. Botte, "La libre composition des prières liturgiques," *Questions Liturgiques* 282 (1974) 211–215.

L. Bouyer, "L'improvisation liturgique dans l'Église ancienne," *La Maison-Dieu*, no. 111 (1972) 7–19.

Y. Congar, "Autorité, initiative, coresponsabilité: Elements de réflexion sur les conditions dans lesquelles le problème se pose aujourd'hui dans l'Église," *La Maison-Dieu*, no. 97 (1969) 34–57.

———, "Initiatives locales et normes universelles," *La Maison-Dieu*, no. 112 (1972) 54–69.

H. Dalmais, "Tradition et liberté dans les liturgies d'Orient," *La Maison-Dieu*, no. 97 (1969) 104–114.

E. Dekkers, "Créativité et orthodoxie dans la 'Lex Orandi'," *La Maison-Dieu*, no. 111 (1972) 20–30.

G. Fontaine, "Créativité dans la liturgie d'aujourd'hui," *Notitiae* 8 (1972) 151–156.

D. Hameline, "La créativité: Fortune d'un concept, o concept de fortune?" *La Maison-Dieu*, no. 111 (1972) 84–109.

J. Hoffmann, "Pourquoi un droit liturgique," *Bulletin du Comité des Études* 59 (1969) 443–456.

W. Kelly, "The Authority of Liturgical Law," *The Jurist* 28 (1968) 397–424.

F. McManus, "Liturgical Law and Difficult Cases," *Worship* 48 (1974) 347–366.

F. Morrisey, *The Canonical Significance of Papal and Curial Pronouncements.* Canon Law Society of America, n.d.

A. Roguet, "De generibus literariis textum liturgicorum eorum interpretatione eorumque usu liturgico," *Notitiae* 2 (1966) 106–117.

J. Rotelle, "Liturgy and Authority," *Worship* 47 (1973) 514–526.

A. Turck, "Le problème de la loi: Réflexions pastorales," *Paroisse et Liturgie* 47 (1965) 3–13.

T. Vismans, "Liturgy or Rubrics?" *The Church Worships.* Concilium 12 (New York 1966) 83–91.

INDEX

A